Editors

Kay Field, M.A.

Edward Kaufman, M.S.W.

Charles Saltzman, B.S.

Emotions and Learning Reconsidered

INTERNATIONAL PERSPECTIVES

Foreword by

Rudolf Ekstein, Ph.D.

GARDNER PRESS, INC.

NEW YORK LONDON MONTREAL SYDNEY

Gardner Press, Inc.
19 Union Square West
New York, NY 10003

Library of Congress Cataloging in Publication Data

Emotions and learning reconsidered : International perspectives / editors, Kay Field, Edward Kaufman, Charles Saltzman ; foreword by Rudolf Ekstein.
    p.   cm.
A selection of papers of the 5th International Conference on Educational Therapy held in Chicago on August 25–27, 1989.
    Includes bibliographical references (p.) and index.
    ISBN 0-89876-205-7
    1. Remedial teaching — Congresses.   2. Learning disabled—Identification — Congresses.   3. Learning disabled—Rehabilitation — Congresses.   4. Learning, Psychology of — Congresses.   5. Teachers — Training of — Congresses.   I. Field, Kay.   II. Kaufman, Edward.   III. Saltzman, Charles, B. S.
LB1029.R4E46 1993   93-13082
371.9'043—dc20   CIP

9 8 7 6 5 4 3 2

To children and adolescents everywhere
with learning problems
and
to their teachers and therapists
who have shared their
struggles and triumphs

Contents

Contributors

Muriel Barrett, M.A. Educational therapist, Tavistock Clinic; co-author of *Attachment Behavior and The School Child: An Introduction to Educational Therapy,* London, England.

Michael F. Basch, M.D. Professor of Psychiatry, Rush Medical College, Chicago; psychoanalytic education faculty, Institute for Psychoanalysis, Chicago; in private practice, Chicago Metropolitan Area.

Mia Beaumont, M.A. Educational therapist, Tavistock Clinic; educational therapist and Team Coordinator, Hornsley Rise Child Guidance Clinic, London, England.

Linda A. Cozzarelli, M.A. Teaching staff, Psychotherapy Institute, Berkeley, California; consultant, Ann Martin Childrens' Center, Piedmont, California; in private practice, Berkeley.

Anna-Marit Duve, Ph.D. Psychologist, Nic Waal's Institute, Oslo, Norway.

Marlene R. Eisen, Ph.D. Clinical psychologist; faculty, Teacher Education Program and Illinois School of Professional Psychology, Chicago.

Sydney B. Eisen, M.D. Clinical Associate Professor of Pediatrics and Psychiatry, Northwestern University Medical School; Director of Training in Child Psychiatry, Children's Memorial Hospital, Chicago; in private practice, Chicago Metropolitan Area.

Rudolf F. Ekstein, M.S.S., Ph.D. Training Analyst and Senior Faculty at the Los Angeles Institute for Psychoanalytic Studies. He is currently Clinical Professor of Medical Psychology, University of California, Los Angeles; Annual Guest Professor, University of Vienna, Department of Child Psychiatry. Dr. Ekstein has authored numerous books and over 500 papers in the fields of psychoanalysis, psychology, psychoanalytic education and the application of psychoanalytic thinking to problems of education.

Kay Field, M.A., Director, Teacher Education Program and Clinical School Services Program, Institute for Psychoanalysis, Chicago; co-editor of *Learning and Education: Psychoanalytic Perspectives*; in private practice, Chicago Metropolitan Area.

Paula Fuqua, M.D. Advanced Candidate, Institute for Psychoanalysis, Chicago; Attending Psychiatrist, Michael Reese Hospital, Chicago; in private practice, Chicago Metropolitan Area.

Robert M. Galatzer-Levy, M.D. Psychoanalytic Faculty, Education Institute for Psychoanalysis; lecturer in psychiatry, University of Chicago; co-author of *The Essential Other*; in private practice, Chicago Metropolitan Area.

Doris J. Johnson, Ph.D. Head, Program in Learning Disabilities; Professor, Learning Disabilities, Northwestern University, Evanston, Illinois.

Edward P. Kaufman, M.S.W. Faculty, Child and Adolescent Psychoanalytic Therapy Program, Teacher Education Program, Clinical School Services Program, Institute for Psychoanalysis, Chicago; consultant to various school and child welfare agencies in the Chicago Metropolitan Area; in private practice, Chicago Metropolitan Area.

Nan Knight-Birnbaum, M.S.S.A. Social worker, Barr-Harris Center for the Study of Separation and Loss in Childhood; faculty, Teacher Education Program, Institute for Psychoanalysis, Chicago; in private practice, Chicago Metropolitan Area.

Betty B. Osman, Ph.D. Psychologist, Child and Adolescent Service, Department of Psychiatry, White Plains Hospital Medical Center, White Plains, New York; author of *Learning Disabilities: A Family Affair* and *No One to Play With: The Social Side of Learning Disabilities*; in private practice, Scarsdale, New York.

Charles Saltzman, B.S., Ph.D. candidate. Committee on Human Development, University of Chicago; Faculty, Teacher Education Program and Child and Adolescent Psychotherapy Program, Institute for Psychoanalysis, Chicago; Past President, Illinois School Psychologists' Association.

Rita Sussman, Ph.D. Clinical psychologist; scientific staff, Michael Reese Hospital; faculty, Postgraduate Education Program, Institute for Psychoanalysis, Chicago; in private practice, Chicago Metropolitan Area.

Jane Trevitt, B.A. Teacher-in-Charge, Childrens' Unit (Brookside Family Consultation Centre), Douglas House Annexe (Addenbrooke's Hospital); co-author of *Attachment Behavior and the School Child: An Introduction to Educational Therapy*, Cambridge, England.

Dorothy Ungerleider, M.A., C.E.T. Educational therapist; Founding President, Advisory Board Chairman, Association of Educational Therapists, Woodland Hills, California; author of *Reading, Writing, and Rage*; in private practice, Encino, California.

Colin Webber, M.A. Social worker, Barr-Harris Center for the Study of Separation and Loss in Childhood, Institute for Psychoanalysis, Chicago; in private practice, Chicago Metropolitan Area.

Rolf Zachariassen, M.A. Principal educational therapist, Nic Waal's Institute, Oslo, Norway.

Rudolf Ekstein, Ph.D.

Foreword

many years ago, in Austria, I became acquainted with psychoanalytic pedagogy, having as my mentors Anna Freud and August Aichorn, both of them deeply interested in psychoanalytic pedagogy. There were many others, including Siegfried Bernfeld. These, as well as other Austrians such as Lilly Peller, Maria Piers, Edith Buxbaum, were the people who influenced my work in the United States. All of them were creative contributors to the literature who believed that through the education of teachers one could also make important contributions to psychotherapy and child analysis. What a pleasure it is to see that this movement of a "new" education, while it had its ups and downs, never really stopped, but continued to be developed.

At that time, when I helped to organize such a program for kindergarten teachers, elementary school teachers, and high school teachers, I challenged them to help children go beyond learning for love to the love of learning. There exist educational approaches today in our schools, and even in academia, where we learn for good marks, for the love of parents and teachers, and for the respect of one's colleagues. Those of us, however, who belong to that apparently still new education movement try to help children learn not merely for love, but to love the learning; to go beyond the mere acquisition of knowledge and skills and become active participants in the educational process.

More and more we have become interested in the education of

teachers, not only to teach the curriculum but to study the mind and the emotions of the growing child and to help him to develop the capacity to become an active learner.

I remember how excited I was, coming to America, when I discovered the work of John Dewey and compared it with Austrians such as Bruno Bettelheim, Willi Hoffer, and Fritz Redl. The fruits of the labors of these men and women can be found a generation later in this new contribution: *Emotions and Learning Reconsidered: An International Perspective.* The conference from which these papers are drawn is not the first of its kind. Actually, it was the Fifth International Conference of Education Therapy, which was held for the first time in the United States, in Chicago in 1989.

When I think of the first publication of a similar kind—*Zeitschrift fur Psychoanalytische Pedagogik*, the first periodical of psychoanalytic pedagogy, which was published for eleven years—I find that times have changed. As I go through these early volumes, I find the psychoanalytic pedagogues of that time, the time of my own beginning, did not clearly differentiate between education and child analysis. Anna Freud herself, as well as some of the other early contributors, began as teachers and left the teaching field to become child analysts and therapists. That had very much to do with the political condition of that time. Anna Freud became a teacher after the First World War, when there was hope in the air that school reform would quickly bring about a completely different educational system based on psychodynamic understanding of child development. But school reform in Austria as well as in other countries did not last. The school system became reactionary again and hopes vanished.

At the end of the last century, Ellen Key published a book, *The Century of the Child*, expressing the hope that the twentieth century would change the school system—no more "soul murder" would take place there. Her book, a pleasure to read, was full of hope. It is painful to think that today, almost a hundred years later, the same problems still confront us, often in new disguises. I have had doubts about our ability to solve them.

As I go through the chapters of this new volume, however, I have hope again. The conference was an international event, drawing together a number of organizations from different parts of our country and from many parts of the world. Additionally, it united many different views. I know many of the contributors and their work from having had personal contact with them. Each of them offers us not a static, but a dynamic, flexible point of view. There are no final solutions, no final views, no dogmatic positions.

Edward Kaufman, Kay Field, and Charles Saltzman bring us material not only about teacher and child, parent and child, administration and teacher, but also about a better understanding of the sociological aspects of school systems that are sometimes regressing, sometimes stagnating, sometimes changing, and sometimes moving forward. The volume focuses on work with emotionally disordered children and children with learning disabilities. It is about the exceptional child—sometimes the very gifted child and sometimes the child who is at a dead-end street of learning and will have to be in a residential treatment center. It is about the new, shared educational space using instructional as well as play materials and serving both therapeutic and educational aims. Thus it extenuates the need to combine different kinds of school with individual and/or group psychotherapy. The new focus, the new key is now *educational therapy.*

I wish I could summarize every one of these papers and respond to them separately and thus do justice to these excellent contributions, outstanding research and experimentation in different settings. What a pleasure it was, for example, to read Dorothy Ungerleider's chapter describing a college student's decision to move to another college and helping her to see that this was not an educational disaster but a major step toward identity and adulthood. She quotes Oliver Sacks, who wrote in *The Man Who Mistook His Wife for a Hat,* "Our evaluations are ridiculously inadequate. They only show us deficits, they do not show us powers; they only show us puzzles and schemata, when we need to see music, narrative, play, a being conducting itself spontaneously in its own natural way." That's what she does with her students. Learning becomes music, a narrative, play, spontaneity in finding one's own natural way.

I found an interesting chapter by Muriel Barrett and Jane Trevitt, who use theories by Winnicott and Bowlby in a most creative way. Applying the concept of the mother-child relationship of Winnicott's facilitating environment to the role of the educational therapist, they show how this allows the teacher to become "an educational attachment figure." I liked the notion of the authors going beyond transference and countertransference and working indirectly with these concepts, described by Freud. It helps us move to a new level, a shared educational space using material of an educational type and serving therapy. Michael Basch writes of the learning child's shame (Adler might have said "inferiority complex") and the hope that the successful educator's influence might someday "put us, the psychotherapists, out of business." This optimism might lead us psychotherapists back to education rather than limit ourselves to efforts to repair damage.

I loved Kaufman's chapter on the residential treatment center, and his remembering Ungerleider's reference in her book about her mother, Florence Fink, who had the gift of being an exquisite and willing listener, and giving delightful advice. Kaufman encourages us to think about Frost's poem about "the road not taken"—to take the road less traveled!

Saltzman, in his chapter, discusses the education of "empathic" teachers through careful study of the works of gifted teachers such as Mary MacCracken, Torey Hayden, and Eleanor Craig, all masters who are willing to go on the "road less traveled by." He is right when he says there are a variety of empathic approaches in the education of children. Gifted, empathic teachers go beyond what they learned in academia and discover the child by finding much of the child in their own soul, their own mind. Saltzman urges us to complete the task of finding and placing such empathic teachers in the schools. We still need to consider teacher-pupil ratios before becoming preoccupied with computer-pupil ratios.

Paula Fuqua's contribution involves the problem of supervision and the attempt to help the young teacher to develop a professional self, mentioning Wallerstein and me and our reference to overcoming the unconscious resistance in the supervisee. I would put it differently now, as I believe today my emphasis would be on thinking about learning blocks: to help the student discover new options, to discover the capacity for empathy, to see not only the resisting child, but also the discovering, creative child. I would stress not only the restoration of the self, but also the discovery of the self.

And how rewarding it is to read the chapter by Mia Beaumont as she helps us to use the views and ideas of Klein and Bowlby. She concerns herself with the child's fear of discovering meaning, the fear, of course, of discovering oneself. I enjoyed her comment about words attacking or killing the child; they are merely symbols, not weapons. Marlene Eisen's chapter is useful to all of us who work with parents. It points out their pain in learning that their child has a learning disability. Further, it notes the felt danger they experience in regard to their sense of their child's well-being and their own well-being. She cautions against putting a static label or a self-limiting diagnosis on the child, warning of the danger of misusing the diagnosis of learning disabled (LD) as a battering ram. And, of course, helping the parents of these children deal with whatever their child's limits might be and move toward realizing their optimum potential.

Betty Osman acquaints us with the problem of depressive disorders in childhood that contribute to learning difficulties. Teachers and mental health professionals must work together and learn to take into account the affective as well as the cognitive state of the child in order to stress that learning and psychotherapeutic treatment are indeed a task of cooperation.

This volume confronts the reader with a particular task. When we were beginners, we each belonged to a particular school of thought, identified as we were with our teachers who gave us the fundamentals of teaching or doing psychotherapy. We live in a much more complicated world than the world I recall of my Viennese days, or rather I should say, the way I wanted the world to be at that time. Actually, of course, that world then was also complicated and involved an eternal struggle to move toward truth. When we look at the educational scene in America today, we are not only reminded of the thinking of Freud, Adler, Jung, and the other representatives of the "new" dynamic psychology at the turn of the century, we also deal with the influences of Rogers, Skinner, and all the different schools of behavior modification, as well as with different psychoanalytic schools, classical or modern Freudians, and followers of Kernberg, Kohut, Bettelheim, and many others. The simplicity of the old days has given way to a complex and ever-changing world. We have to cope with the endless political pressures of the school system: problems of funding, the pressure of parents and school boards, and other stresses and strains.

This collection illustrates all of that, but space limitation unfortunately does not permit me to mention more than a few of the contributors. As I read, I find that practically all of the authors attempt to talk to each other, learn from each other, try to find methods of working with children and adolescents and parents in order to improve their work. The book presents an eternal dialectic struggle. It does not pretend to have the final word but it presents new, promising notions of education. As I write these lines, we find ourselves in the midst of a war in the Middle East. Perhaps this book represents that hopeful part of America and other nations that experiment with peace, with peaceful methods of education, of teaching and learning. It has as its focus the development of both the teacher and the educator of teachers. Siegfried Bernfeld, a mentor of mine who wrote the classic *Sysiphus or the Boundaries of Education*, spoke about the task of the good analyst. I want to paraphrase him and say: A good teacher is only he (or she) who remains, all of his professional life, also a learner who never gives up seminars! I would love to use this volume containing the thoughts and the research of my colleagues, in a seminar I am planning for teachers who wish to continue learning. All the people who read and study this book will come away from it convinced that the love of teaching has to be accompanied by the love of learning, and that in the complexity of teaching and learning we can discover and enlarge our sense of what it means to be fully human.

Acknowledgments

many people and organizations contributed their wisdom, their energies, their resources and their encouragement to the conceptualization and organization of the Fifth International Conference on Educational Therapy.

We would like to thank the following people and organizations for their contributions, support, and encouragement: the Institute for Psychoanalysis, the Teacher Education Program, Dr. Ner Littner, Rhoda Pritzker, Muriel Barrett, Rona Brown, Mia Beaumont, James Bensdorf, Marlene Eisen, Glenn Miller, Gloria Needlman, Marilyn Silin, Carole Slucki, Joan Tobin, Dorothy Ungerleider, Dr. Glorye Wool, conference secretary Christine Susman, and many others too numerous to mention.

The Fifth International Conference was realized through the efforts of the Conference Planning and Organizing Committee: Kay Field, M.A., Chair; Edward Kaufman, M.S.W., Coordinator; James Bensdorf, M.Ed.; Lynn Borenstein, M.S.W.; Andrew Boxer, M.A.; Rona Brown, M.S. Ed.; Barry Childress, M.D.; Marlene Eisen, Ph.D.; Robert Galatzer-Levy, M.D.; Glenn Miller, M.A.L.S.; Jerry Olson, Ph.D.; Rhoda Pritzker; Pearl Rieger, M.A.; Charles Saltzman, B.S.; Alex Shapiro, B.A.; Marilyn Silin, M.A.; Morris Sklansky, M.D.; Carol Sonnenschein, M.A.; Paul Stein, M.S.W.; Christine Susman; Joan Tobin, A.B.; Jerome Winer, M.D.; Glorye Wool, M.D.; and the Association for the Advancement of Therapeutic Education.

Special thanks also go to the Forum for Advancement of Educational Therapy (England), National Association of Teacher Therapists and Teachers in Multidisciplinary Settings (England), Association of Educational Therapists (United States), Professionals in Learning Disabilities (Illinois), American Association of Children's Residential Centers (United States), Multidisciplinary Academy of Clinical Educators (New York), Child and Adolescent Psychotherapy Training Program (Institute for Psychoanalysis, Illinois), Northeastern Illinois University, Erikson Institute of Loyola University (Illinois), Learning Disability Program (Northwestern University, Illinois), and Roosevelt University (Illinois).

We are indebted to the following foundations and individuals whose generous financial support helped to make the conference possible: Michael Littner Trust; Oppenheimer Family Foundation; Pan-American Airlines; Pritzker Foundation; Albert and Joyce Rubenstein Family Foundation; Marcia Berkman; Louise Baygood; Mr. and Mrs. Walter Bensdorf; Mr. and Mrs. Richard Elden; Joan Grauer; Irving Harris; Howard Gordon Kaplan; Adele and Edward Kaufman; Phillip Klutznick; Estelle Loeb; Judd Malkin; Edward Neisser; Claire Prussian; Eileen Reynolds; Gunther Rice, Ph.D.; Pearl Reiger; Jennifer Robin; Chaya Roth, Ph.D.; Doris Samuels; Dorothy Sheridan; Allen Siegel, M.D.; David Terman, M.D.; Mr. and Mrs. E. Hodson Thornber; Orah and Daniel Winograd.

We would also like to thank the McCormick Charitable Trust whose generous grant made the publication of this book possible.

Introduction

this book was inspired by the spirit and content of the Fifth International Conference on Educational Therapy that was held in Chicago on August 25–27, 1989. This was the first time that this conference was held in the United States and was attended by a broad array of professionals from Great Britain, Norway, Canada, Israel, Argentina, Venezuela, as well as representatives from various parts of the United States. Throughout the conference, there was a sharing of ideas both formally and informally in the various sessions and small discussion groups, all marked by a spirit of conviviality and collegiality.

This is not a record of the proceedings of the conference but rather a selection of papers that we believe charts the interface between education and mental health. We regret that constraints on the size of this volume prevented us from including other excellent papers that were presented at the conference. We believe that the papers demonstrate the benefits of interdisciplinary collaboration that address the emotional and subjective dimensions of learning largely neglected in educational theory, research, and practice. The international mix highlights the universality of concern about learning and offers advances in theory and technique for remediating learning problems. We have tried in this volume to provide a forum wherein readers in the fields of education, mental health, and human development can share in the international exchange of ideas and experiences that occurred in the conference. Taken together, the papers emphasize progress and recent developments in educational therapy, psychotherapy, learning theory, supervision, and training.

The origin and development of the field of educational therapy took place in parallel yet diverse ways on two continents—America and Europe—during approximately the same period of time, underscoring a widespread interest and universal awareness of the importance of this field. The contribution of this emerging new profession is already well-established, and we foresee a burgeoning of this cross-disciplinary model during the next decade. In the United States, simultaneously and separately, initiatives were undertaken in New York, California, and Chicago. In 1965 the Institute for Psychoanalysis in Chicago established the Teacher Education Program, whose overarching theoretical framework was based on contemporary psychoanalytic theories of learning and development. Common to both the European and American programs are the emphasis on the development of the whole person and the recognition of the complexity and diversity of the educational process. All call attention to the emotional, subjective, and relational factors in the teaching-learning process, with particular emphasis on issues of motivation and meaning. Implicitly and explicitly these programs and the authors of the papers in this collection are committed to an empathic stance wherein the educator strives for attunement to the inner experience of the learner.

The papers are grouped into four unavoidably overlapping categories: research and theory, diagnosis and assessment, interventions, and training.

Kay Field, M.A.

A Selective History of Educational Therapy:

1940–1991

Two men, each having lost his way, chanced to meet in a
forest. Spying the other, each was elated, hoping that his
new-found companion would know the way out. To no avail.
But there was reason to rejoice. Said one to the other, "For
certain I know that the way I have come will not lead us out.
But together, friend, we can find the way."

the above tale bears a metaphoric relation to the
origin and development of educational therapy
in recent decades. Like the two travelers, teach-
ers and therapists see the child with learning problems from different perspectives. One looks to the external world of people and things in the
environment and tells us how it appears to a fixed focus camera; the
other looks to the internal reality, the subjective experience of the learner, and tells us how the world is perceived by a particular learner at a
specific time and place. In effect, like the two travelers, educator and
therapist create what Schon calls "a hall of mirrors" in which reflection
is possible. While the educator and therapist see different landscapes,

both come to realize that either one can be successful in teaching or treating the learning-disabled child only if what the other knows is respected. *Educational therapy* is a term that announces such a cross-disciplinary endeavor, a dialogue inspired by questions of concern to both professions: What impels or impedes human learning, be it in the family, the classroom or the consulting room? How, when and why do some children become passionate about learning while others avoid or resist it? Both questions reflect the emotional/subjective elements in the learning process.

The history of a profession, particularly one that seeks to break new ground, is embedded in the biographical narratives of its founders and practitioners. Educational therapy is such a ground-breaking profession. Therefore, I have organized this historical review around the stories or case histories told by six individuals who have played significant pioneering roles in conceptualizing and developing educational therapy in the United States and abroad. All except one have contributed chapters to this volume. Included in the six are Mary Kunst, Ph.D., of Chicago, Illinois; Anna-Marit Duve, Ph.D., and Rolf Zachariassen of Oslo, Norway; Muriel Barrett of the United Kingdom; Dorothy Ungerleider of Los Angeles, California; and the author, Kay Field, also of Chicago. I make no claim that their histories typify the thinking of myriad others who have contributed to this emerging field of practice. My summary of their material may have misinterpreted it. I hope not; but if I so, the full responsibility is mine. I want to take this opportunity to thank them for telling their stories and to express the hope that their recounting will inspire and benefit others. I also wish to thank all my colleagues and students, from whom I have learned so much. Their voices, too, are reflected here. Ungerleider reminds us in her account, "The history of educational therapy is more an oral than a written one; most of what is known is not yet in print." This multidisciplinary approach is rooted in the observations, insights and improvisations of educators and clinicians.

The purpose of this chapter is to present a portrait of educational therapy as it emerged and developed in four geographic locations: the United States (Chicago and Los Angeles); the United Kingdom (London); and Norway (Oslo). In this overview we identify some of the connecting themes that characterize this hybrid model of educational practice and consider their implications for learning in classroom and school.

Educational therapy has come to have dual meanings both specific and general in scope. In the narrow sense, it describes a specialized modality of therapeutic intervention devised for children and adolescents of average or better intelligence who present severe problems in learning and going to school.

In the broad sense, it stands for an emerging paradigm of interdisciplinary inquiry, training, and practice located at the margins of education and the clinical disciplines of psychiatry, psychoanalysis, psychology, and social work. Its overriding aim is to bridge the gap between conflicting controversial approaches to children's learning problems. It seeks to dispose of the deeply entrenched artificial "teach versus treat" dichotomy that has effectively separated educational and clinical approaches to learning problems, isolating cognitive/intellectual from affective/subjective issues and assigning the former to educators, the latter to clinicians. Educational therapy aims to chart the diverse landscapes of human learning which educator and therapist need to explore together.

The order of these case histories is roughly chronological. I say "roughly" because coinage of the term *educational therapy* emerged in different countries around the same time, albeit with somewhat different definitions and theoretical orientations.

The Emergence of the Term *Educational Therapy* (The Michael Reese Hospital Psychiatric Clinic, Chicago): 1940s and 1950s

Mary Kunst, a psychologist, working as a tutor of learning-impaired children in the milieu of a psychiatric hospital in Chicago during the 1940s and 50s was among the first to coin the term *educational therapy* to describe the nature of her work. Under the tutelage and supervision of Maxwell Gitelson and Emmy Sylvester, both psychoanalysts, her view of her role and approach to children's learning problems were shaped in large measure by the explanatory frameworks coming out of psychoanalytic ego psychology. She saw herself as a psychotherapist, with a special interest in and knowledge of learning process dynamics. According to Kunst,

> Educational therapy may be thought of as a form of psychotherapy involving a combination of educational, psychological and psychiatric skills. The educational therapist integrates the tutoring with the healing process whenever the child is psychologically ready. Communication between therapist and child is effected by play activities as well as by conversation. Through spontaneous play and creative activity, the child reveals more about the nature of his conflicts than he is able to verbalize. In like manner, the therapist may be able to reach the child's emotions more adequately by entering into his play than is possible by verbal means.

In addition to her private practice in psychotherapy and educational therapy, she taught and supervised classroom teachers and allied mental health professionals concerned with the education of children "who avoid or resist learning in school." In 1965 she became a founding faculty member of the Teacher Education Program at the Institute for Psychoanalysis in Chicago (to be described below), which applied many of the basic developmental/psychodynamic concepts and remedial techniques of educational therapy to teacher training. Kunst's thinking about the role of the psychoanalytically trained educator reflects one of the most honorable traditions in psychoanalysis: its affinity for collaboration with education. It is little known that Anna Freud and Dorothy Burlingham, her long-time collaborator in such ventures as the war nursery in London during the Second World War, had earlier directed a Montessori school in the 1920s and 30s. The roster of consultants and psychoanalytic pioneers connected with this school reads like a *Who's Who* in child analysis, including Blos, Redl, Bettelheim, Erikson, and others. A separate effort was made by August Aichorn, who developed a group educational program designed primarily for delinquents. It was as a result of this early work that Ernst Kris, Siegfried Bernfeld, Willi Hoffer, Fritz Wittels, Marie Bonaparte, Lou Andreas Salome, and others began the series of volumes entitled, the *Zeitschrift fur Psychoanalytiche Pedagogik* in Vienna, which evolved into the Anglo-American venture, *The Psychoanalytic Study of the Child.*
While some of the papers in this annual series emphasized the earlier psychoanalytic approach to the study of education, others documented the teacher's unique contribution to development through enhancement of the child's tie to reality in a manner which takes developmentally determined fantasy into account. Understanding the child's place in the group and helping children to learn more effectively in school are central concerns in the history of psychoanalytic thought.

The work of Dr. Kunst, as educational therapist, psychotherapist, clinical teacher of educators and related disciplines is emblematic of this tradition.

Educational Therapy in Oslo, Norway: 1952–Present (Summarized from the writing of Duve and Zachariassen)

In 1952 Anna-Marit Sletten Duve (see Chapter 7, this volume), then a teacher of mentally retarded children in the public schools, was invited by Nic Waal, a child psychiatrist, to join her newly founded Child Psychiatric Institute in Oslo, Norway. It was a situation not unlike that in which Mary Kunst found herself during the same period in Chicago. There, too, psychodynamic theory dominated professional discourse and practice in child psychiatry, and ego psychology was beginning to emerge. As an educator "dissatisfied with the limitations of educational testing methods that were restricted to measures of ability and achievement." Duve found in the atmosphere of the clinic and in the dialectic of clinical discourse fresh insights and new challenges to rethink and redesign educational methods for assessing children's learning problems. Like Kunst, who had been encouraged by psychoanalysts Gitelson and Sylvester, Duve was encouraged by Dr. Waal, "who herself had been trained in clinics in the U.S. and who was convinced that suitable techniques were lacking."

This collaboration inspired Duve to design a diagnostic instrument which became known as the AMS test, named by some of the children after the initials of the test's author. It is an observational method for teachers working with emotionally disturbed children with severe learning problems, which

blends ideas from psychoanalytic ego psychology and Lewinian field theory with concepts associated with pedagogy, that is, with the kind of instructional situations found typically in schools. This unique method of observation is based on the deliberate creation of a setting and a progression of tasks that form a close analog of the child's familiar classroom situation. How the child copes with these stimulus demands provides the data for the diagnosis, a method which is quite similar to the administration of projective tests like the Rorschach and the TAT. AMS then is a method which is positioned between direct observation of the child in his natural setting and the relatively strange and austere setting of the clinician's office. (Saltzman)[1]

The AMS method of assessment helped to build a bridge between child psychiatry and education in Norway, and in so doing it enlarged the scope and effectiveness of child psychiatric evaluations and "elevated teaching to full standing as a treatment or intervention available for prescription" as well. In Norway, today the clinical teams in child psychiatric clinics include, in addition to the traditional trinity (psychiatrist, psychologist and social worker), an educational therapist equipped with a repertoire of instructional methods and assessment techniques like the AMS. Zachariassen (co-author of the chapter referred to above) illustrates the application of psychodynamic perspectives to education in his work with children and parents at the Nic Waal Psychiatric Institute.

Educational Therapy in the United Kingdom: 1960–Present (Summarized from report by Muriel Barrett—personal communication, 1989)

In the early 1960s Irene Caspari, an educational psychologist (in what was then the Department for Children and Parents of the Tavistock Clinic), founded and developed the first training program in educational therapy, which she described simply as a "form of treatment for children with learning difficulties." The program was designed for qualified teachers with a degree in psychology. Remedial teaching with the individual child and small groups of children referred by neighborhood schools was an important component of that program. The children were seen once or twice weekly, either in the clinic or in their schools. Caspari, in consultation with colleagues, recognized while supervising trainees' work, that many elements of this remedial teaching process were similar to aspects of their own work with children. This recognition and acknowledgment of the therapeutic value of remedial teaching, led to the use of the term *educational therapy*.

Realizing that teachers disinterested in becoming educational psychologists would nevertheless benefit from a deeper clinical understanding of children, Caspari established a part-time evening course to study "the interrelationship between teacher, teaching method and child." This course was called "Psychological Aspects in the Treatment of Severe Reading Disability." Teachers discussed their work with colleagues in the group. At this early stage, the theoretical input was informally introduced.

In the early 1970s the course was renamed "Psychological Factors in Learning Difficulties." From the teachers' case presentations it became apparent that they had to give more consideration to family dynamics when reviewing the emotional development of children in order to assess how both factors were influencing scholastic achievements. "Social and economic pressures and the disintegration of family life seemed to indicate a need to consider the wider implications of a child's learning problems." Thus began a broadening of the educational therapy perspective to include work with families. A few participants in this course received further personal supervision from Caspari, who in 1973 established the Forum for the Advancement of Educational Therapy (FAET). A year later her paper on educational therapy was published as a chapter in *Psychotherapy Today* (1978) edited by V. Varma.

As Caspari defined it, "Educational therapy is based on empirical evidence suggesting that some emotional disturbance is present in most cases. The problem of treatment is, therefore, approached with particular regard to the child's emotional needs and great importance is attached to the understanding of the child's feelings, and of his emotional reactions."

Caspari was careful to add that "this kind of approach does not . . . exclude other etiological factors, such as inadequate teaching, . . . or some kind of neurological dysfunctioning put forward by supporters of the hypothesis of specific developmental dyslexia, such as Newton, Critchley and Vernon (1970). Other workers in the field look specifically for perceptual difficulties, such as Frostig (1968, 1967), Tinsley (1967), and Nardoo (1970 & 1972). It merely assumes that amongst the variety of possible factors some degree of emotional instability will be present as well" (p. 48).

Caspari specifically described the method of treatment as resting on the Freudian hypothesis that unconscious mechanisms are very important determinants of human behavior. "To this extent," she said,

> educational therapy can be described as a psychoanalytically oriented
> type of treatment. . . . focuses on a particular aspect of dysfunction, *viz:*
> inability to read, spell or do arithmetic. . . . It shares with most kinds of
> remedial teaching the special emphasis on carefully planned and pro-
> grammed instruction. . . . [It is] based on the understanding of the child's
> behavior in the relationship with the therapist and this understanding
> can . . . be used in many different ways.

In each course professional practice, clinical training, and individual supervision of the teacher-learners were closely linked components of the program. Given the dramatic societal changes affecting
the lives of children and parents during recent decades, it was inevitable
that all these programs placed special emphasis on work with families
in their training programs.

That same year (1974) Caspari presented a paper in Philadelphia,
"Parents as Co-Therapists," describing the treatment of reading disability using a family approach. This paper was the result of her work
with Dorothy Heard, Muriel Barrett, and David Campbell representing
the psychiatric and psychological disciplines. The gradual extension
of the training parameters to include other related disciplines led Caspari, Barrett and Heard (1975) to explore the potential for a multidisciplinary training (emphasis added), "using educational therapy as a
method of helping families in which there were children with learning
difficulties."

While the training program did not get off the ground, their discussions led to a series of multidisciplinary workshops, seminars, and
clinical work, organized by the department's Educational Therapy program. The concept of educational therapy with families and how this
knowledge could contribute to the amelioration of the learning problems
of children attracted more and more interest, and work with families
continued to develop. Following the death of Irene Caspari in 1976, the
emphasis on family work continued to grow. A symposium was published to commemorate the ideas she continued to generate until the
end of her life.

Barrett later organized a part-time course, "The Psychological
Factors in Learning," and introduced a weekly theoretical component.
This later evolved into a foundation year for those wishing to apply for
a daytime clinical course entitled, "The Advanced Course for Remedi-

al and Specialist Teachers" (also organized by Barrett). Concurrent with their work involving individual children, the inclusion of families became an integral part of educational therapy training for psychologists and remedial teachers. Such training was also available in an advanced course for experienced psychologists and social workers. The 1980s were a time of continuing growth and consolidation of this emerging training paradigm. It was furthered by the publication and presentation of papers which disseminated the concepts of educational therapy to a wider audience. Heard and Barrett (1982) published their work with thirty-five families of severely reading-disabled children. Their understanding of family dynamics was based on Bowlby's attachment theory and the techniques employed by educational therapists. Following Barrett's departure from the Tavistock Clinic in 1984, training in educational therapy was discontinued, but the concept of educational therapy was then advanced by FAET and subsequently extended through the establishment of the National Association of Teacher Therapists and Teachers in Multi-Disciplinary Settings (NATTATIMS), now the National Association of Teacher Therapists (NATT). Barrett and Trevitt describe training in educational therapy today in their recent book, *Attachment Behavior and the School Child: An Introduction to Educational Therapy* (1991) and note that since 1986 FAET and NATT jointly organized a training program in educational therapy at Regent's College, London, open to experienced teachers and educational psychologists working in diverse settings.

In the view of Barrett and Trevitt (1991) educational therapy is unique in its use of metaphor to examine feelings about learning educational material. This approach differentiates it from, for example, remedial teaching or child psychotherapy. The educational therapist, they emphasize, seeks to reawaken the child's capacity for play and learning to rediscover the skills he does possess.

In 1984 Barrett inaugurated the first annual meeting of educational therapists, which drew colleagues from other parts of the United Kingdom, Scotland, Norway, and one person from the United States. The following year this event was hosted by the Notre Dame Clinic in Glasgow, Scotland, where colleagues from Norway, Spain, Britain and Colombia attended. Oslo, Norway, was the site of the third annual conference, which was hosted by members of the Norwegian Association of Educational Therapists trained in the Nic Waals Institute (mentioned earlier). In 1988 this event became an international conference, jointly organized by FAET and NATT. It was held in London and attended by teachers, psychologists, art therapists, and psychotherapists from seven countries. Barrett notes it was at this conference in 1988 that they discovered, quite by chance, that educational therapy was being established in Norway at the same time as in England. In 1989 the Fifth International Conference was held in Chicago and was hosted by the Teacher Education Program of the Institute for Psychoanalysis. This event was attended by over three hundred teachers, psychologists, social workers, psychiatrists, psychoanalysts, pediatricians, language therapists, special educators, and nursery school directors, from the United Kingdom, Norway, Israel, South America, Central America and many cities in the United States.

The Teacher Education Program of the Institute for Psychoanalysis in Chicago: 1965–Present

The history of the Teacher Education Program of the Institute for Psychoanalysis in Chicago, now in its twenty-sixth year, demonstrates the utility of educational therapy, conceived as a multidisciplinary paradigm for the professional preparation of educators. Many have noticed how student learning difficulties seem to produce what can only be described as "teaching disabilities." A learning-disabled child's deep sense of personal inadequacy and failure becomes, in effect, his teacher's failure as well. The impetus for initiating the TEP in 1965 came out of the despair and the hope of a group of teachers from three inner city schools. In fact, there were several in that founding group who felt about their profession as their pupils did about school: on the verge of dropping out. It might be said that those who came to the Institute to develop an educational program responsive to their needs had done just that, dropped out of the accustomed channels of teacher education. Their presenting problems touched on familiar management issues and themes: How may the "acting out" child be maintained in a classroom? How can teachers assist parents in helping their children? How can we be both mothers and teachers to these children, and should we even try? How can teachers have a clearer understanding of themselves, and assess their own mental health and their ability to cope with certain types of problems? Despite familiar elements in their voiced concerns, new emotional undertones and subjective referents in their questions were apparent. These teachers were calling attention to the psychological realities of their classroom lives, which Sarason, Davidson, and Blatt (1962, 1986) called, "an unstudied problem in the preparation of teachers." The TEP was founded by teachers for the purpose of studying this unexplored and largely ignored panorama in the education of children and their teachers.

Looking back over the twenty-six-year history of the TEP, several more or less distinct milestones in its development can be discerned, each marked by corresponding changes in the title, goals, curriculum, methods and student composition of the program. These milestones represented the dynamic interplay between developments occurring within the program—what we (students and faculty) were discovering about learning and about ourselves in the program—and what was happening in the external world of the schools.[2]

During the first three years (1965–1968) the project was called, for lack of a more precise title, "Mental Health in the Classroom." It consisted of informal, loosely structured case seminars usually conducted by a clinical leader (social worker, psychologist, psychiatrist, psychoanalyst) and focused on case material drawn from the teachers' own classrooms. The clinical rather than the pedagogic skills of the faculty (e.g., skills in listening, observing, communicating, empathizing) accounted for the excitement, pleasure, and interest pervading the seminars. It seemed that teachers were discovering in the seminars what Kubie (1958) once called "the fifth freedom, the right to know (and acknowledge) what one feels," a right largely denied or actively suppressed at all levels of education. Teachers and faculty were discovering the truth so elegantly expressed by Greene (1981): "Learning, in one dimension is a search for some kind of coherence, some kind of sense. Learning is also a process of effecting new connections in experience and imposing diverse patterns on the inchoateness of things."

But with the "effecting of new connections," unforeseen problems and concerns began to surface signaling a need to change the format and the structure of the program. Problems over the long entrenched dichotomy between teaching and treating emerged when faculty began

to wonder about drawing the line between these two modalities of intervention. Teachers also responded to this issue. They began presenting
the most grossly damaged and intractable children, who clearly required
the kind of help that only a therapist could provide. Faculty wondered
whether this "collusion" with the clinician's psychopathology interest
might reflect a teacher/faculty learning problem—indeed, a resistance
to learning about learning. So we began to think more specifically
about the mental health tasks and competencies essential for effective
teaching, about the methods by which cognitive and affective modes of
learning could be integrated in the teaching/learning process, and about
the undergirding explanatory frameworks. A curriculum was designed,
and with it came a new phase in the development of the program. The
title of the program was changed to the "Teacher Training Program,"
reflecting these shifts in its content, scope and direction.

The basic assumptions of the program at that time were as follows:

1. The psychological realities of the educational situation require the
   teacher to be simultaneously an educator in the pedagogic sense
   and a mental health agent in the clinical sense, a "psychological
   tactician" of the learning process (Sarason, Davidson, and Blatt,
   1962). Teaching and learning are understood to be inherently affect
   laden with important consequences for both teacher and learner.
   Each teacher is subject to many pressures, both internal and external, to which she responds with many feelings. Her teaching effectiveness will be significantly enhanced if she can understand her own
   reactions to pupils, colleagues, parents and/or superiors (Fleming,
   1969).
2. Teaching requires an understanding of children's needs as well as
   the inner laws that govern mental functioning, and a recognition that
   the teacher's function is determined by both of these.
3. Teachers will be better prepared to cope with the exigencies of the
   classroom and better able to carry out their professional goals as they
   grow in self-understanding and acquire the skills of introspection
   and the capacity for empathy.

The implementation of these assumptions into a viable educational program for teachers has been the subject of ongoing study and
dialogue between faculty and students. It became increasingly clear
that "training" was an inappropriate way of describing the program

because what we were aiming for was the development of a new epistemology of teaching and learning in the educational situation. With this realization the title of the program was changed to the "Teacher Education Program." The intent was to conceptualize a psychodynamic model of teacher education that complemented in specific ways, but did not supplant, existing educational models informed by other disciplinary perspectives.

The next stage in the development of the TEP came in 1983 with the establishment of the Clinical School Services Program. While the TEP had been designed specifically to meet the clearly identified, but largely unmet, needs of classroom teachers, it was attracting increasing numbers of allied special service personnel, who were no better prepared for serving the particular needs of children and families, or for supporting and counseling teachers. To address this interdisciplinary challenge a new design of professional education was established, called the "Clinical School Services Program." The purpose was to train a new category of leadership personnel in special education, to be known as educational therapists, or consultants in special education. The candidates for this program were drawn from the ranks of existing special service personnel: learning disability specialists, guidance counselors, school psychologists, social workers, speech and language therapists, remedial reading teachers, and the like. The broad goals of this program were to develop professionals competent to identify high risk children of all ages from preschool through high school, those professionals to be skilled both as teachers and as clinicians, able to help children with learning problems, behavioral and emotional disorders, and capable of providing classroom teachers the assistance they require. A distinctive feature of the program lay in its approach to the total ecology of the school and its focus on the totality of the troubled child, his possibilities as well as his disabilities, his strengths and his weaknesses. It was designed to bring an integrated, developmental approach to the multiple dimensions of human learning in the home, the classroom, and the consulting room. This program represents our conviction that what is needed in education today is a cadre of professionals who can study the developmental and psychological factors affecting children and teachers relative to the larger context of the modern school.

The most recent stage in the development of the TEP/CSSP occurred in 1991 with the development of a new master's degree pro-

gram in Human Development and Learning to be offered jointly by the
Institute for Psychoanalysis Teacher Education Program in affiliation
with DePaul University School of Education. The purpose of this degree
program is to prepare professionals for leadership positions in the burgeoning field of human development and learning. The affiliation offers
a means of drawing upon the special knowledge, expertise and resources
of the two institutions to break new ground helping children with learning problems and their families.

This new multidisciplinary program prepares educators, administrators, and mental and physical health professionals to work in many
different settings. Graduates may serve as members of clinical teams,
work as consultants on learning problems, become educational therapists,
work with children and families in community agencies, or otherwise
advance their career goals. Our aim is to help these professionals serve
children and their families more effectively. A major focus of this program is on developing professionals equipped with knowledge and
skills to serve at-risk children and their families in a wide range of educational settings, from inner city to suburban public and private schools,
as well as in remedial and therapeutic contexts.

The preceding histories of educational therapy bear the imprint of
the clinical cultures in which they originated and developed—the Tavistock Clinic in London, the Nic Waal Child Psychiatric Institute in
Oslo, the Institute for Psychoanalysis Teacher Education Program in
Chicago, and the Child Psychiatric Clinic of Michael Reese Hospital,
also in Chicago. In each instance, the contemporary theories and propo-
sitions of clinical psychoanalysis and development research provided the
overarching theoretical frameworks.

History of Educational Therapy in Los Angeles: 1970s–Present (Summarized from article by Dorothy Ungerleider)

The following history from an account prepared by Dorothy
Ungerleider (founder and organizer of the Association of Educational
Therapists in Los Angeles, California, in the 1970s) departs in a num-
ber of ways from the models described above, although there are many

important points of convergence as well. Referring to educational therapy as "a profession," she proceeds to delineate some of the concepts that define its practitioners. Ungerleider states at the outset that "the origins (of educational therapy) are firmly rooted in the 150-year-old history of special education." She goes on to say that the Association began in 1970 when a small study group of private practitioners, frustrated by their professional isolation, began to meet monthly in Los Angeles to discuss questions arising from their practices and to explore new developments in research and remediation. The group was diverse, with members trained in different specialties and representing many geographic regions.

Ungerleider divides her account into two parts: the first delineates the various theoretical strands that have informed practice in special education and in the subarea of educational therapy, in particular. As part of this she offers a simplified chronology of the conceptual and professional development of educational therapy, organized around the insights and ideas of leading figures in special education. The second documents the history of the Association from its modest beginnings as an informal study group in 1970 to its status as a national professional organization with 325 members spread over eleven states and Australia, Canada, Israel, Japan and Venezuela in 1983. I will attempt to summarize material from each section which, I believe, best conveys how these professionals think about their work.

In her discussion of the controversies that divide practitioners, Ungerleider calls attention to the troublesome issue of professional identity that confronts those who use the title, "educational therapist." Despite the general consensus among practitioners that "educational therapy" refers to a melding of the clinical/psychotherapeutic with the pedagogical/educational, the operational titles that they give themselves (therapeutic tutor, psychopedagogist, special teacher, reinforcement therapist, clinical teacher, remedial therapist, language therapist, multidisciplined teacher and learning therapist) suggest an underlying discomfort and conflict over the term itself. Ungerleider defines educational therapy as follows:

> The educational therapist plays a unique role serving as a case manager and client advocate interfacing with parents and a multitude of professionals on a regular basis. The educational therapist has been trained in areas which emphasize the development of supportive relationships with

all professionals involved in the educational development of learning disabled individuals and is skilled in the facilitation of communication
between the individual, the family, the school and involved professionals.

This question of professional identity appears to be a recurring
issue, which is inherent in this hybrid field of practice. For example,
Ungerleider notes that "the Frostig-trained members [of the Associa-
tion] called themselves 'educational therapists' because Dr. Frostig had
provided the label, and gradually the others adopted this title because it
seemed to describe best what they did with their learning disordered
students." Nonetheless as the association grew, members of the study
group began to experience difficulty over use of this title. Frostig based
her philosophy of educational therapy on her early experiences with
August Aichorn in Vienna. "He also taught me to take into account all
the forces in the past and present life of the child and how they are perceived by the child, because these contribute so heavily to the child's
development. In other words, Aichorn was concerned with what we
now call 'lifespace'" (Frostig). When asked to define themselves, members of this initial group could not agree upon a uniform self-description.
Ungerleider invokes the old dichotomy between teaching and treating,
referring to DeHirsch's warning that "the educational therapist who sees
himself as a psychotherapist is bound to fail in both roles" (DeHirsch cited
in Ungerleider). According to Ungerleider, "an attitude prevailed that it
was too soon to see the teacher as any kind of therapist." She goes on
to quote Anna Freud who "acknowledged that the teacher should try to
understand the problem child by varying her demands on and behavior
toward him or her," cautioning meanwhile that "if this presupposes as
close a relationship between the child and the teacher as between a child
and a therapist, then it transgresses the limits within which the teacher
can work. The teacher is neither a mother nor a therapist." On the other
side of this dichotomy, Ungerleider recalls that "remedial pioneers like
Margaret Rawson knew that 'to teach' meant to teach the whole child,
with the teaching done in a way that was therapeutic" (Rawson, personal communication, May 22, 1986). In support of this view, she refers
to the way another pioneer, Ray Barsch (1960), attempted to promote the
concept of educational therapy, that is, education concerned with the
total organization of human beings with emphasis on the connection
between movement and cognition (movigenics). The chronology of

major contributors to the field of educational therapy compiled by Ungerleider reflects the deep dichotomy that pervades both the special education
and the clinical literature, and the daunting integrative task this poses for
practitioners who claim the title "educational therapist."
    Citing the two volumes edited by Hellmuth (1966, 1969), Unger-
leider calls attention to another aspect of this split that further divides
the profession. These publications trace the evolution of educational therapy from two directions:

1. *Psychoeducational Model,* which addresses perceptual and lan-
    guage disabilities and is influenced by the work of Straus and Lehti-
    nen (1947), Cruikshank (1961), Myklebust (1964), Kirk (1962),
    Kephart (1971), Mallison (1964), Frostig (1976), Barsch (1968).
2. *Mental Health Model,* which deals with the special educational
    needs of emotionally disturbed children in (a) a therapeutic milieu
    (Bettelheim [1966], Ekstein [1969], and Redl [1966]; and (b) an
    engineered classroom (Hewitt, [1966], Rhodes [1966], and Gard-
    ner [1975]).

    It is little wonder, given the vast but fragmented state of knowl-
edge about learning and the persistence of the teach or treat dichotomy
that so burdens practitioners in special education, that the Association
of Educational Therapists felt constrained to banish the resultant ambiguity by formulating their own definition and their own working rules.
They defined the purposes of their organization as follows: "(1) to
define educational therapy. . . . the role, responsibilities, ethics, and
standards of practice; (2) to spell out criteria for training and to provide
a support system for colleague consultation and continuing education."
Toward these ends, the Association has published a newsletter; organized study groups and workshops for continuing education; established university courses on principles of educational therapy; devised
a qualification procedure for the level of certified membership; initiated a community service program stimulated by the need for volunteers
to serve the Juvenile Justice System; appointed an executive advisory
board; and set the wheels in motion for a changeover from local to
national status. Their hope is that their "growth will allow the principles of educational therapy to influence the training of educators, regular or special, and allow AET a voice in national educational policy."

Conclusion: Connecting Themes

The preceding histories testify that educational therapy today is a house with many gables and rooms enough to accommodate many theories and professional disciplines. Given such diversity and the relatively recent origin of this modality of intervention, one finds not one but several versions of its history and different definitions of its purposes and methodology. The histories read like a veritable "Rashomon" tale, or do they? A closer reading reveals some connecting themes common to all, which may help chart the topography of the new space opened up by this hybrid endeavor.

Educational therapy embodies a vision of learning and teaching that compels us to rethink many deeply ingrained, taken-for-granted notions about the nature of the human learning process in education and in psychotherapy. Positioned at the margins of these two disciplinary cultures, educational therapy occupies a space where "those feelings and intuitions which daily life doesn't have a place for, and mostly seems to suppress" (Donoghue, 1983) can be acknowledged and studied. The prevalent belief that academic learning is solely an intellectual endeavor that has to do with the transmission of knowledge and skill from teacher to student presumes a one-way process—a "jug to mug" model of learning—and denies the emotionally charged nature of learning in the classroom, and the intimate complementarity and reciprocity in the teacher-student relationship. Educational therapy directs attention to the underside—the inherent subjectivity of the teaching/learning process— and offers a means to study and utilize these phenomena to facilitate and enrich student learning.

The process through which learning occurs in the classroom, though widely observed, is imperfectly understood and rarely examined. Neither teachers nor learners evidence much concern with theory about the process which so profoundly affects them both. Except for the educational therapist, one finds little interest in exploring organized explanations of learning dynamics within education. Instead the literature is dominated by work addressing the content and structure of education rather than its process. Educational therapy directs attention to the process aspects of learning, and to the utility of theory for making sense of its inevitable ups and downs. Renewed interest in the self of the learner has led to increased appreciation of the role of the subjective agenda and the empathic mode of understanding the student's experience of the curriculum (Jones, 1962).

While educational therapy focuses mainly on the therapeutic remediation of learning problems and the factors that interfere with learning, it also illuminates those contributing to the facilitation and enhancement of learning. This history of educational therapy demonstrates its generative capability and its potential contribution to our understanding of the teaching/learning process in the context of healthy growth in learning as well as in its pathology. Maintaining and cultivating its roots in teaching, illuminating the nature of good teaching in the context of healthy growth in learning will ensure its continuing vigor and vitality and prevent it from becoming an elitist specialization. As Barrett and Trevitt have pointed out, "the principles upon which educational therapy is based are relevant to all who work with children" (Barrett & Trevitt, 1991).

Notes

1. For a full description and discussion of this diagnostic tool, see Chapter 7, Duve and Zachariassen, adapted by Saltzman, this volume.
2. The chapter (Part IV, Section 1, this volume) on teacher education by the author, elaborates the implications of this learning experience.

PART

I

Theory of Educational Therapy

Introduction

I t should be immediately evident that the segregation of papers under the rubric of "theory" is somewhat arbitrary and provisional. Theory at high as well as low levels of abstraction inevitably informs all discussions of professional practice. The papers assembled in the sections on diagnosis, treatment, and training describe professional activities informed at every step by theory.

The body of theory presented in this section prompts several observations. To the extent that it defines a field of practice, it is clear that the field so defined is a portion of a larger field, one that includes practice informed by neurological-behavioral and cognitive-behavioral theories. The views these latter practitioners, who tend to emphasize technique and behavioral outcomes, are more fully represented in other sections of the book.

Since Freud's original formulation of object relations in libidinal terms and his concept of transference, object relations theories within psychoanalysis have proliferated. There now exists a virtual family of such theories, some near and some quite distant and hardly recognizable cousins of Freud's original conceptions. European practitioners have found useful the work of such theorists as D. W. Winnicott, John Bowlby, and Melanie Klein. In contrast, American educators and therapists have been strongly influenced by the work of Heinz Kohut and his followers, promulgators of self psychology, or the self-object theory of motivation, as it is sometimes called.

Drawing upon the theoretical contributions of Heinz Kohut, the work of psychologist Sylvan Tomkins, ideas from the field of cybernetics, as well as the recent observations of infant researchers, Michael Basch elucidates the role of chronic shame in producing problems in living and learning. Affects rather than drives become the salient components of motivational systems. Tension regulation and growth in competence through relationships with empathic self objects replace drive discharge via relationships with libidinal objects as the focal issues tracked by educators and therapists alike.

Paula Fuqua, like Basch, also turns to self psychology as a conceptual framework for understanding the process of human learning. She examines learning as a lifelong endeavor, taking place in formal as well as informal settings. Beginning with the notion that learning involves change or a disruption in an ongoing system, she elaborates a model that initially seems to align itself closely with that of Piaget and less closely with that of Freud. Unlike Piaget, however, Fuqua makes ample room for the influence of affect on human learning. Fuqua's learners are always involved in human relationships, and learning is always seen as influenced by those relationships. Teachers, like parents, are seen as managers of the disruptions to the equilibrium of the self of the learner, titrating the optimal level of stimulation for each learner. Beyond this, Fuqua lists four other functions teachers in formal educational settings provide. Extrapolating from Kohut, she examines teacher-pupil interaction and group psychological processes as an ever-shifting constellation of self-object relationships, which sometimes facilitate and sometimes impede learning. Fuqua demonstrates the utility of her self psychologically informed model finally in an extended example involving the supervision of a psychiatric resident learning psychotherapy.

Characterizing neurotic interferences with learning to read succinctly as the child's fear of meaning, Mia Beaumont reminds us of the enduring utility of some venerable psychoanalytic understandings of learning blocks that marked Freud's work as the preeminent system for exploring motive and meaning in human psychological functioning. Beaumont's perspective, however, extends beyond Freud to include the contributions of British object relations theorists such as Klein and Winnicott. These ideas are brought to life by a rich assortment of vividly described personal experiences. No clearer exemplification of the practice of educational therapy in the form she describes can be found than that which is evident in her own work.

Muriel Barrett and Jane Trevitt construct a theoretical rationale for educational therapy, a form of dynamic interaction, by tracing the pattern of interactions between the infant and its earliest care givers. Drawing upon the work of Bowlby, Ainsworth, and others, Barrett and Trevitt underscore the fateful significance of early attachment behavior for the infant's emotional and cognitive development. Children who have formed secure attachments will be able to tolerate the separation when they reach school age and will be able to form an appropriate attachment to the teacher. Those children for whom the attachment process has been distorted in some way are likely to experience difficulty in forming such relationships with their teachers, and consequently will learn less effectively. Basic to school success is the ability to establish a "good enough" relationship with a new attachment figure. It is this premise that the authors establish in the first of two papers.

In their second paper, the implications of this theoretical principle for the practice of educational therapy are explored. Educators and, when necessary, educational therapists, provide in their view an opportunity for a second chance at developing the appropriate adaptations that make play and learning possible. Children arrive at school with patterns of attachment behavior and attempt to replicate these with their teachers. Being able to identify particular patterns of anxious attachments, the teacher or therapist is then in a position to present a second chance by providing a deliberately contrasting relationship. Beginning with an empathic response to the child's effort to establish a familiar, although dysfunctional, kind of relationship, the therapist attempts to establish a history of more satisfactory experiences, with herself as a new object. Readers familiar with the early literature of psychoanalytic therapy and pedagogy will be reminded of the venerable advice that those transferences that facilitate progress need not be interpreted or otherwise interfered with, whereas those that do, need to be dealt with directly.

Michael F. Basch, M.D.

1

The Contribution of
Developmental Research and
Clinical Psychoanalytic Theory
to an Understanding of Learning

beginning with Freud, psychoanalysis suggested that development is based on the opportunities for discharging sexual and aggressive instincts. Freud proposed a deterministic system in which our course of development—from oral, through anal and phallic phases, culminating in the Oedipus complex—was a given that could not be altered, and that normal development always depended on the resolution of an inevitable oedipal conflict. Sexuality, and later aggression, were the two forces that determined all our motivation, and hence all our learning. This has been changed in the last forty years by the discoveries of workers in the field of infant research, and discoveries by psychoanalysts about the nature of unconscious human motivation. In both fields it has been shown, first, that issues of attachment, autonomy, and creativity are not simply extensions of the sexual instinct; second, that so-called aggressive instinctual behavior is more often than not a reaction to the frustration of failure in communication; and finally, that affect, not instinct, is the immediate motivator for action.

I have elsewhere (Basch, 1988) summarized the evidence that indicates that the basic motivation of human behavior is not the discharge of instinctual energies but the achievement of competence. Our brains are information-generating and information-processing systems that strive to create order out of the myriad of stimuli that impinge upon our sensory organs at any given moment. Using what cyberneticists call feedback mechanisms, the brain utilizes the information provided by the effects of its interaction with the environment to modify its behavior accordingly. Every human infant is born with certain inborn perceptual preferences and, as the environment impinges upon it, uses this innate propensity to generate what are called patterns of expectation. In everyday language we call these patterns of expectation "experience." The infant then, as he or she will do throughout life, builds up anticipations with which it meets future events, and in this way develops programs or scripts for dealing with the world in its various aspects. This is what we call "learning."

How does the infant know whether to reach out toward a particular situation or to avoid it? This is where affect comes in. It was already noted by Darwin (1872) that infants exhibit the full range of affects that we see in adulthood—a curious phenomenon, since infants are clearly not capable of the kind of cognitive discrimination that comes only in later childhood and in adulthood. The psychologist Silvan Tomkins (1962–1963, 1970, 1981) picked up on Darwin's work and suggested that in early infancy affect is a matter of stimulus intensity and patterning and does not involve reflective activity.

The affects of interest and joy (contentment) are the positive affects. If the intensity of stimulation is within an optimal range, the infant's interest is aroused; if there is an excess of stimulation that is suddenly decreased, the smile of joy (contentment) appears on the infant's face. The two-step process that leads to contentment takes place as follows: First, signals that are coming in but are not yet organized create overstimulation or disorganization; then, when these signals are matched with patterns of expectation, there is a sudden decrease in the intensity of stimulation; when that happens the baby smiles. In other words, it is the ordering process of the brain, which (when successful) generates a smile of contentment. So, for example, the infant attempting unsuccessfully to get his thumb into his mouth finds himself frustrated, that is, overstimulated, and gives evidence of distress. When the thumb is finally properly located between the lips, a smile of joy and contentment is noted; particular pattern of expectation associated with contentment has been matched successfully and order has been restored. We have the same experience when, having found ourselves confused by a problem, we then have an Aha! reaction when things fall into place.

When there is an overstimlation that does not result in ordering, negative affects appear. At first there is distress, and if this is not alleviated, anger follows, and if the over stimulation continues, fear evaporates.

So, as I hope you can see from this all-too-brief sketch, the infant functions from the beginning of life like a self-programming computer. It takes in stimulations, arranges them using inherited perceptual preferences, and as these innate abilities are modified by the environment, develops programs for adaptation. It knows what to avoid because some patterns of expectation are associated with negative affect, and it knows what to patterns of expectation associated with the positive affects of interest and contentment.

There is one negative affect in addition to distress, anger, and fear that I have not yet mentioned, and that is shame. Shame has been called the "keystone affect" (Broucek, 1982), because it is the affect that is associated with incompetence (White, 1960). Shame as Tomkins (1962–1963) has, suggested, and as the experiments of Papousek and Papousek (1975) and Broucek (1982) have demonstrated, occurs when a pattern of expectation associated with competence and, therefore, with contentment has been activated but meets with an obstacle that prevents fulfillment. So, for example, the infant anticipating the usual joyous reunion with his mother after awakening from a nap, reaches out to her with a broad smile and cries of excitement, only to be greeted by an angry face, which he does not realize has been caused by the fact that he has soiled himself during his sleep. This is a disorganizing experience for the infant. The pattern of expectation is not running its course, and yet the excitement he felt at her approach does not simply In this situation, as the infant grapples with the conflict between hope and reality, he must break off contact and put an end to his disappointment. His head is averted, his eyes cast down, and his face is suffused with a rush of blood indicative of thwarted excitement.

This, when we experience it in adulthood, is the emotion of shame. Shame is a protective mechanism that puts an end to activities that are not going to lead to the fulfillment originally expected (Nathanson, 1987). We see this in adulthood when we call happily to another person whom we have identified as a friend, only to find that it is a stranger's face that greets us. We have committed a faux pas, and although we may have by that time learned to dissemble the outward manifestations of shame—the averted head, the blushing, the eyes cast down—the inner experience is a very familiar and unpleasant one.

Shame, as I said, is a protective mechanism. It feels most unpleasant, but, optimally, it prevents us from going on with behavior that could only lead to further distress. Optimally, having been shamed, the infant or child should have the opportunity to undo the damage when the parent, seeing his distress, reestablishes contact and thereby restores his self-esteem—he is once again competent in the area of attachment. But there's the rub. If shame is not aborted and a sense of efficacy restored, one becomes ashamed not just for having done something that signaled incompetence, but one develops a chronic sense of shame about one's whole self. Not just "I have done something wrong," but "I am worthless."

The psychoanalyst Heinz Kohut (1971, 1977, 1984), in his study of narcissistic personality disorder, demonstrated the effects of chronic, pathologic shame on the sense of self of his patients. Kohut discovered the self-object theory of motivation, which fits very well with the work of developmental researchers that I have briefly sketched above. Kohut described how the infant, because of his relative cognitive and motoric helplessness, frequently requires the intercessions of the care givers around him. Not only do infants need physiologic support to still hunger and thirst, they need what he called the "psychological oxygen" that an empathic response to their needs can supply. Empathy, as Kohut used it here, consists of the parents' ability to put themselves in, the place of the distressed, frightened, or angry infant—or, for that matter, the interested or joyful infant—and respond appropriately to the need expressed by the particular affective display of the baby. It is the parental intervention in completing the infant's pattern matching that generates what Kohut called a "selfobject" experience. By "selfobject" he meant that the infant does not identify, for example, his mother as such; he registers only that there was a need and that it was fulfilled—the mother functioning as an extension of his self, meeting the need for organization, order, and competence that the infant himself is unable to achieve. From the objective point of view of the observer, the mother has done something for the infant; from the subjective experience of the infant, he wanted something and he got it, order is restored, and he has proven himself competent. When appropriate self-object experiences are not forthcoming, the infant experiences chronic incompetence and with it a chronic sense of shame. Most commonly then, chronic shame is the result of repeated self-object failure during early development.

Seen most dramatically in the patients with narcissistic personality disturbances, but present in most of the patients we see in psychotherapy, a shame-imbued self cannot continue to develop normally. The efforts expended in avoiding shame, or what is anticipated will be occasions for shame, preclude greeting the possibility for new experiences with reasonable interest. Chronic shame, in other words, seriously interferes with learning.

As Kohut demonstrated in his clinical work, what needs to be done for these patients is first to immerse oneself emphatically in their shame-ridden world and to convey to these patients by one's understanding that they are still seen as individuals worthy of respect and care. Then, eventually, when patients feel reasonably secure in the therapeutic situation, one explains to them in fractionated and acceptable amounts, what one has understood about them, eventually helping them to gain insight into the empathic or self-object failures that led to their difficulties.

So, as I have suggested, one of the greatest obstacles to learning in childhood and adulthood is the problem of chronic shame. It is a challenge for the educator to differentiate between the child who has an organic deficit that interferes with learning, and the child who appears to have such a deficit but is actually suffering from the inhibition that shame—a chronic sense of shame—has foisted upon him or her. In either case, shame must be reckoned with in any child who has learning problems. Although shame can be the primary issue, the child with an organic deficit will also, secondarily, develop a sense of shame as he becomes increasingly aware of his lack of competence, and that sense of shame will interfere with his benefiting from attempts to help him with his basic problem.

It is in dealing with the child's shame that the work of the psychotherapist and the educator becomes intermingled. Just as we psychotherapists have to educate our patients eventually to what is going on within them, so too does the educator have to understand and respond to the child's sense of shame psychotherapeutically, the educational task is to be joined successfully. The antidote for shame is the experience of competence, especially competence in human communication. It is the educator who has the opportunity to evaluate the child's shame-proneness and subsequent withdrawal from the educational task and to introduce, bit by bit, those opportunities for communication that may very well undo some of the earlier damage.

A significant obstacle to both therapist and educator in dealing with an individual's shame-induced difficulty is the sense of shame that a shamed person generates in us. This is what is technically called countertransference in the field of psychoanalysis. The effects of the vicious circle of incompetence, leading to shame, and shame leading to further incompetence, presents us with individuals who cannot learn readily, who cannot benefit from our ministrations. As a result, *we* experience incompetence, shame, and a need to defend ourselves. One of the most obvious ways of protecting ourselves is to turn away from these patients, or students, as the case may be, and to write them off as too limited to benefit from our efforts. Only if we can understand and thereby overcome our own feeling of helplessness and the subsequent shame that a shame-prone individual's inability to function generates within us can we ultimately help such a person.

This is not, by any means, easy. The child beset by chronic shame who comes into the classroom is not necessarily just going to sit there in a withdrawn, depressed fashion. As a matter of fact, that sort of child is worse off than the one who tries to demonstrate some level of effectiveness by being unruly, disturbing others, or being openly oppositional to the teacher. This latter sort of child is at least still hopeful of achieving self-esteem, albeit in a self-defeating way. The obstreperous, unruly child, however, makes the teacher feel even more incompetent than the depressed child does; he shames the teacher in front of the rest of the class by openly demonstrating the teacher's inability to carry out his or her functions, and in doing so invites active or passive retaliation. If not helped at this stage of development, such a child usually grows up to be an adult who can only continue to resort to self-defeating patterns throughout life. It is not unusual to find that antisocial adults have just such a history.

I continually encounter shame-induced difficulties in the psychotherapeutic situation, but that is a very privileged and unusual kind of relationship in which the patient is, at least to some extent, aware that there is something wrong, and has come to the therapist to do something about it. The child in the classroom may present a much more difficult problem. In many cases, however, the teacher does have an advantage over the therapist. The adults that I see have developed a chronic, well-defended pattern of dealing with shame that, although it gets them into difficulties, is deeply imbedded and has come to have secondary gain for the patient and is therefore more difficult to relinquish. The child, being in his or her formative years, may still be in a position to develop more readily what Kohut called compensatory structures. That is, given the relative malleability of the still-immature character, the child is ready to share with a teacher those experiences that can offset the damage done by the empathic failures of the early years of development.

If psychoanalysis has taught us anything, it is that it is never too late to influence positively the patterns of expectation that form an individual's character—the sooner, the better; therefore, it is the educator who has the opportunity of exercising an early positive influence on the shame-damaged child and, one hopes, someday putting us, the psychotherapists, out of business.

Paula B. Fuqua, M.D.

2

A Model of the Learning Process
Based on Self Psychology

earning is something we do in school, something we do in therapy, and something we do day to day. It is integral to the very act of living. Without learning we would not adapt or grow, we would become stagnant and rigid. Ultimately, we would die. The primitive man who did not notice that the lion lay in wait behind rock every day, or that certain plants caused vomiting while other, were easily digested and life sustaining would quickly disappear from the list of our forefathers. The modern political refuges who came to our city but could not learn our language, our monetary system, or the routine of bus and subway travel, would soon be hungry and without shelter, barely existing. We must learn in order to survive and thrive. The process of learning goes beyond structured educational settings to the very fabric of our existence.

Yet with all we have to recommend the activity, we still find ourselves resisting the process at times. Even as you are reading now with the hope that you will hear something new and enlightening, you must be looking simultaneously for the familiar landmarks of ideas already mastered, signposts pointing toward familiar ground. Too much newness all at once is overwhelming to us, and even when we seek out new knowledge, we find ourselves avoiding the process while simultaneously stifling the urge to pursue it.

To illuminate this paradox, I would like to propose a model of the educational process based on self psychology. While none of the elements in the model is wholly new, I believe the model unifies many facts about learning we already know in isolation. It provides an overarching structure for understanding and a systematic road map for approaching new learning situations, as teacher, supervisor, or therapist. It also provides a way to understand our reluctance and failure to learn. The emphasis in this model is on actualizing the initiative of the learner and on seeing the learning process as an optimizable unfolding of inner potentials, in contrast to approaches that emphasize an externally motivated experience, or one that sees the learner as suffering from a dysfunction that must be overcome in order to master what must be learned. Psychoanalytic approaches to learning, in particular, often take the latter approach. The assumption that all learning would come easily if it were not for some conflict creating resistance seems to have been the guiding principle in understanding the process of psychoanalytic supervision, for example (Fleming and Benedek, 1966; Ekstein and Wallerstein, 1958). I believe a shift to a self-psychological model will offer a more positive basis from which to conceptualize the whole process of education and at the same time provide a more extensive psychoanalytic theory of learning than we have had heretofore. In the past, as David Rapaport (1960) has observed, classical psychoanalysis has not had a serviceable learning theory of its own, and in my view it has taken to cannibalizing Piaget as a stopgap measure. The shift to a theory based on the self as an organizing concept provides us with an opportunity to extend the psychoanalytic theoretical model to encompass learning and to fill this gap. I will specify both the new approach and the structure that arises out of it.

What do I mean by learning? For my present purposes I will say that learning is the incorporation of new facts, perceptions, and ideas. It is also the mastery of new processes, styles, and formats of thinking and interacting, both with each other and with the environment. Put more simply, we learn content and we learn processes. In the category of content, I would put knowledge of the names of U.S. presidents, awareness that a water molecule is a combination of two hydrogen atoms and one oxygen atom, and the perception that Chicago is located along the southwestern shore of Lake Michigan. In contrast to "things" learned, processes we learn are ways of approaching matters. In eighth-grade cooking class I learned to wash the glasses and shiniest objects first so these objects would not be clouded by the grease from the pots and pans washed later. In college I learned sophisticated processes of thinking and problem solving: comparing and contrasting, the use of syllogistic logic, and how to think inductively. One also learns physical skills, which I would include under processes learned.

An essential aspect of learning is the addition of something new to an existing structure, producing a necessary change in that structure. The structure that is modified is both the body of knowledge already held by the learner and his self system. What is learned changes what was preexisting. This has profound and extensive implications for the activities of teaching and learning. I will come back to this point later.

What does self psychology have to do with all this? To answer, let me backtrack a moment and describe a few of its fundamentals. In 1971 Kohut described persons as striving for an overarching feeling of cohesion as opposed to a subjective feeling of fragmentation. A person with a sense of self-cohesion feels lively, effectual, and confident. A person who is fragmented complains of listlessness, disorganization, inability to concentrate or think straight, feelings of depletion, and difficulty following through on things. Sometimes, she also feels enraged. The universal urge in the psyche is to try to reinstate a sense of cohesion whenever it is disrupted.

Self psychology developed out of a clinical need to go beyond Freud's earlier theory that the unfolding of the psyche was the result of conflict generated by sexual and aggressive drives. Kohut (1977) elaborated his model, describing the experience of self-cohesion as a dynamic equilibrium, a tension arc between the opposing poles of a person's ambitions and ideals. Empirically, he observed that a state of self cohesion is developed and maintained best when a person has available to him both adequate mirroring (affirming admiration for his real qualities, talents, and accomplishments) and idealizable others whom he can admire and emulate. Mirroring may also include emotional states that are experienced as mergerlike or twinlike. The "significant other" who supports these states is experienced as a part of the person's own self, like a part of one's own body. The descriptive term for this mirroring person and for the person who provides a focus for idealization is self object.

Self-cohesion includes, but is not confined to, one's subjective idea about one's attributes—one's subjective identity. Am I tall or short, clever or dull, sexy or prim? It also arises out of one's goals and values. Am I an ambitious yuppie, aspiring to great wealth or a free-spirited intellectual? Firmly religious or skeptical? Liberal or conservative? Finally, are all these qualities solidly ensconced or fluctuating and easily changed? A cohesive self is one in which the basic substructure is relatively firmly defined, and one in which modifications can be introduced without endangering the overall structure. The essential structure of the self, including the ambitions and ideals, goals and values, is also called the nuclear self.

Within this model, learning represents a potential disruption of a stable, cohesive self because it is an attempt to incorporate something new. This quality of newness is a defining characteristic of learning in my view, not a side effect. It demands a change in the self structure, and by implication this means that if the self structure is not changed, nothing has been learned. How the learner and his environment relate to this potential disruption has a great deal to do with the ease with which one learns. It will be obvious right away that too much disruption will push the learner toward a more fragmented, less cohesive state and that he will have to spend his energy reestablishing an acceptably stable state before he can continue to learn. This factor of destabilization is often what leads us to resist learning.

On the other hand, it is also true, though less obvious, perhaps, that one can suffer from too little novelty in one's life as well as too much, for both biological and adaptive reasons. It is well established that babies from the beginning seek novel stimuli in acceptable quantities (Stern, 1985). This fact illustrates that there is a biological need for a certain amount of newness to sustain the baby's lively engagement with the world. It is adaptive because, as I pointed out earlier, there is survival value in learning. Thus a cohesive self is not a static structure but an ongoing, stable dynamism. Just as we need some food to go on living, we need some newness. Too little food starves us and leads to decline; so does too little novelty (Moraitis, 1988). Too much stimulation also impairs our ability to cope in different ways. So a cohesive self is not a rigid self, and maintaining self-cohesion is not a task with an end point, but an ongoing, continually active process, like metabolism.

It is probably also true that the particular amount of newness that each person requires and the amount that is excessive is different for each person (Thomas and Chess, 1977). We all have our individual set points based on temperamental variables that have an underlying genetic basis. A comfortable learning situation is one in which the self structure can be modified in a sufficiently stimulating, enlivening way without endangering the stability of the overall, evolving structure.

Socioculturally, we have many customs, that help us tolerate the process of disruption and reintegration involved in learning. These assist in keeping the disruption at optimal levels. When Joe, a recent high-school graduate, goes off to college, for example, he has a ready-made role to assume. As he leaves family and high-school achievements behind, he is provided externally with a new set of expectations and behaviors (the college-student role), which will serve to organize him until he develops his own modified internal equilibrium. Part of the student role is that it is okay not to know, without feeling like a failure, because one is just beginning to learn. One does not have to be humiliated by ignorance. Since humiliation disrupts self-cohesion, the inbuilt, partial protection from this untoward event promotes effective learning.

Another aspect of the college-student role is that one belongs to a group of other students in the same situation who function as mirrors and twins, stabilizing one's self perceptions. In addition, the group ideal supports learning. For example, when I was in medical school, we all aspired to become academic practitioners. There was contempt for the LMD—local medical doctor, usually the referring general practitioner. This depreciation was clearly undeserved, but it enhanced our continued striving to learn more and belong to the elite. Peer social pressure intensified the identification with our teachers. The group norm and an aspect of the medical, student role was ongoing learning. It was admirable to quote the latest journal article on your patient's illness during rounds. This set of expectations provided a structure that supported the absorption of much new information within an assigned identity which shored up whatever crumbling states of self cohesion we medical students were experiencing. In contrast, the norms in my high school were anti-intellectual. Those who stood out academically were thought to be weird by other students. Here there was a bias against learning beyond a certain moderate amount. This eroded individual efforts. "Excessive" learning had a destabilizing effect on one's self-cohesion because it put one at odds with one's peers. This has a potentially powerful negative effect on learning during the adolescent period when peer approval is so important in identity formation. The culture and role expectations were undermining to learning and in that sense nonadaptive.

Training and indoctrinating experiences like Marine boot camp and "brain washing" take advantage of the need for self-cohesion in a very different way. Instead of supporting a minimum of acceptable, ongoing continuity of the self, these experiences seem to do everything possible to break it down. They remove familiar clothing and personal possessions and take the person out of his usual physical surroundings. Within such circumstances, the impelling need to reestablish an equilibrium makes it possible to ingest massive doses of information, new forms of behavior, and a new identity as one strives to reorganize with whatever is at hand.

To the extent that college, too, is away from home and friends, the effect is similar. The college experience also breaks down existing structures and roles to make way for something new. It is easy to see that this dissolution might promote some students becoming more active, curious, and flexible learners. Others less secure might be too disrupted by being away from home and might have more energy to learn if in a familiar environment, living at home and attending classes at a commuter college.

The stability of the self structure depends on affective as well as cognitive factors. This point is important because many learning theories, including Piaget's, omit affect, whereas self psychology makes a place for it to have an important effect on self-cohesion and therefore on the whole learning process. This seems to fit better with the ordinary experience of countless teachers and learners than a purely cognitive theory does.

Within the framework I have described, the teacher's role can be conceptualized as the "manager" of the disruptions to the self of the learner, keeping them at an optimal level as much as possible in order to foster the process of incorporation of whatever is to be learned. This practically impossible task includes five elements:[1]

1. The teacher assesses the student's baseline biological capacities as much as they can be known. This means observing the student's temperament and, when possible, getting a history of the infantile period. Was he quick or slow to adapt to new situations, to strangers? Was he a curious, active baby or a placid one? It means noticing the student's later achievements in learning situations and attending to the student's self report both about his past and his present in regard to what can be inferred about underlying biologic givens. The teacher tries to understand the impact of these biological and genetic factors on the student's ability to maintain a cohesive self organization, especially in the learning situation. The obvious example is the learning-disabled student, who may have a short attention span on a constitutional basis, which leads to failures, low self-esteem, and a concept of himself as damaged and inadequate. This discouraged person will be reluctant to take on new challenges that might expose him to further failure, overwhelming shame, and fragmentation. Here a responsive teacher will adjust the learning challenges to manageable levels that can be successfully completed, as she attempts not only to help the student master as much material as he can, but also to help him achieve and maintain an acceptable level of self-cohesion by avoiding failure, shame, and fragmentation in the same process.

   Inversely, with a student who has an exceptional memory, for example, the teacher will attempt to protect the learner from understimulation, which can also lead to boredom, feelings of depletion, and even fragmentation. Here we may find the bright underchallenged student who starts talking to his neighbors in class, making rude gestures, and generally disrupting things as he tries to restimulate and enliven himself when he doesn't have enough to do. Again, the teacher will intervene to give him more appropriate stimulation.

   In the case of an older or adult student, the biological assessment may be informal eyeballing, but some speculation about the temperamental baseline is still useful.

2. The teacher assesses the climate and stability of the student's peer and family relationships outside the classroom environment. Are

the parents divorcing or has there been a recent death, illness, marriage, or birth in the family? Is the student supported by a well-
developed network of friends? Is he distracted by burdensome
financial worries? Every teacher knows how events outside the
learning situation can affect a student's self-cohesion and capacity to learn. I do want to stress additionally that these events need
to be evaluated in terms of their effect on the self-cohesion of the
learner. Many apparently interfering outside situations are handled well by particularly stable persons with adequately firm self
structures, and, conversely, some things that would seem inconse-
quential to us can be enormously interfering.
3. The teacher, evaluates the student-teacher relationship. Is there
trust on both parts? Is there a good alliance around the tasks? What
is the transference on either side, especially in regard to self-object
needs for mirroring, twinship, or idealization? This relationship is
a very important parameter to be aware of, particularly in respect
to whether it is promoting enough stability to learn but not so much
as to suppress it. A highly structured teacher with many rules and
expectations may shore up the eroding self of some students,
enabling them to learn effectively, while others may find the same
approach stifling. The match between student and teacher is enormously important. The occurrence of transference is probably
ubiquitous, and the important question is not whether it is there
(because it usually is) but whether its character is facilitative or
undermining.
4. The teacher assesses and influences the group dynamics within the
classroom, if such there be. One wants to decide how best the class
can function as a unit. Is a quiet atmosphere helpful or inhibiting,
for example? Is there one student who needs so much attention
that he disrupts meaningful continuity for others, or one who is so
disturbed that he makes the rest of the class too anxious to learn optimally? If so, it is the teacher's job to intervene. An example comes
to mind from my college years of a student who, looking back on
it, must have been a paranoid schizophrenic. He had a well-worked-
out delusional system involving a complicated plan to restructure
the U.S. Postal Service. He was in many of my philosophy seminars. On the slightest pretext he would hop up to the blackboard to
diagram his plan, interrupting class discussions in courses like

ethics or medieval philosophy, which had nothing to do with the post office. What a challenge for the teachers! Somehow they managed to contain him tactfully and skillfully and thereby to preserve everyone's chances to learn, including the unfortunate disrupter's.

One can assess group dynamics in terms of their effect on each individual and attempt to compromise among the many different needs involved, but Pajak (1981) has pointed out that one can also regard the group as a more or less comprehensive whole. The common need of all for the expression of a proud self and the shared possession of ideals and even admired heroes creates a cohesion at the level of the group. This conceptual leap to a single cohesive unit makes the task of the teacher as a manager of multiple selves in a group at least conceivable. Otherwise a group process is so complex that it becomes a fragmenting task even to enumerate the many ongoing effects on the individuals in the class (Stone and Whitman, 1977).

5. Finally, and perhaps most important, the teacher both assesses and affects the internal psychological world of the student. Again, this is from the point of view of his self-cohesion and kind of maneuvers the student routinely engages in to maintain his stability. How vulnerable is he in general? Does he need large or small amounts of praise and encouragement when he does well? What happens when the student's narcissistic needs are not met? Can he tolerate a great deal of tension and disappointment or almost none? If his tension tolerance is small, for example, does the student need smaller, shorter assignments to learn effectively without getting overwhelmed?

The teacher evaluates these five areas in more depth than I can encompass here, often without thinking about it in a formal way. The purpose of my listing them is to make the approach explicit so that we may apply it more thoroughly and consistently. Once a teacher has made an evaluation, she formulates a teaching plan based on what she has gleaned. Her teaching tools (parameters of intervention) are her own behavior and the amount, type, and format in which she presents material. Obviously, this is a general systems approach,[2] but it is filtered through its effects on the intrapsychic world of the learner. The system is the self of the learner.

At this point, one may well ask, "But what is 'optimal' disruption?"

How are teachers to know? To borrow from Marian Tolpin (1971), how did Goldilocks know when the porridge was just right? Retrospectively, the teacher can see whether the student has learned something. But in the moment, this is not very useful. I believe that what is an optimal amount of destabilization is individual for each student and student-teacher pair. The biological baseline and what has worked before are clues. Finding the right mix is an art just as it is in doing therapy, and an essential part of that art is trial and error. What is optimal is what works, and assessing what this is, trying things and readjusting, is the ongoing dynamism of teaching, just as it is the dynamism of doing psychotherapy or of maintaining one's own self stability.

Of course, this means checking continually, not just when a course or other learning experience has ended. This is what quizzes for example. They are as much a check of the teacher's functioning and a clue to readjustment as of the student's achievement. If Professor Thomas sees that Ms. Novak has not understood the supply and demand curve, he will readjust his teaching plan in relation to her, taking into account his comprehensive assessment of the ways her self-cohesion is maintained optimally. This might result in any number of changes. Perhaps he will present a more thorough explanation in class using more visual aids, recommend further reading, or suggest that she transfer to a class in which she is separated from her boyfriend, who is distracting.

It must not be forgotten that the self-report of the learner is as important as test performance assessing what works. Is the student enjoying the process or hating it? Is he bored, pleasantly stimulated, or overwhelmed and panicking? This belongs in the category of the intrapsychic world of the student. If the student feels zest and enthusiasm for what he is learning, he will probably remember it longer and feel motivated to go on to further study in the same area. On the other hand, even if he gets an A in calculus but feels deadened by a monotonous or understimulating approach, he will be less likely to try to incorporate learning about calculus into any ongoing version of his functioning (i.e., into his permanent self structure). He will be less likely to want to be an engineer, for example.

Within the matrix of the student-teacher relationship the teacher evaluates and modifies his or her behavior viewed in terms of its self-object functions for the sake of promoting learning. This means the teacher assesses whether the student needs compensatory mirroring or an idealized role model (Wolf, 1988). The teacher tries to stabilize the student's self-cohesion so that the student can learn more effectively. But in addition, he or she examines the five dimensions I have outlined and formulates an overall interpretation of available information and a plan for effective interacting based his or her knowledge of the impact of all the known factors on the self—cohesion of the student. Acting as a self object in concrete encounters with the student is only one part of this overall task, although it may be the point where all the other understanding comes to bear most intensely.

Here is an example of a situation in which a doctoral student in English literature had a weakness in her self structure based on long-standing pathology. I choose this example because it is taken from my own professional experience, which is mainly with adults. I believe the same principles would apply in a modified way to any student at any age.

Ms. Masters was always unsure that she really had earned her previous good grades. She grew up devoted compliantly to a needy mother who was preoccupied with appearances. She faced the mandate to do an original piece of research with trepidation. Her subjective idea about herself did not include being smart and capable. Her teachers, while reassuring, left her to flounder on her own as far as concrete suggestions were concerned. Ms. Masters panicked. She finally found a faculty member who would sit down with her and scrutinize her emerging ideas. Ms. Masters' thoughts and ideas then became acceptable; that is, she identified with the teacher's cohesive identity as a scholar to shore up her own identity temporarily. In Kohut's terms this was a fortuitous, growth-promoting, temporary merger transference with an idealized self object, stabilizing Ms. Masters self-cohesion until she could develop a further identity of her own as an adequate scholar. With this help she was able to continue, and develop an *original* idea. Her self structure had crumbled when faced with the challenge of confronting the "not yet known." Her compliant defenses, developed in her relationship with her mother, didn't work in these circumstances. Provided with reinforcement via an adequate, idealized self object, Ms. Masters was able to function successfully. This was not psychotherapy in the usual sense; it was meant to help her learn and be intellectually creative. Yet I cannot help but think that her successful dissertation might have had a mutative effect in solidifying her subsequent scholarly identity. In fact, Ms. Masters has gone on to establish herself as a successful scholar and academician in the English literature department of a major university.

I believe that the model I propose is particularly well suited to address learning as an outgrowth of the self rather than as the result of either conflict or deficiency. The urge to learn is part of the urge for increasing adaptation via the desire for novelty and change that is our genetic heritage. This is as true of a child as it is of an adult. Does this mean I think a child would come to want to learn to read and do arithmetic on his own if given the chance and the proper support to follow through? Yes, I do. In fact, one can think about the idea that learning temporarily disrupts self-cohesion for the purpose of maintaining it at a higher level from the perspective of infant development. One of the major reasons that early development is able to proceed at such an enormously speedy pace is that there is so little preexisting structure to be disrupted as new skills and bits of information are accrued. When there *is* internal structure, it is less complex than in later life. For example, compare Baby Gloria's learning her first words and the letters of the alphabet with her brother John's struggle to learn Spanish in high school. She has no prior language skills to contend with. He has a well-developed knowledge of English to somehow disengage while he struggles to remember strange new sounds and spellings. It is this very difference, of course, that is the rationale for learning foreign languages in the earlier years.

Despite the relative lack of structure in infancy, there is *some* structure, which does get disrupted with the acquisition of something new. This accounts for the common observation mothers make that their children become disorganized and fussy for several days before completing a new developmental step. Susie, eleven months old, suddenly won't go down for her nap and cries when she is bathed, though she used to love splashing energetically with her boats and ducky. Jane, her mother, is dismayed. Things seemed to be going so well and Jane was beginning to think that she had gotten this motherhood thing figured out finally. Now all is again in disarray. Then suddenly Susie starts drinking from a cup and loses interest in breast and bottle. Gradually over the next week her behavior returns to its former smooth level. The rough spot was a temporary fragmentation of Susie's existing rudimentary self structure caused by a biological thrust that introduced new skills and interests. The psyche, temporarily and partially overwhelmed, gradually accommodated the new capacities and they become "old," incorporated into a newly revised and restabilized self structure. The more sudden, intense, and thoroughgoing the biological thrusts, the more fragmenting to existing structure they will be and the more disorganization will result. This is similarly true in adolescence, when the biological changes that affect sexual function and cognitive capacity as well as evolving social expectations can also be disruptive. Although the details of what is changing and the level of underlying, pre-existing structures are very different in adolescence and infancy, the basic process of change is the same.

My approach places a great emphasis on the "newness" of learning. In this regard there is a spectrum of newness, which is also addressed by Piaget's distinction between assimilation and accommodation. Assimilation is the incorporation of new information and experience into existing schemata, and accommodation is the modification of existing schemata to conform to new experiences. The assimilation process is less "new" and less disruptive to self-cohesion. The learning of new vocabulary would be an instance in which relatively little internal change is required as more details are added to a preexisting schema. Adding bits of data to a computer program is an analogy. Coming to understand the relationship of physical cause and effect as the infant does over the first twenty-four months of life is an example of accommodation, the infant's internal schemata changing in response to the impingement of externals (as maturing neurological capacities make this possible, of course). Here the analogy is to putting an altogether new program into the computer. If there is a difference between my approach and Piaget's, it lies in the greater emphasis I would place on the learning process as a spectrum of internal structural change, starting from zero, progressing to low quantities of change Piaget would call assimilation, and proceeding further to higher amounts of change that Piaget would then call accommodation. My model is more "analog," his more "digital."

Another difference between a self-psychological theory and Piaget's theory is that the existing metapsychology of self psychology encompasses affect. When we speak of a cohesive self we include an affective dimension, *prima facie* as part of the nuclear self. Piaget does not include affect as an essential part of learning; learning is purely cognitive.

It also follows that in my position there is a relative hierarchy of newness. What is newer and more globally and structurally mutative involves more learning than that which is less new. In such a scheme there will obviously be a relationship between knowledge and creativity, since both revolve around the novel. Arbitrarily, knowledge is what goes inside, creativity is what comes out. By these definitions, newly discovered knowledge represents a creative expression on the part of the discoverer.[3] Within this framework, one can understand the genius as someone who, through particular biological capacities or previous experiences, has a personality structure (state of self organization) uniquely suited to tolerate the new without fragmentation and with minimal disruption.

One such personality type, perhaps the healthiest, is the person whose stable self-concept includes constant change. Such a person will be more suited to learn and to be creative than a person of exactly the same biological capabilities whose self-concept includes little change. This fortunate sort of person always likes to look at things a different way and does not find the dizzying view of things turned upside down too upsetting. The physicist Richard Feynman seems to me to be such a person, based on his biography.

There are other types of genius as well, however. The vulnerable artist whose inner life always seems in disarray may stabilize himself by creating paintings that objectify his inner states, providing an external focus for needed mirroring. Here the process of creativity is not the result of a stably functioning self structure, but the result of the process of attempting to create a stable self. A sculptor, for example, may create a work full of sharp lines and tension, hoping to express his emotional state and generate a response both empathic and appreciative. As a concurrent effect, the artist may provide us with a new perspective produced out of his unique inner life, such as the new way of seeing light that the Impressionists introduced.

A third type of creative genius may have grown up in a repressive home and kept his thoughts and ideas secret, thereby safeguarding their uniqueness and idiosyncrasy. When the ideas are shared later in a novel, painting, or new scientific theory, we see the creativity involved. Those who are familiar with Franz Kafka's life might agree that he fits in here. Of course, there are artists, writers, scientists, and other creative geniuses with very different dynamics to their creativity. My point is that all must have found a personality structure that tolerates a great deal of novelty one way or another.

Sometimes the creative person needs some externally stabilizing resource to face his radical new insights without fragmenting or withdrawing, just as Ms. Masters did during her dissertation work. Kohut has written about this in the case of Freud, who needed Wilhelm Fliess as an idealized self object in order to develop and tolerate his own creative insights via his self analysis (Kohut, 1976). Fliess's facilitative function for Freud as described by Kohut is similar to the function of the teacher in my scheme. The presence of a self object stabilizes self-cohesion so that the disruptive change in structure initiated by the creative process can be tolerated until what is new becomes "old" intrapsychically. Since really radical new ideas inevitably erode the idealizing pole of self structure by virtue of overturning previously cherished beliefs, it is usually true that there will be some compensating modicum of idealization in the relationship to a stabilizing self object whatever the need for mirroring.

Conceptually, I have sketched a model of the learning process in the foregoing paragraphs. It can be described paradigmatically in the following statements:

1. Learning is biologically driven and is adaptive (within limits).
2. Learning is defined as a change in self structure. This occurs at a physicochemical level and at a conceptual (organizational) level.
3. Learning is facilitated by some structural disruption.
4. Learning is interfered with by too much disruption.
5. The individual tolerances for the amount of disruption that is optimal are (a) biologically determined and (b) experiential insofar as the previously existing self structure is concerned.
6. Learning can be the result of (a) a need to increase novelty or (b) a need to increase cohesion and therefore to decrease the amount of change by incorporating the changes into a new stability.
7. Learning is facilitated by the presence of a knowledgeable self object who helps manage the level of structural change, disruption, and so forth.

I would now like to turn to the process of supervision of psychotherapy as an example of a learning process to which the model of the teacher as a manager of states of self-cohesion in the student can be helpfully applied. In using my model, the supervisor must assess all the parameters I have listed above.

1. He will formulate as best he can the biological baseline capacities of the therapist-supervisee.
2. He will garner some idea of the supervisee's current outside life situation on his tolerance for change and novelty.
3. He will evaluate both the actual current and potentially developing relationship between himself and the supervisee in regard to its effect on self-cohesion. This means understanding his own expectations and needs from the student (as well as vice versa) and understanding the way the two interact in a dynamic matrix.
4. He will assess the group environment if there is one. This would apply to instances of group supervision and case conferences and might include persons outside the room at times, such as an administrator, who may have a great effect on the supervisee. It also involves the goals and values of the professional groups to which the therapist belongs, which may affect the learning process.
5. He will try to get some idea of the internal world of the supervisee. In what way does he usually insure his self-stability? What type of self objects does he need and how tolerant is he of disorganization, of not knowing, and of disappointment in cherished beliefs? Does he seem to need a lot of positive reinforcement or does he get along pretty well with minimal amounts of affirmation?

One gathers this data in a very ordinary way. It surprises me that I have not seen the following recommendations in the literature. Perhaps they are too basic even to be mentioned, yet I know of many instances where these suggestions have not been followed, so it must be important to point them out.

To begin with, it is my practice to ask the supervisee to tell me about himself and to offer to tell him about myself. I ask about his professional development and interests, where he has been trained, what he has found helpful and disappointing in his education up to this point, and what his special interests and future plans are. What is his special expertise and where is he hoping for guidance? I ask about his personal life in a nonintrusive way. Where was he born and where did he grow up? Is he married? Does he have children?

I also tell the supervisee about my own background—my personal and professional development—in a similar manner. Sometimes I find it a good idea to be the first to start because this may put the other person at ease if he is feeling defensive about being scrutinized. Through this process we can begin to find where our matches might be and whether or not I can help him in the way he wants and needs. Obviously the center of this process is around the initiative of the student, and all the activities one engages in are pointed toward supporting a process generated out of his initiative. One assumes the supervisor has mastered the material being taught (in this case, the knowledge and skill of doing therapy), but conveying information is not the goal of his activity. It may at times be the chosen technique to achieve the goal, but the goal is to support the ongoing interest, curiosity, striving, mastery, and creativity of the supervised therapist. Barring a disaster, the patient's progress in therapy serves mainly as an indicator of the progress of the therapist.

The emphasis in a self-psychological approach is on actualizing the goals of the supervisee. This contrasts with much of what has been written in the psychoanalytic literature. Ekstein and Wallerstein (1958) and Fleming and Benedek (1966, 1983) all see the task of the supervisor as one of overcoming unconscious resistances in the supervisee. Their emphasis is negative in the sense that learning blocks or problems become the focus. In my view this approach has a judgmental cast to it and leads to a defensive approach on the part of the supervisee. In contrast, Dewald and Dick (1987), also psychoanalysts, see the need for praise and reward when supervisees do well (mirroring) and the need for the supervisor to function as a master to an apprentice and to think out loud to illustrate the therapist's functioning (idealized self object). These are more humane ideas, consistent with a self-psychological approach, though they are presented from a classical base by Dewald and Dick. In that theoretical framework, their suggestions seem somewhat *ad hoc*. What I am adding is the expectation that a consistent effort be made from the beginning to understand *in extenso* just what particular types of interactions are most helpful to the supervisee in actualizing his own goal of mastery and his own self-cohesion. By adding the theoretical superstructure of self psychology to Dewald and Dick's ideas, one gains a coherent rationale for their suggestions.

As in the activity of teaching in general, the supervisor also "checks" on how effectively the student is learning. This is as it is

done in the classroom, but by asking the supervisee, what his concep-
tualizations are and how the supervision is going; that is, what he feels
about the relationship, what is helpful, and what is not.

Here is a case that illustrates some of the above points. Dr. W.
came to me as a second-year resident transferring to his current program
from a hospital in another city. He was in his late twenties and belonged
to a fundamentalist religious sect. On our first meeting, when I introduced myself and suggested we share information about our backgrounds, interests, and past professional experiences in order to get to
know each other, Dr. W. blurted out that he had come to Chicago
because his fiancée was here and that they had broken up a few weeks
after he arrived. To make matters worse, a teacher he admired had just
left his program precipitously. He was devastated and anxious. Like
Dr. W., I can't say I handled this with total presence of mind. Although
it was true I had invited this, I was surprised to have so much difficult
personal information and feeling emerge so suddenly and openly. My
post facto interpretation was that what he was telling me was that there
was so much going on in his life outside work that he could not focus
very well on the task at hand. He was temporarily losing his stable self
organization and could not muster the usual social defense of "not wearing his heart on his sleeve," as Winnicott termed it.

Another supervisor did the appropriate thing. He asked Dr. W.
whether he wished to be in therapy with him rather than in supervision. Dr. W. said, "Yes," and that is what happened. I maintain that this
was helpful not only for Dr. W's general well being, but for his ability to learn as well. Until his outside life was stabilized, until the supports to his self-esteem were reactivated and his self-cohesion
reestablished, he could not go on to function.

As the supervision with me continued, the activity of helping him
to unify his therapist self at various levels seemed to be what was needed. He began by bringing up his confusions about theory, and I attempted to help him organize with minilectures and suggested readings.
When I saw that my attempt to give him alternatives without prejudic-
ing the case one way or another was leading to confusion in his clinical work, I took a more organizing stance than I am used to. I suggested
he take careful process notes, and I began to tell him how I would see
the patient's material and intervene primarily within my own paradigm.
It had become clear that it was too confusing at his stage of development

to give multiple alternative ways of seeing things. At the same time, I emphasized that he ought to filter all I had to say through his own perceptions. If something did not fit, it was just as well to discard it. In this way I was functioning as an idealized self object and providing him with a more stable self structure in his role as a therapist via a potential identification with me, while maintaining the opportunity for him to take over as much as he could—based on his own initiative—whenever he was ready.

Though Dr. W. rarely invoked his privilege to take over, he seemed to be becoming a very good listener with his patients. We dealt mainly with material from one patient and met on a weekly basis for about a year. When the first case terminated successfully, we focused on a second case in depth. With the first patient, Dr. W. had gradually developed a sense of continuity about what was going on. Since the patient seemed to need a relatively silent but attentively mirroring paternal self object, this worked out pretty well.

Later in the supervision, Dr. W. told me he found himself often missing transference references and reactions of his patients to his absences. I asked him why he thought this was happening and he said that he felt guilty about going away. This was such a burden that he fended off his awareness of any patients' reactions that might precipitate his guilt. I was impressed with his self—reflective insight and pleased with this clear evidence of his attempts to take initiative as a learner and as a therapist. I responded with a discussion of how difficult this issue was for all therapists at times. I talked about the reasons therapists sometimes feel intense, unachievable urges to rescue their patients and thus come to feel burdened, what patients sometimes do to elicit this type of reaction, and some of my own experiences along those lines. I was again acting as an idealized self object, I believe, providing a model of the therapist as someone who makes mistakes, is imperfect, but is continually striving for better understanding and more optimal capacities.

One day Dr. W. asked me, "When do you feel effectual as a therapist?" I took this to be further evidence of his striving for this feeling, which would indicate a cohesive therapist self. I replied honestly that I thought it took a long time because it took so many years for people to change fundamentally, and one had to see this happen to be fully convinced that it could. Meanwhile, one could get evidence from one's own treatment and to rely for the time being on faith. I added that many of my colleagues had felt the need for ongoing supervision after they finished their residencies, perhaps out of the same concern he was expressing. I did feel that I had become convinced of the power of therapy and of my capacities to do it over the years. He was very reassured to hear this, and I believe this helped stabilize his sense that one could feel confused or unsure without failing or fragmenting.

In the meantime the resident got married. In general he seemed to have no more problems in his outside life that interfered with his learning process. Within the supervision, my function as an idealized self object seems to have been to (a) help fend off fragmentation and (b) help him begin to establish a sense of initiative in regard to his functioning as a therapist. Along the way I provided a great deal of information, but none of this was nearly as valuable as my promoting his own curiosity and self-analytic explorations. Not all of the five areas I mentioned above were at issue here. (2) His outside life certainly did have an effect on his self-cohesion and his ability to learn as we have described. (3) There was also a relevant group environment in the sense that I had to evaluate Dr. W. for the purposes of his training program. We did this together because I felt this was more in keeping with the fact that it was *his* training. There were other supervisors too, one of whom became his therapist and thereby helped him greatly, particularly from the perspective of enabling him to feel stable enough to resume learning. (4) In terms of Dr. W.'s relationship to me, he seemed to turn to me for direction and guidance, first with theory, later clinically, and often even personally. For instance, when he sometimes felt injured by the comments of his residency director, he would bring it up with me spontaneously for discussion. I concluded that he primarily needed an idealizable self-object type of relationship. There was little attempt on his part to show off his good work or to confound me with his cleverness, which I would take to be a sign that more of a mirroring type of relationship was needed. Rather, he sought out comfort and guidance. This is applicable to (5), his inner characterological structure, which involved a rather shaky sense of stability buttressed by idealized relationships, as his serious religious commitment to a sect with an authoritarian superstructure also illustrates.

Other types of supervisees need other types of relationships. It is common that a therapist will need praise and approval for her successes as much as guidance where she seems to err in other cases. These people dig in and get inspired when told they are doing good work. I cannot cover all the many possibilities here. The purpose is mainly to illustrate the self-psychological model of learning I have proposed, with an example from supervision which I hope will promote further thinking and discussion on the topic.

Notes

1. This is consistent with current thinking about science and the philosophy of science, which emphasizes the creativity and imagination of the scientist over methods of deduction or induction in developing new theories.
2. A system is a complex of components in interaction. It can be a closed system, as the system of deductive logic is, for example. (All A are P; X is A; therefore, X is P.) In contrast, a biological system or a psychological system is an open system (Von Bertalanffy, 1967). Things can be added or deleted while, an underlying identity remains. One may grow or decline, lose teeth or limbs, learn new things or suffer total amnesia, yet one remains the same person. There is a physical continuity though all the molecules of the body turn over, and psychological continuity though the mental contents may change.
3. This is consistent with current thinking about science and the philosophy of science, which emphasizes the creativity and imagination of the scientist over methods of deduction or induction in developing new theories.

3

Reading Between the Lines:

THE CHILD'S FEAR OF MEANING

"The trouble with reading," said Jamie, "is that I've never really got my mind on it. Where my brain's going right now is to inventing. I like to look at the pictures to understand, and with the picture I can make it up myself. I think it sounds interesting how I do it. If I looked at the writing, it might say 'The valve is connected to the battery,' and I might not like it because it would upset me. The wrong valve might be connected to the battery."

Educational therapy has helped Jamie to unravel his reasons for not reading and has also enabled him to learn to read. His reasons could broadly be classified as internal and external. The ostensible cause is that Jamie's parents are divorced and have decided that Jamie should choose with whom to live. Jamie has been given the power to decide, and he realizes that he will hurt one of his parents whatever he decides to do. To him this means hurting half of himself. It is interesting that when Jamie starts to read, he normally stops after reading a couple of words and complains that part of his body hurts. It is as though he is suggesting that reading for him represents a part of himself that is too painful to contemplate. The internal reasons seem to be related to Jamie's omnipotent view that his most acceptable creations come from inside himself. By not reading he also avoids the dilemma of being loyal to one parent at the expense of the other. Additionally, reading faces him with the possibility of finding out something that he would rather not know.

"What really worries me," he said, "is when my dad left my mum and took me with him—was it because he refused to let her have me, or was it that she didn't want me?" Somehow, for Jamie, the written word has become imbued with a quality that it does not possess. Reading for Jamie is not a symbolic representation of a story. It has another, more powerful meaning.

Jamie cannot read because he is reluctant to recognize words as symbols. For him they are real. As Bettelheim and Zelan (1981) suggest, "The child, like primitive man, is convinced that words have magic power and that by manipulating words, one can manipulate simultaneously whatever these words symbolize. The child about to learn to read is at a stage in his intellectual development where the separation between a symbol and what it symbolizes is still a tenuous one that tends to break down in moments of emotional involvement."

If a child cannot bear or does not wish to use words as symbols, if he cannot or does not wish to understand that words on a page are only words representing a story, then he cannot begin to learn. The task of the educational therapist is to help the child realize that the written word is not a concealed weapon to be used for or against himself.

Educational Therapy

Educational therapy makes use of psychoanalytic insights to help children like Jamie unravel their deep-seated reasons for not reading. It is a technique pioneered by Irene Caspari at the Tavistock Clinic in the early 1970s. It is similar to psychotherapy in that a child is seen regularly over a period of time in a confidential setting, and the educational therapist understands that everything that the child does and says during a session is a form of communication. It differs in that part of the session is normally taken up with some reading, writing, or mathematics. The educational therapist will use these tasks in two ways: as information about the child's underlying preoccupations and as an indirect way of communicating with him. It is necessary to understand how a child sees the written word in order to disillusion him if necessary. Communicating through the educational task distinguishes this method from child psychotherapy.

Emotional Factors Inhibiting Learning

The way in which the child sees the written word and his reluctance to recognize their symbolic representation can be connected to a number of emotional factors, frequently interrelated. For reasons of clarity, however, it may be helpful to itemize them and then elaborate on how each one of them affects the child's view of learning.

1. Anxieties about family relationships
2. Symbiotic relationship with parent
3. Lack of assertiveness
4. Lack of curiosity
5. Anxiety about discovering and finding out
6. Anxiety about being overwhelmingly greedy
7. Infantile omnipotence or self-idealization,
8. Worries about the danger of words
9. The effect of loss on learning
10. Lack of boundaries and confusional states found in sexually abused children

Since they are closely connected (1) and (2) will be considered together.

Anxieties About Family Relationships and Symbiotic Relationship with Parent

Possibly one of the most important factors inhibiting learning is the part that the symptom of nonlearning plays in the family. At Hornsey Rise Child Guidance Unit there is a weekly workshop specifically set up for families of children with learning difficulties. Dr. Peter Loader, who runs the workshop, has developed the ideas of Britton (1989) and related them to nonlearning as a family symptom.

It often seems that the child has difficulty with "the initial recognition of the parental sexual relationship which involves relinquishing the idea of sole and permanent possession of mother" (Britton, 1989), There may be external and internal factors that are making it hard for the child to recognize the parental couple. However, until he can tolerate the position of being "a witness (of his parent's relationship) and not a participant" (Britton, 1989), he is going to remain inextricably merged with his mother. For the nonlearning child this relationship often results in a lack of assertiveness and curiosity, which may be due to complacency and satisfaction about the symbiotic relationship and a desire to remain in this position. On the other hand, it may be caused by anxiety about the precariousness and quality of the maternal connection (as in the case of Jamie).

The child may feel that it is essential for the good of the family for him to remain a baby and to enjoy all that this entails—hugs, kisses, and sharing mother's bed. This way he can keep daddy away from mummy or he can stop mummy feeling depressed and lonely. In this case the child sees reading as a wrench that forces him apart from his mother so that he has to individuate and grow up. In order to learn you have to risk taking a step forward on your own.

Many children seem to feel that they are being helpful to other members of the family by not reading. They see their continuing illiteracy as a way of keeping the family together. If parents are likely to split up, then reading is seen as a way of avoiding the split. The child may also think that if he learns, he will overtake either his mother or father and become cleverer than they are. If he overtakes his mother, then, she may feel sad and depressed about being left behind. She presents as the least powerful member of the family, and the child may think that she finds this particular position unbearable. If he overtakes his father, all his oedipal feelings and fantasies about ousting his father may be too powerful for him to cope with. He may imagine that overtaking his father is a way of killing him off.

Lack of Assertiveness

Strongly connected to a symbiotic relationship with the parent is the child's lack of assertiveness. I would say, if I were to generalize, that most of the nonreaders who have been referred to me over the last twelve years have been unassertive, incurious boys who are heavily involved with their mothers.

Assertiveness is very necessary for learning. In order to be able to digest words, the child (like the toddler) has to chew them, mull them over, and commit them to long-term memory, as opposed to the baby who spits out the lumps in the soup instead of chewing and digesting them.

Lack of Curiosity

A lack of assertiveness is often combined with a lack of curiosity, which is related either to complacency and self-sufficiency about the symbiotic relationship, or to a fear of finding out about an event that is supposed to be a secret.

Anxiety About Discovering and Finding Out

Bowlby (1988) suggests that cognitive disturbance is formed by the child being told that what happened did not really happen, that what is true and real is untrue and unreal. He gives examples of a boy who saw his father kill himself with a shotgun but was told later that night that his father had died of a heart attack. A girl who discovered her father's body hanging in a closet was told he had died in a car accident, and two brothers who had found their mother with her wrists slit were told she had drowned when swimming. When the children described what they had seen, the surviving parent had tried to discredit it, either by ridicule or by insisting that the child was confused.

Many people can remember occasions in their own childhood when their parents invalidated what their eyes and ears knew they had seen or heard. Parents often behave in the same way with their own children when a disturbing event, which they wish the children had not seen, takes place.

"Daddy wasn't really angry when he threw the geranium pot at me. It was only a joke." One can imagine confusion of a child who has been violently assaulted or sexually abused by a trusted parent if he is then told that he dreamt it or that it did not happen. Bowlby (1988) suggests that the result of being told that what actually happened did not happen, or being told to forget about what happened are (a) a chronic distrust of other people, (b) distrust of the child's own sense, and (c) a tendency to find everything unreal.

One of the main features for the child is the confusion that follows the result of not being able to trust his senses. If a child is told that he did not see, hear, feel, touch, or smell what he knows he did, then in a way he becomes "blind, deaf, numbed, and unfeeling" (Sinason, 1988). It is striking that children with learning difficulties often draw pictures of people with blind eyes, no ears, and no hands. A boy who drew pictures of people with blank eyes told me how his mother, disguised as a monster, came into his bedroom, pulled back the sheets, pulled off his pajamas, and sucked his penis . . . but perhaps it was just a nightmare, he added. For a second child it was accepting the fact that his mother was having a relationship with a woman who lived downstairs. For another it meant remembering his one assertive act as a toddler, when he had defended his mother by banging his drunken father on the head with a toy train. The father subsequently left the family and the mother went into hospital suffering from a depressive illness, while the boy was taken into care for a few months.

Anxiety About Being Overwhelmingly Greedy

In families where one or other of the parents are seen to suffer from a depressive illness or there is a handicapped member of the family, children often feel anxious about taking in the written word because they imagine that their excessive demands may become insatiable, and so they have to limit their learning. They must be parsimonious with themselves in case there is nothing left and mother/teacher collapses. They see learning as represented by food that is about to run out. It is the one bag of food in a country of famine.

A ten-year-old boy, whom I saw for three years—apparently conceived after a violent argument between his parents—felt that he should not have been alive at all. His mother suffered from a postnatal depression, followed soon after by a hysterectomy. He saw his mother as old and depressed, with nothing left to give him. When reading a book entitled *The Baked Bean Queen*, he misread it as *The Burnt-Out Queen*, and instead of reading the word "nobody" he replaced it with "no baby." His stories and drawings suggested that he was a lonely, despairing boy who was unable to take in sustenance from anywhere. I think in many ways the normal situation was reversed and that he saw himself as providing food for his mother. He drew a terrifying picture of a female crab with a bleeding boy between her claws. The crab, he said, wanted to eat somebody because she was too hungry. She had not had food for years because everyone got away from her. Another picture was of a fish tank where fish were being fed. They were fed too much food and grew so fat that they died because they burst. So, he added, it was better to let them starve to death. His stories repeated themes of boys and animals who were unable to have food because there was none there.

Another child from a large family with two handicapped brothers thought that I would die if she came to see me too often. If she had a session where she felt metaphorically well fed, she would absent herself the following time because she thought she had taken too much from me. This is what she said in one of her stories: "A long time ago there was an old woman and she was beginning to die and she said to herself, 'I will go into the kitchen and make dinner.' But she fell over on her way to the kitchen because she was too weak and ill and she could not make dinner." Another story of hers was about a puppy dog who was sad because he could not eat his banana. "He had been naughty because he had not listened to me and so he did not get a banana. He was so hungry that he could not listen."

Infantile Omnipotence, or Self-idealization

Another form of defense that causes difficulties in learning is that of self-idealization, or infantile omnipotence. Children with this disorder know everything. They are stuck at the toddler "I'm the king of the castle" stage. The defended part of them says they cannot learn because they already know everything and there is nothing left to learn. Reading and learning presents them each time with what they do not know, and they find this mortifying; words are seen to be pins that puncture their balloon of self-idealization, and often this is so intolerable that they cannot bear to look at what they do not know.

In my experience, children who are put in the position of having to act as partners to their mothers or fathers often use this form of defense. Because it is so frightening to be treated as an adult when only a small child, it becomes necessary to adopt an omnipotent defense for survival.

Worries About the Danger of Words

Some children see the written word as dangerous. Taking in learning is like taking in food. The child who has rejected his mother's food will often reject the written word: he feels they are both poisonous. This may be caused by excessive envy. Klein (1946) suggests that the child envies the mother's capacity to produce good milk (or the teacher's capacity to teach) and then becomes anxious about his envious, attacking feelings and imagines that he has projected them onto his mother. So now his mother is filled with rubbish rather than good milk, and he cannot therefore take anything in from her because he believes it has now become unpalatable and dangerous for him.

I would like to give an example of what a child I saw thought about words. Because of his extreme anxiety and fear of words, he found it very difficult to hold any in his mind. The only words he could remember were "the mummy" and "Michael." I had been reading *Fuzz Buzz*, a series from a phonic reading scheme that tells the story of some little creatures. He had not read further than Book One when he stopped and said he did not want to read any more because the Fuzz Buzz might jump out of the page and eat them up and he did not want to draw them because they might jump out of the page and the words might kill him.

"Has anything like that ever happened to you?" I asked.

"Yes, when I was a baby, I came out of my mummy's tummy and I ate her up."

"When was that?" I asked.

"When I bit her I ate her all up."

"Yes, but she's still there now." I replied.

"Yes, but she hits me when she's angry and she eats me up inside her tummy."

"It feels as though she's eating you up?" I inquired.

"No," said Michael adamantly. "She has eaten me up."

"How do you think you got into your mummy's tummy in the first place?"

"She must have eaten a big boy like me who turned into a little boy inside her tummy all chewed up."

"What about a daddy?" I suggested. "Do you think a daddy could have put his seed inside the mummy?"

"If he had, it wouldn't be a seed. It would be a bomb."

"How is it that you are here with me now?" I asked.

"Oh," said Michael. "Someone sewed me together, but I'm all empty inside."

The Effect of Loss on Learning

Loss, in my experience, is one of the most inhibiting factors in learning, particularly if the loss is that of a still-born sibling and happened before the birth of the referred child. If the parents have failed to mourn that death, the effect on surviving and subsequent children can be catastrophic (Lewis and Page, 1978).

It seems that the child regards the mother's body as the container of all knowledge and learning, but it can also be dreaded as a place of destruction, which could be a basic factor in inhibiting the desire for knowledge. As Klein wrote in 1931,

It is essential for a favorable development of the desire for knowledge that the mother's body should be felt to be well and unharmed. It represents in the unconscious the treasure-house of everything desirable which can only be gotten from there; therefore, if it is not destroyed, not so much in danger and therefore not so dangerous itself, the wish to take in food for the mind from it can more easily be carried out. (p. 241)

Beaumont (1988) has also addressed this issue:

If the mother's body is proved to be "a place full of destruction" because it produces still-born infants, rather than live, healthy ones, or that it appears too fragile to withstand fantasied attacks from other born or unborn siblings or the unborn foetus, then the wish to take in food for the mind must surely be imbued with all sorts of dreads and inhibitions. (Beaumont, 1988)

Children in this position often dread learning to read because in their minds knowledge comes from the dreaded but also envied place where the dead babies rest, so to them, learning belongs to the dead babies. One girl I used to see would often begin the session by turning her face to the wall and saying, "All books is baby's stuff."

Lack of Boundaries and Confusional States Found in Sexually Abused Children

In families where there are too few boundaries, children often feel at the mercy of their own violent and greedy impulses. They feel that their parents are too weak to say no to their excessive demands, which provokes such panic and overwhelming fear that it is impossible to learn. If a child is allowed to be as demanding, aggressive, or seductive as he likes, then he also feels open to attack from the uncontrollable impulses and desires of adults, either real or imagined. It is as though the child has an internal text that is so exciting and preoccupying, he cannot see the words on the page for what they are.

When looking at a child who has been sexually abused, many other factors need to be taken into account—self-disgust, guilt, triumph, anxiety about the mother's disgust, and low self-esteem. The confusion over boundaries, however, is probably the factor that will most affect his learning. It is as though the child who has been abused, particularly within the family, does not know where he begins or ends. He sees himself as an object attached to an adult for the gratification of that adult, so learning for himself as a separate person does not make sense.

A ten-year-old boy who was allowed to do exactly as he liked gave me a vivid description of his psychological state. "My brain is like a hotel full of different rooms. One is full of willies, one is full of bums, one is full of snot, and one is full of shit and they all run into each other so I can't tell what is what."

Discussion

The importance of the inhibiting emotional factor has to be understood before any change in the child's learning can take place. This will normally entail working with him over a period of time within a confidential setting so that a trusting relationship can be built up.

In many instances the inability to symbolize words is caused by the child's intolerance or fear of the parental, sexual couple. For some children the physical gaps between the printed word can signify loss and separation from the mother, caused by "prior failure of maternal containment." (Britton, 1989) In educational therapy the child has the opportunity to explore symbolically what this means to him.

Close attention must be paid to the way the child uses print and copes with the gaps between the words, to his miscues, his hesitations, his comments about the vocabulary, pictures, and characters in the story. As in psychotherapy, it is also important to be aware of the transference and countertransference.

The therapist must see the world from the child's point of view without being judgmental or moralizing. Many children find it easier to communicate through metaphor, in the form of a story, through drawings, or in their play. The child has to be shown that he is understood by staying with the metaphor.

A four-year-old girl told me a story while playing with a toy crocodile. The story was about a crocodile who stole a baby kangaroo from its mother and ate the baby kangaroo all up. The mother kangaroo was so angry that she beat up the crocodile, whereupon the baby kangaroo peed on the mother kangaroo's head. I said that I expected the baby kangaroo was angry with the mother kangaroo for allowing the crocodile to eat her in the first place. The little girl agreed and placed the baby safely back in the mother kangaroo's pouch. She then disarmed the crocodile by clamping plasticine in its jaws and on its legs. This is a child whose father has been issued with a court order forbidding him entry to the house after assaulting his daughter.

Conclusion

At the outset of this paper it was suggested that a child's reading difficulties could be seen as a neurotic symptom. In order to understand the precise nature of the child's problems, it is often appropriate to offer individual educational therapy. This form of treatment enables the child to discover that his view of the printed word is askew. It helps him to learn that words will not literally attack and kill him. Letters are symbols, not weapons. In understanding the child's world, the therapist can change misconceptions to more realistic conceptions, and the process of reading and learning can begin.

Muriel Barrett, M. A.
Jane Trevitt, M.A.

4

Educational Therapy and

Attachment Theory:

CONCEPTUAL FOUNDATIONS

e ducational therapy is an intervention that
considers the effect of a child's emotional
development on his cognitive learning. We
believe it is important to understand the origins of the learning process
by studying the interactive behavior of an infant with his* primary care
giver, usually mother.*

The concept of attachment behavior is taken from the work of
John Bowlby (1969, 1973, 1980, 1988). It is built on the notion of a control system aimed at achieving certain goals, the primary one being the

---

* For simplicity's sake, we have identified all the children discussed as "he"
and parents or other primary care givers, teachers, and educational therapists
as "she."

activation of the infant's behavioral system toward seeking the proximity of his mother, his "attachment figure." Separation from, or the loss of, an attachment figure is an integral part of this concept.

Secure attachment behavior facilitates the infant's emotional and cognitive development; anxious attachment behavior (as defined by Ainsworth and Wittig, 1969) is likely to inhibit both.

With the help of diagrams, we focus on the foundations for healthy learning and outline the basic stages in the interactional process that allow for the establishment of a "secure base" (a term first used by Ainsworth in 1969) for both mother and infant.

Patterns of Secure Attachment Behavior

First we need to think about the situation in which the new infant and the mother find themselves at the birth, in an entirely new, "unknown" relationship. The pair are rarely isolated but are members of an already-established family system, all of whom have to adjust to accommodate the newcomer. Initially the infant is totally dependent on his mother to meet all his needs. (See Fig. 4.1.) The sensitivity with which she is able to do this, recognizing and responding to the baby's gradually emerging ability to communicate his feelings and requirements, sets the pattern for interactional learning, both hers and his. An important part of this process is the mother's maintenance of clear boundaries to ensure that her infant is "held" in the Winnicottian sense (Winnicott, 1965).

The infant will be able to trust his mother's emotional availability, confident that she will comfort him when he is anxious or upset. He

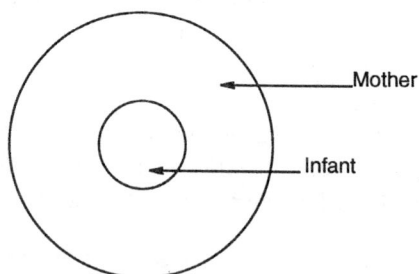

Fig. 4.1. Mother and dependent infant.

gradually learns that the overwhelming feelings of aggression, fury, and despair that he experiences when his needs are not instantly gratified can be survived with the help of his mother, his "attachment figure" (Bowlby's concept).

The infant begins to discover, at an unconscious level, the boundaries of his own "skin" which later will enable him to recognize his own personality as distinct from that of his mother (Bick, 1968). This process also involves the mother and is dependent on her ability to allow the individuation to take place. (See Fig. 4.2.)

Bowlby (1969) states that at some stage in the development of the behavioral systems for attachment, proximity to mother becomes a set goal. The wish to maintain closeness can be observed when an infant, at the stage when his smiles and actions denote a distinct preference for his mother's presence, cries if she leaves him momentarily to move to another room. The mother who is able to accept her infant's wish for proximity and can assuage his anxious feelings enables him to feel secure in what soon becomes reciprocated interaction.

Exploratory Behavior

Bowlby regards this as a class of behavior in its own right. The exploratory behavior of the newborn infant can be observed *as* he feels his mother while feeding or being nursed. He explores her nipple (or the bottle teat) with his mouth and tongue, feeling her with his hands and fingers as she holds him close. The infant begins to discover his own control systems and how he can influence his mother's responses to him as he feeds, and he develops eye contact with her. A "sense of

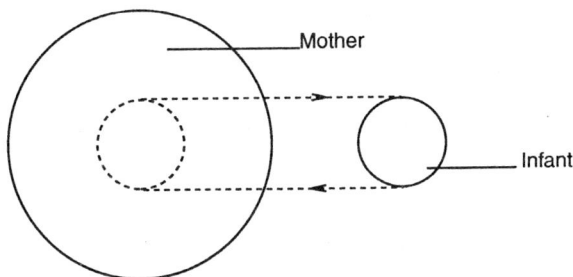

Fig. 4.2. Goal-seeking behavior.

self" (Stern, 1985) extends through body-awareness such as thumb sucking, touching of genitals and toes, and holding toys.

The infant becomes increasingly responsive to his mother and other members of his family unless he is tired. Gradually the exploratory behavior becomes more complex. It is inextricably linked to attachment behavior. When the infant feels secure, he is able to explore with confidence. If this behavior is encouraged and the earlier experiences are confirmed, the process continues.

The capacity for play between mother and infant develops within what Winnicott (1971) describes as a "potential space." The mother's consistent response sets a pattern of her reliable emotional availability. She also encourages her infant to accept limit setting, not only to avoid danger but also as an introduction to the idea that another's goal-directed system may be different from his own. (See Fig. 4.3.)

Thus, the infant's goal-seeking behavior develops and with it his emotional and cognitive skills. With his mother's approval he can begin to struggle with the things he finds difficult and learn ways of managing himself and his world within their shared space.

Internal Working Models

The establishment of a secure attachment will allow the infant to build a memory of self-interacting with a preferred attachment figure, an inner representation of her that he can carry around with him in his

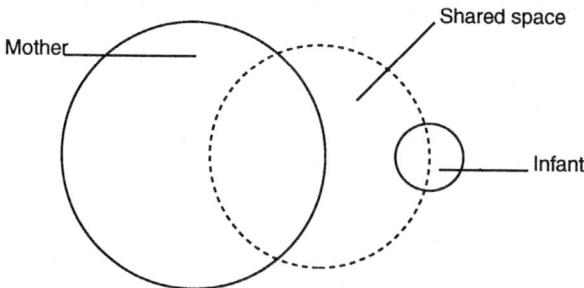

Fig. 4.3. Interactive behavior.

head: an "internal working model." (This concept of Bowlby's has been further discussed by Main, Kaplan, and Cassidy, 1985.) It enables the infant to experience himself as a worthwhile individual interacting with a trusted adult.

Updating

The infant's inner and external adventures bring new "structures" that are added to and modify his internal working models. They allow the map of self, interacting with others to be adjusted. Bowlby refers to this experience as "updating." Internal working models act as a reference point for future interactions and evermore complex situations. If children are secure in the knowledge that they are loved and are validated as individuals within their family systems, then it becomes possible to carry forward these feelings into new encounters such as school. They can transfer and update their feelings of well-being about self-interacting with mother in the belief that these feelings will be carried forward to their interactions with a first teacher. (See Fig. 4.4.)

The secure child and his mother will be able to tolerate the separation when he reaches school age. If all goes well, he forms an appropriate attachment to his teacher. He can relate to his peers and is able to wait for help and actively seek attention when he needs it.

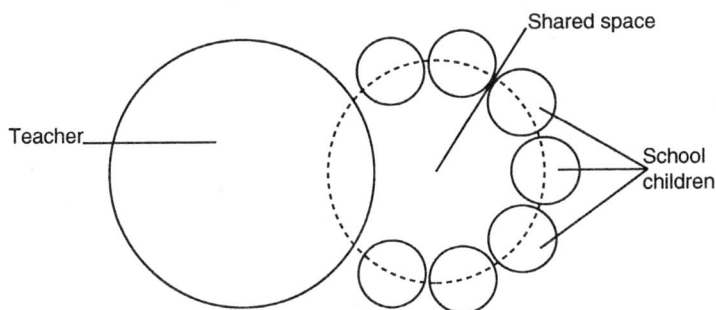

Fig. 4.4. Attachment behavior in the school system.

Anxious-Attachment Behavior

There are some children, however, who form anxious attachments. When the process of attachment has been distorted in some
way, problems arise in making relationships and in future learning patterns. Loss is the single most significant feature in the lives of these
children. The majority of learning-disabled children have experienced
unexpected separation from, or loss of, an adult or adults who hold particular significance for them.

Three examples of early distortions of attachment behavior are
illustrated in diagrammatic form in Figures 4.5, 4.6, and 4.7.

If a mother (or other primary care giver) is unable to tolerate the
infant within her space, this may result in total rejection of him. His basic
needs are met without reference to his feelings. This mother cannot
be emotionally available for her child, which can lead to his rejection
of her. He may develop inappropriate attention-seeking strategies or his
behavior may become increasingly withdrawn.

If a mother is unable to allow her infant to explore independently, he has few opportunities to learn that he and his mother can survive
separately. The resulting relationship is sometimes referred to as symbiotic, or "smothering mothering." Because the child's needs are met
almost before he has become aware of them, he rarely experiences frustration. He has therefore had no chance to develop problem-solving
strategies nor to discover that frustration and anger can be survived.
This can result in omnipotent behavior: these children never discover

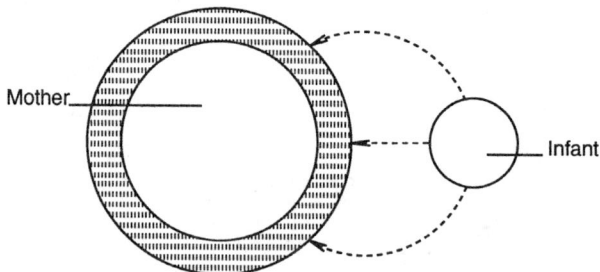

Fig. 4.5. The rejecting attachment figure.

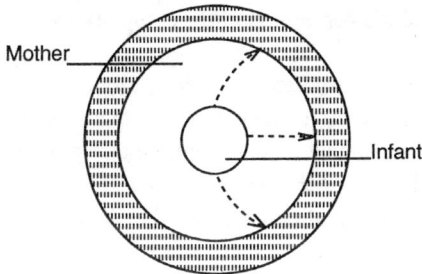

Fig. 4.6. The over-protective attachment figure.

that their wishes are not commands. Without any experience of individuation the child cannot develop a realistic sense of self.

If the mother and her infant have no shared, fixed point or reference, they are left in a state of internal isolation, spinning in uncontained space. The efforts of the mother and her infant to make contact are frequently mistimed, which leads to a mismatch in their approaches to one another. There is no apparent opportunity for the formation of any attachment, since the mother is emotionally unavailable. The infant is excessively anxious and has no meaningful strategies for interacting with others.

How then do these anxiously attached children manage the transition into school? The first step away from home for many children is into a play group or nursery school. Sroufe (1983) suggests that this experience can offer a child a new opportunity to form a trusting relationship with an emotionally available adult in the new setting. He considers it is possible that a "specific attachment person" (a teacher)

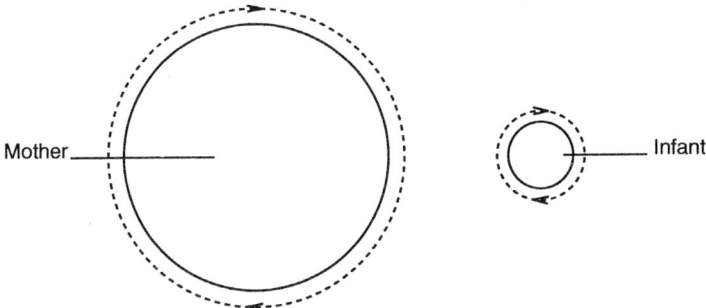

Fig. 4.7. The "spinning" attachment figure.

can modify the child's perception of his earlier experience (see Figs. 4.5, 4.6, 4.7).

The children referred to us for educational therapy appear to be anxiously attached. They have not had the opportunity to explore from a safe base or to know that a consistent, emotionally available adult is close at hand. The complex origins, often cross-generational, of the situations described cannot be considered in detail here, but we believe that loss, unresolved parental grief, depression, illness, and deprivation are among some of the factors that are involved. It is important to note, however, that although the problem may originate with the mother, it does seem likely that some infants are less energetic at overcoming resistance or are particularly vulnerable in some other way.

We believe that those children who have been unable to establish a good-enough relationship with an attachment figure do not have the basic foundation essential for effective learning.

Muriel Barrett, M.A.
Jane Trevitt, M.A.

5

Educational Therapy and

Attachment Theory:

APPLICATIONS

i n our study of the interactive behavior between attachment figures and infants, we began to recognize certain patterns in the interaction. We discovered that similar patterns of behavior could be discerned in our interaction with learning-disabled children. This led to the realization that in our role as educational therapists we became "educational attachment figures" who could offer learning-disabled children an opportunity for "second-chance learning" (Barrett and Trevitt, in press).

In order to clarify this statement we use diagrams to compare the two dyads: mother/infant and educational therapist/learning-disabled child. (See Figs. 5.1, 5.2, and 5.3.)

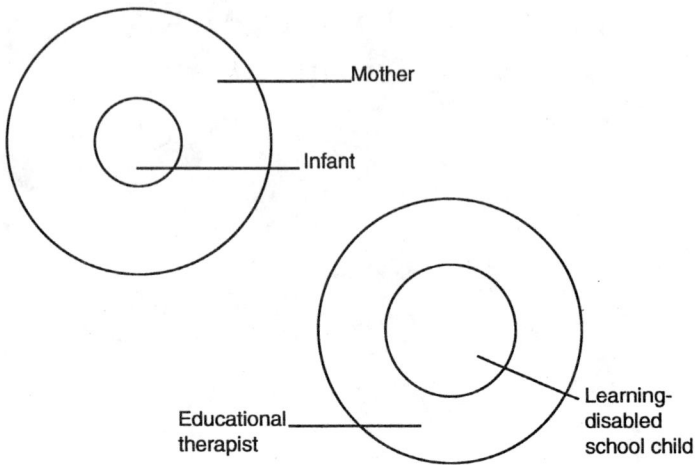

Fig. 5.1 Preparation; interactional introduction; initial dependence.

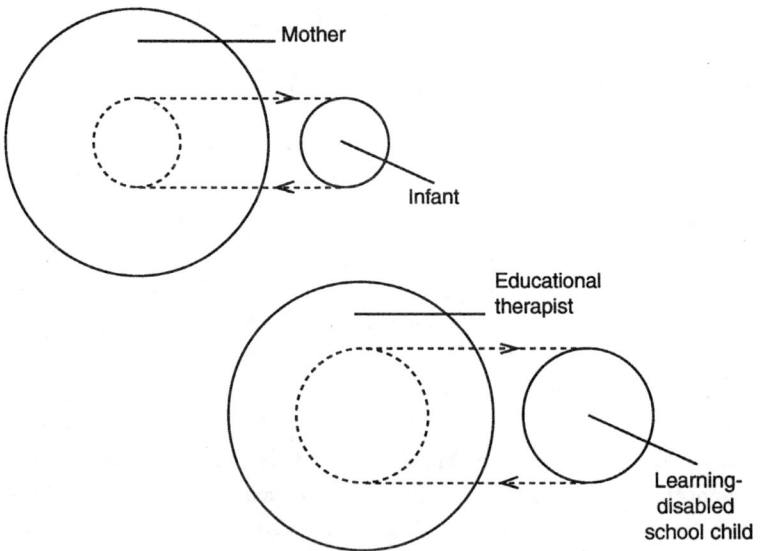

Fig. 5.2. Establishment of a secure base; consideration of feelings; exploratory behavior.

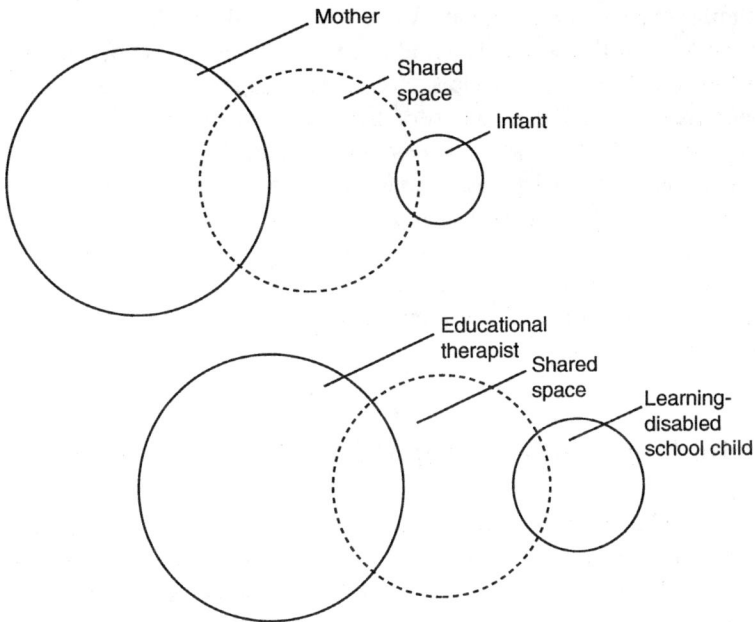

Fig. 5.3. Establishment of a shared space; play and learning;
development of internal working models.

The aim of the adult in both these dyads is to think about the child (preparation) and acknowledge what is happening in the here and now (secure base). When the infant/child is ready to acknowledge feelings on his own behalf he extends his explorations and becomes less dependent on the adult (exploratory behavior). Both members of the dyads are active in creating a playing and working space where respect for personal boundaries is explored. Throughout the process of the interaction a memory of a good-enough experience becomes possible. Cognitive tasks are achieved and problem-solving skills are developed until the infant/child is ready to assume age-appropriate autonomy (internal working models and updating).

Bowlby's concept of updating has helped us to realize that when anxious children enter school, they carry forward an image of themselves as worthless. These children are likely to have internalized an image of their mother that leads them to believe that a teacher will have similar expectations of them. Unlike secure children, they will not have learned that a failed first attempt may be overcome by further efforts (goal-seeking behavior). Secure children know that their mothers have confidence in the ability of the teachers not only to develop their cognitive skills but also to be emotionally available to provide comfort and empathic understanding when things go wrong. We use the term back-dating to describe what we see as the negative updating of anxiously attached children. They frequently become socially isolated, either withdrawing into themselves or channeling all their energies into negative attention-seeking, acting-out behavior, bullying, or taking on the role of the victim.

Children Referred for Educational Therapy

Children who have experienced inconsistency in their lives are left in a state of confusion. It is our task as educational therapists to help them make some sense of the world within the session so that they can begin to discover connections between cause and effect, a basic ingredient for learning. Many of the children referred to us are preoccupied with their longing to return to an infantile state of dependency. The links previously referred to between loss and learning disability in children seem also to affect their parents, many of whom are suffering unresolved grief. This may relate to the death of important family members, including miscarriages, still-births, and cot deaths. There are increasing numbers of children who are experiencing the trauma of their parents' separation or divorce, with all the changes and uncertainties that this can bring. The difficulties of adjustment to single-parent status or reconstituted family groupings can easily be overlooked as these become increasingly a part of "normal" life. This has been the experience of children referred for educational therapy who have formed anxious attachments.

Transitions form a natural part of everyone's life experience, and for securely attached children and their parents they do not generally present insurmountable problems. Normative life events such as the birth of a sibling or moving can result in the temporary suspension of a child's learning in school. This is usually recognized by sensitive parents and teachers. However, equally familiar events such as a transition to a new class or school or the unexpected departure of a teacher are less obviously stressful. For anxious children such events can prove overwhelming. For a few children, the experience of these changes may even confirm a self-perception of "badness."

The Educational Therapist

Our knowledge of attachment theory has helped us to understand families and peer groups, but we have chosen to focus on our work with individual children. We examine the links that we see between the first experience of interactional learning that takes place between the mother and infant in the home and the second-chance learning experience that we offer to anxiously attached children. Some of the latter have lost their capacity to play as well as to learn, and one of the important tasks of the educational therapist is to bring those children into a state of readiness to play, as a first requisite for learning.

In our role as educational therapists, in addition to becoming educational attachment figures, it is essential that we make use of our teaching skills. (The third aspect of the role, that of consultant, we shall not address here.) We always work within our professional boundary, never assuming the role of mother. We are aware of the phenomena of transference and countertransference (described by Freud, 1926). Instead of taking on the characteristics of a witch (transferred from another figure) that the child is projecting onto the therapist, the therapist and child look at the witch together. When helping a child to understand his feelings we make extensive use of the metaphor.

The way in which a mother prepares appropriate food for her infant, milk, not whiskey, is analogous to the preparation of appropriate "educational food" by an educational therapist for the learning-disabled school child (Caspari, 1974).

Securing a room on a regular basis where there will be no interruptions is essential. It has an educational bias, with materials such as books, games, sand, water, building bricks, and puppets. These materials will be used by all those children who are seen by the educational therapist. Each child keeps his own specific play and work materials in a secure box, which often becomes a symbolic container for his feelings.

Identification of Learning Disabilities

As already mentioned, we are examining links between a child's emotional development and his cognitive learning. While we recognize that the children under discussion cannot be placed rigidly into any one classification, we have found that generally they fall into three broad groups. We have identified these as follows:

1. Children with no basic skills (those who have not started to acquire basic skills)
2. Children with suspended learning (those who have managed for a while until some crisis, often a transition or impending change, precipitates a suspension of their ability to manage)
3. Children who are resistant to learning (those who, in spite of having all the necessary academic knowledge and skills, fiercely resist using them, often destroying their books and refusing to allow themselves to work)

The Process of Educational Therapy

The following three examples exemplify learning-disabled children who exhibit the anxious attachment behavior described earlier. Their intellectual ability was not in doubt, but they could not use their potential capacity for playing and learning. Each child had met his therapist once before in a family interview.

David

David was seven years old and had no basic skills. He was reported to be uncontainable at home and in school. He lived with his mother and older brother. His mother and father, who were separated, were in open conflict over the management of the boys.

First Session: David resembled the infinitely-falling infant described by Winnicott (1965). His arms and legs were all over the place, and he was very tense and restless. When his therapist collected him from the waiting room he appeared to be running up the walls. He greeted her without any apparent anxiety, racing ahead up the passage with no idea of which direction they were heading. He burst into the prepared room, scattering all the things from his box with only a cursory glance at the contents. His clothes flew in all directions, compounding the sense of confusion and chaos that surrounded him. He appeared uncontained and inaccessible.

Adam

Adam was nine years old. His learning had become suspended. Like David, he was the younger of two boys, living with their mother. The father was a violent man who drank heavily and was only intermittently at home. Mother's decision to go to college as a mature student precipitated the crisis. Adam, who had always been very reluctant to go to school, gave up going out altogether. His mother had to push him on her bicycle when she was obliged to leave the house, since he refused to walk outside. Mother described him as a "growth on her side."

First Session: He shuffled slowly into the room and flopped on a chair. He resembled an oversized, sleepy baby, huddled in a fetal position. His long hair, cut roughly round in a bowl-shaped fashion, fell down over his face, like the coat of an old English sheep dog. He seemed unavailable and resistant.

Nathan

Nathan was ten years old and resistant to learning. He was the eldest of three children in an intact family, but his father was only home on weekends. Nathan was expected to be the man around the house in father's absence. He was unable to achieve any scholastic task, though he had no discernible learning disability.

First Session: When Nathan arrived he had his parka zipped right up to his nose and his hood pulled down to meet it. It was not possible to see his eyes. His limbs were curiously sticklike and his movements restless and jerky. He climbed up the stairs one at a time like a toddler, despite considering himself an accomplished sportsman. He appeared very apprehensive and guarded, fiercely defended.

We can see from these accounts the various ways in which these three children made the transition into their first session. All transitions mean a loss of the "known" and facing up to the "unknown." Progress in cognitive learning involves the loss of infancy and dependency, and confirms the inevitability of growing up. It is important that negative and ambivalent feelings be accepted, and the child needs help in managing his behavior relating to these feelings within the session. All three children revealed their desperate need for the establishment of a secure base. They were "held" by the educational therapist, within the boundaries of the session.

Subsequent Sessions

The process of establishing a secure base continues, and the child gradually builds a memory of the earlier sessions. The here and now of the present is accepted by the child. The therapist's belief in his capacity for change introduces the possibility of a future.

We will use a further description of our three children to illustrate their use of the playing/working space, in which their tentative explorations began.

David

David (with no basic skills) remained in perpetual motion, exhausting to watch, until his eye lit on a kaleidoscope on a shelf. He immediately became absorbed and apart from twitchy limbs, he was at rest. He repeatedly shook the kaleidoscope and then looked at the patterns he had made. He would hold it out for the therapist to look, always taking it away before she had done so! She felt exhausted just to be in the same room with him. Suddenly it occurred to her that the scraps of colored paper in the kaleidoscope were flying about in the same hectic movement that she was observing in David—but they became still together, forming a complete pattern. She mused aloud about the confusion of the tiny pieces that were "all over the place" and yet could come together to make a very satisfying pattern. David stopped moving, then he solemnly turned around and for the first time made eye contact with her. "Yes," he breathed, pausing again. David momentarily recognized that order could come out of chaos in the playing space.

He began to explore ways of containing his all-too-fragmentary parts within the playing space. He endlessly punched holes in pieces of colored paper. Initially, these were scattered like confetti with his wild movements. Gradually he began to find ways of containing them: he made paper boxes and envelopes and, most important of all, he discovered he could use tape to collect them together and keep them safe. He was learning the way from the waiting room to the therapy room and he felt proud. Progress was slow, but as his play became more purposeful and less random, so he began settlement for short periods to "educational" tasks in what was becoming the working space. Again he used scraps of paper, but this time he put letters on them and began to assemble words, the first of which was his name. His internal working models became more positive as he updated his previous perception of adult behavior.

Adam

When Adam (the child who had given up learning) was referred to a children's psychiatric unit for help, his capacity for playing and learning had been suspended for about a year. For several sessions there was little or no possibility of movement for either child or therapist as Adam struggled to get her to take on a mothering role. He still was a large, lumpy boy and his tenth birthday was looming: the thought of being "one and zero" overwhelmed him. It was only possible to acknowledge and stay with his distress at growing inexorably older when his avowed wish was to remain a baby, preferably not even one year old.

Once he got started, Adam was able to work directly in the metaphor by dictating and illustrating his story about a helpless, "rubbished" kitten. The kitten faced one disaster after another, always being swept along without any possibility of influencing the direction in which he was taken. Gradually over the months the kitten became stronger and began to discover ways in which he could influence the outcome of events, until finally he had control over his life as a young cat. The relationship between this cat and his owner became a positive one; both were able to maintain appropriate boundaries for themselves.

Nathan

Nathan (the resistant-to-learning boy) continued to struggle. All his energy was taken up with maintaining his defenses. Although it was possible to develop some interactional behavior with the therapist in the sessions, it was never very meaningful. His ability to make any attachment seemed to be seriously damaged (although it is worth remembering that Bowlby reminds us that children remain attached to their parents regardless of their behavior). The therapist was away ill for a time, and on her return, Nathan politely greeted her. (His mother had said in the first family interview that he always said what people wanted to hear.) However, he expressed his displeasure by farting repeatedly. The therapist mused about how angry he must have felt with her for being away. Uncharacteristically, he made real eye-contact and nodded sadly. He was then able to relax and work more appropriately.

Endings

We referred earlier to the significance of transitions for anxiously attached children. The management of transitions inevitably forms a part of the educational therapy process. The preparation of children for breaks is very important. Their previous painful experiences of separation and loss from significant attachment figures make even short breaks difficult to tolerate; however, reunion with his educational therapist, in he, role as educational attachment figure, following a break confirms the child's belief in himself.

David: Family circumstances precluded the continuation of treatment for this boy. He found ending the work with his educational therapist very difficult to understand. This loss was slightly ameliorated by the deputy head teacher taking on the role of "specific attachment person" for David in school.

Adam: He appeared to use the achievements of his story about a kitten, as well as his own interactional experiences, to update his inner working models. He was able to move away from working in the metaphor by addressing his feelings directly. Adam made links between the experiences of the characters in his story to his own. The milestone of his tenth birthday, which had loomed so large, became manageable. His transition from the unit back into school presented no problems.

Nathan: After a period of two years his therapy was concluded. The process of ending proved to be the most important part of the work. Nathan was able to allow himself to face some of the realities previously unacknowledged. He started to talk about the feelings of sportsmen when things went wrong for them, how they had to keep their feelings to themselves, "to be good sportsmen." We looked together at the more demonstrative behavior of the players, and the expression of their feelings. Nathan was able to share the difficulties that he experienced playing team games because of his terrible anguish and anger if he was not perfect. He was able to describe how he couldn't trust his teammates enough to pass the ball to them. (By this time he was leaping up the stairs wearing only shorts and a T-shirt; his jacket was left at home.)

As the goal-seeking of these three boys increased, they were able to "make use of" (in the Winnicottian sense, 1965) the educational therapist. They understood the nature of the "space" that was being provided in which they could play and learn. As for most children with whom we work, their boxes became symbolic containers of feelings as well as concrete evidence of educational tasks achieved.

Children undergoing educational therapy are gradually able to make better use of their experiences within their own classrooms, but planning for the end of the therapy should involve discussion with the child, his parents, and teachers.

We have focused our attention on working with individual children to emphasize the earlier patterns of play and interactional learning, believing that these patterns can be inhibited or facilitated by the behavior of attachment figures. If the children experience attachment behavior, the patterns may be repeated in play and learning at school. Educational therapy is an intervention that aims to change these patterns and offers a second-chance learning opportunity.

PART

II

Diagnosis

Introduction

diagnosis in this collection of papers is revealed as a complex process requiring multidisciplinary, multimodal techniques. The diagnostic question is never simply one of classification but an inquiry into the how and why of a child's functioning. Diagnosis provides the conceptual foundation for devising intervention strategies and for evaluating their effectiveness.

Doris Johnson describes in capsule form the conceptual underpinnings and technical repertoire of contemporary multidisciplinary practice in well-staffed psychiatric clinics and public schools. This popular approach, which in the case of American public schools is mandated by federal regulation, is predicated on the understanding that problems in human learning invariably are multiply determined and that sound preventative and remedial intervention can be devised only after a thorough multidisciplinary study of the problem has been completed. The approach simultaneously embodies biological, psychological, sociological, and cultural perspectives. It provides a cross-sectional as well as a developmental view of the problem being experienced by the learner. It draws data from many sources: teachers and parents, some anecdotal, some quantitative. The subject of the inquiry may be observed or tested with instruments yielding quantitative as well as qualitative data. When brain pathology is suspected, a variety of sophisticated brain-imaging procedures may be employed in determining the diagnosis. Within each domain numerous techniques and instruments are available to the diagnostician, allowing for considerable flexibility. A multidisciplinary team evaluating a series of learners may then produce a wide variety of diagnostic protocols, each reflecting choices made by the professionals responding to the unique set of features in each case.

A highly original approach to the assessment of school-related learning difficulties is described by its originator, Anna-Marit Duve, and a current practitioner, Rolf Zachariassen. Although the method has been frequently reported in European journals, it is fairly safe to say that most American professionals are not yet familiar with it. Conceived at a time when psychoanalytic ego psychology was a familiar, if not dominant, point of view in child psychiatry, the method reflects an eclectic blend of theory, including ideas from Kurt Lewin's field theory and David Rapaport's formulation of the principles of mental functioning. The technique creates a way station between the clinic office, strange and unfamiliar to the child, and the familiar or natural setting of the classroom. The clinician, who seldom ventures into the classroom for direct observation of the child, has in this method a simulation of the classroom environment, complete with physical appurtenances of blackboard, books, globe, et cetera, and an examiner who enacts the role of the teacher. How the child adapts to or copes with the various demands made upon him in this setting will be revealed through measures and observations from which inferences can be drawn about his likely behavior in his schoolroom. While the method lacks the authenticity of naturalistic observation, it comes closer to it than the ordinary practice of observing and testing a child in the clinic office, where little effort is made, via decor or procedure, to replicate the schoolroom's atmosphere, even though the clinician typically generalizes his findings to that situation.

Betty Osman discusses the convergence of evidence and theory in the fields of psychiatry and education, establishing the frequent coexistence of depression and learning disabilities in children. Recognition that this is indeed the case required some clinicians to abandon the view that young children, by virtue of their incomplete development, lacked the necessary psychological structure to experience depression, and for some educators to realize that emotional factors could play a secondary, or even a primary, role in the development of school learning difficulties. Whether a depression is primary or secondary (i.e., reactive) can only be determined by a comprehensive assessment in which varied measures and observations sample a broad spectrum of cognitive and emotional processes. Additionally, a thorough history of the child's development by establishing chronology will often help the clinician to discern cause and effect sequences. A diagnostic assessment that is relatively complete and accurate will show the current configuration of cognitive and emotional factors, their interplay, and how this pattern has evolved over time. The realization of a comprehensive diagnosis enables both the educator and clinician to formulate strategies of intervention that will address all of the child's needs.

Rita Sussman visualizes, for heuristic purposes, the normally achieved and maintained integration of emotional and cognitive experiences as a puzzle whose pieces interdigitate and resist minor disruptions. In contrast, integrative deficiencies are visualized as puzzles whose individual pieces merely abut one another without interlocking, a system that is consequently more vulnerable to disruption. Her discussion proceeds by way of a succession of provocative questions intended to alert the practitioner to think seriously about the meaning and causes of learning difficulties, the mix of cognitive and emotional factors influencing a problem, and the implications of these formulations for designing interventions.

Doris Johnson, Ph.D.

6

Diagnosis of Learning Problems

the purpose of this chapter is to present an overview of the process involved in the evaluation of learning problems. Since there are many reasons for learning difficulties, it is essential to conduct a comprehensive study that includes a case history, objective testing, and observation. Learning problems may arise because of mental deficiency, sensory impairments, emotional and/or motivational factors, lack of experience, poor instruction, or specific learning disabilities such as dyslexia or other language disorders.

Whenever an individual experiences problems, one looks for reasons and, in most instances, the diagnostician looks for patterns of problems. That is, if certain conditions such as hearing impairments or mental retardation are suspected, one expects to find particular patterns of behavior, strengths, and weaknesses. Mentally retarded children, for example, typically have a history of delayed development and below-average performance in all areas of learning, including social skills and adaptive behavior. In contrast, those with dyslexia may show no evidence of problems prior to school or in nonacademic skills; their problems arise when they are learning to read and write. All hypotheses, however, must be verified with both formal assessment and observations.

Case History

The case history is one of the most important aspects of the diagnostic process (Myklebust, 1954). From the history, the diagnostician can obtain valuable information regarding the parent's perceptions of the problems, their feelings about the child, their expectations, and the child's overall development. It is helpful to interview both parents to determine their perceptions of the problems and whether they have similar values regarding child rearing. Often families go to numerous professionals to obtain answers about the child's problems, and opinions may differ. Their responses to the evaluations and recommendations can be revealing.

The case history should provide information about early development including play, social skills, language, schooling, and any special services. Children who began having problems during nursery school because of hyperactivity or an inability to play normally have a longer history of negative experiences, reprimands, and possible failure than those whose problems were identified later in school. The relationships between cognitive and affective behavior are also important. For example, the child with delayed language has fewer means to express feelings and to participate in certain family communication. These same children may have difficulty participating in early preschool experiences, story time, and early reading. In addition, if language is delayed, parents may talk less to their children, thereby reducing stimulation. Discipline also may be problematic. Parents may wonder whether the child cannot listen and attend or whether he refuses to comply, so they may alternate between being overly indulgent or punitive. A comprehensive diagnostic study should address these issues and provide information that will help parents understand the problems and manage their child's behavior.

Good medical histories are essential because they provide some evidence about possible causes of the learning problems. Information regarding prenatal history, events surrounding the birth, and postnatal illnesses or accidents are all relevant. The prenatal history should include questions about the use of drugs, tobacco, and alcohol as well as specific illnesses. Many low-birth-weight babies are born to mothers who were substance abusers. Children from deprived environments may have been born to mothers who received little or no prenatal care or who were themselves undernourished. Such conditions may interfere with the development of the fetus.

After birth certain illnesses may have an impact on language acquisition and learning. For example, many young children have repeated episodes of otitis media (ear infections). If these infections occur at a time when children are acquiring language, they may have difficulty listening to instructions or perceiving all the phonemes in words, leaving them with "gaps" in their vocabulary and general listening comprehension. More acute illnesses such as meningitis or encephalitis may also create learning problems. In these cases it is important to know whether the child regressed and whether the behavior changed following the illness. In some instances the child may have cognitive, language, or motor problems; in others, there may be no long-term organic effects, although periods of hospitalization may result in anxiety, loss of trust, and other emotional consequences.

Finally, the history should include information about any learning, mental, or emotional problems in the family. There is substantial evidence to suggest that at least some specific learning disabilities may be familial (Hallgren, 1950; Pennington, 1989). Occasionally, three or four children in the family may have dyslexia, or there may be a history of two or three generations of individuals with academic problems.

The age at which parents, teachers, physicians, and other professionals express a concern is important diagnostically. Some physical handicaps are evident at the time of birth. Other conditions may be identified during the first few weeks or months of life, as is the case with deafness. Fortunately, many special services are now available for handicapped infants and toddlers. For example, children with severe and profound mental retardation and low-incidence handicaps are eligible for Special Education as soon as they are diagnosed.

Those with less obvious problems may not be identified until later in childhood or when greater stresses are placed upon them academically, socially, and emotionally. They require careful study by multidisciplinary teams in order to meet their needs and determine the breadth and scope of their problems. Failure at any age level, whether it arises from cognitive, psychological, or social factors has long-term consequences. Hence, every effort should be made to prevent problems before they become too severe and to provide intervention that fosters both learning and self-esteem. As a practitioner in the fields of speech and language pathology and learning disabilities, I have long been concerned with the impact of language, learning, and communication problems on ego development. Indeed, one of the reasons for my pursuing the postgraduate Child Care Program at the Institute for Psychoanalysis and a Ph.D. in counseling was to gain a better understanding of the relationships between learning and emotional problems. One cannot ignore the impact of a learning problem on self-esteem (Raviv, 1987) and on independence. Often an inability to read and write will result in a reduction in overall social maturity. Since adults with severe reading and writing disabilities may need to have people take care of their financial accounts as well as their correspondence, every effort should be made to offer early intervention in order to prevent more serious academic and social problems from developing.

Multidisciplinary Studies

Because of the complexity of most learning problems and the many reasons for such difficulties, a comprehensive evaluation and multidisciplinary staffing are required (Public Law, 94–142). This generally includes the classroom teacher, specialists who evaluate sensory acuity, psychologists, special educators, and social workers. In certain instances, consultants from medicine and psychiatry may be needed to complete the diagnosis and make recommendations.

Failure in school and difficulty learning may also arise from environmental and emotional factors. With the increase in cultural diversity in our schools, diagnosticians should be aware of certain linguistic and social factors that may interfere with a child's performance in the traditional curriculum. The transition from home to school can also be a traumatic experience for some children, so information about responses to instruction, temperament (Keogh and Bess, 1991), and social-emotional development are essential.

The remainder of this paper is devoted to a more detailed discussion of the broad areas of learning that should be included in a study. Emphasis will be given to school-age children, but some references to preschoolers and adults with learning disabilities also will be included.

Mental Ability

In most cases of suspected learning problems, mental ability should be evaluated carefully with both verbal and nonverbal tests (Wechsler, 1974, 1989), since cultural, language, perceptual-motor handicaps, and other factors can interfere with performance (Carlisle and Johnson, 1989). Generally, it is advisable to select intelligence tests that do not require skills in the area of expected difficulty. For example, one would not give a verbal IQ test to a hard-of-hearing child or a performance-based test to the physically handicapped. Diagnosticians should be equally concerned, however, about subtle types of processing disorders that might interfere with the measurement of potential among children and adults with learning disabilities (Johnson and Blalock, 1987). For example, many have problems with word retrieval and recall that interfere with their ability to convey knowledge and with social interaction (Johnson and Croasmun, 1991). Others have perceptual motor deficits that interfere with tests such as Block Design and Mazes or with self-help skills. Residuals of these problems may persist and interfere with various occupations.

By definition, children and adults with specific learning disabilities have at least average mental ability; some may even have superior ability. Often, however, they exhibit considerable "scatter" because of their deficits; hence, diagnosticians should be somewhat cautious in using global IQ measures that do not allow one to examine patterns of strengths and weaknesses. Often measures of adaptive behavior and social maturity are used in conjunction with standardized tests of intelligence. Some people perform better in real-world, naturalistic settings, whereas others are better on highly structured tests.

Language delays and other learning difficulties may be related to the child's overall mental ability and level of development—that is, the child may be slow in all areas of development—so information is obtained from the parents and pediatricians about the youngster's rate of development including sitting age, walking age, language acquisition, toilet training, play, and general social maturity. Slow learners and mentally retarded children typically have a history of slow development. Those with severe problems will usually be identified early, whereas those with mild to moderate difficulties might not be detected until they enter school. Generally, Special Education services are available for the mentally retarded so they can be taught at a level that is appropriate for their overall level of functioning. If such children are pushed beyond their ability levels, they may become frustrated and lose a sense of self-esteem. On the other hand, expectancies should not be too low lest they fail to actualize their potential.

Background and Opportunity for Learning

It is difficult to determine the specific impact of cultural deprivation, lack of opportunity, and quality of instruction on a child's learning. Nevertheless, from the case history we obtain information about language stimulation at home, noting whether the parents read to the child, whether more than one language is spoken in the home, and the types of experiences they provide.

In addition, we need to know about the child's general physical condition, health, and quality of care. Many studies of high-risk populations indicate there are higher percentages of problems in low socioeconomic areas. Sigel (1971) also reported that certain disadvantaged children had difficulty on classification tasks that required picture interpretation. Thus, we must be aware of the ways in which experience or lack of exposure to certain media may be reflected in school performance. Various aspects of a child's language, such as vocabulary, grammar, and articulation, may appear to be deficient, when in reality they are the forms used in the culture and should not be considered as disabilities or problems. Parental expectations, the makeup of the family, and any marital or family disruptions should be considered in the diagnostic process.

Emotional Status

Information regarding emotional status is obtained from interview, observations of the child with familiar and unfamiliar people in naturalistic settings, and from watching reactions to success and frustration. If projective tests are used, they should be selected carefully, since perceptual and language disorders may impact on the individual's response. When children are evaluated by studying their play, diagnosticians also should be aware that those with language disorders often have generalized symbolic problems that interfere with pretend behavior, gesture, and other forms of representation (Cable, 1981; Roth and Clark, 1987). In addition, children with attention disorders may be disruptive in group settings.

When social-emotional problems are noted, efforts should be made to determine whether they are a result of primary or secondary disorders. Many children with language and learning disabilities, for example, are frustrated, angry, or depressed because of repeated failures. Others may be limited in their ability to express their feelings because they do not have the vocabulary to do so. Parents may find it difficult to discipline these youngsters because they are not sure whether they misunderstand or are deliberately misbehaving. Clinicians can help parents and teachers by informing them of the type of vocabulary and sentence structure the child can understand and remember.

Children with attention disorders require careful observation across contexts to determine as much as possible about their ability to function in various settings. Often they should be seen by physicians to determine whether medication is advisable. If so, we strongly recommend double blind studies, in which parents and teachers participate but are not told whether the child is given medication or a placebo. Behavior is charted over time across contexts to determine whether the child responds successfully to the medication. If medication is not recommended, children with attention-deficit disorders (ADD) or other attention problems often need quiet, structured environments in order to live and learn to the level of their potential. Adults with residual attention problems also experience frustration in noisy situations at work. Some become irritable because they cannot tolerate excessive noise and stimulation. They, too, may need a modified work schedule and environment.

Certain types of learning disabilities interfere with social perception and interaction (Johnson, 1987). Those with nonverbal disabilities, for instance, are somewhat like individuals with acquired right-hemisphere damage, who have problems with facial recognition or spatial orientation. Others are similar to people who have had closed head injuries in that they lack initiative, are disinhibited, and have difficulty maintaining social interaction and close relationships.

Sensory Acuity

Auditory and visual acuity should be checked carefully, since even minor disturbances can interfere with language and learning. Although hearing is generally screened by school nurses, whenever a problem persists, the child should be seen by a physician and a qualified audiologist. Children with repeated ear infections or allergies are of particular concern because they may have temporary reductions in auditory acuity. Young children who have had many infections during the preschool years may have language delays or difficulty following directions.

Visual acuity and other visual functions are equally important and should be carefully studied by an ophthalmologist or visual specialist. It is particularly important with young children to watch for conditions such as amblyopia or ocular imbalances. By school age, both far- and near-point vision should be examined, since children are expected to read material from the blackboard as well as books.

Professionals who test children with learning disabilities should be aware of possible difficulties reading various eye charts, since there may be problems in reading letter names or with spatial orientation. What appears to be a problem of visual acuity might be a perceptual disorder.

Cognitive Processes, Language, and Academic Achievement

In this country the term *learning disability*, is used to designate children and adults who have at least average mental ability and no primary sensory deficits, motor handicaps, or emotional disorders but who have a discrepancy between potential and achievement (Federal Register, 1977). The children are motivated to learn and have had adequate stimulation but are not performing at the level of their ability in one or more areas such as listening, speaking, reading, writing, spelling, and mathematics because they do not process information normally. Since it is a heterogeneous population, a comprehensive psychoeducational study is done, which includes a case history, assessment of sensory acuity, both verbal and nonverbal mental ability, emotional status (as indicated above), as well as tests for auditory receptive language (listening), oral expressive language (Wiig and Semel, 1984; Carrow-Woolfolk and

Lynch, 1982), reading (both decoding and comprehension), written language, mathematics, and various areas of nonverbal behavior. Tests and procedures for evaluating these areas of learning can be found in Salvia and Yssldyke (1988), Silver (1989), and Swanson (1991). In addition, psychological processes such as attention, perception, memory, and conceptualization are investigated to determine whether there are patterns of deficits that interfere with achievement and language. One rarely sees an isolated area of underachievement such as reading. For example, we would expect an auditory comprehension problem to interfere with verbal expression, reading comprehension, mathematics reasoning, and social skills (Johnson and Myklebust, 1967; Donahue, 1983). Similarly, when studying visual processes we want to know whether perceptual problems interfere with reading, writing, arithmetic, and/or nonverbal learning tasks such as drawing or spatial orientation. In adults, we want to know how such problems might interfere with work or everyday life.

We also try to determine whether the problems are primarily verbal or nonverbal. Verbal disorders usually interfere with language comprehension and expression, reading, writing, and some aspects of mathematics. Comprehension problems typically interfere with expression. Thus, children who have difficulty understanding words will have a limited vocabulary. Similarly, those with reading disabilities cannot write more than they read, even though they may be able to copy words.

Nonverbal disabilities occur less frequently but debilitating for social perception, play, and self-help skills (Johnson and Myklebust, 1967; Johnson 1987). As stated above, some individuals with these problems are similar to those who have sustained right-hemisphere disorders. At times they have difficulty with facial recognition, interpretation of body language, understanding prosody (the inflection and rhythm patterns of language that convey meaning), spatial orientation, and visualmotor skills. Often such children are loners and do not know how to interact with others but may do quite well academically. Consequently, they may be thought to have primary emotional or behavioral problems when, in reality, their social difficulties result from an inability to perceive or interpret nonverbal communication. In recent years, as clinicians have recognized the importance of such problems, some professional organizations and government committees have recommended new and broader definitions of learning disabilities to include social skills deficits (Kavanagh and Truss, 1988; Bryan 1991).

Intervention

The general goal of intervention for children with learning disabilities is to help them actualize their potential and to acquire skills they have not learned from regular instruction. Most schools and professional organizations recommend a "cascade" of services that include special classes, resource rooms, itinerant services, and consultation (National Joint Committee on Learning Disabilities). There is currently a strong emphasis on mainstreaming and integration of exceptional learners in the regular class. Nevertheless, some children require more intensive services to actualize their potential. Some need help from other specialists, including counselors and psychiatrists, to help them deal with feelings of frustration that result from repeated failure. Therapists should, however, work closely with special educators or vocational counselors to become familiar with the kind of problems the children or adults experience in school, at home, and at work. With appropriate intervention and guidance, many in this population can become competent, independent adults.

Research and Current Trends

In recent years, with the development of new technology, a great deal has been learned about brain-behavior relations (Kavanagh and Truss, 1988; Gray and Kavanagh, 1985). For example, computerized tomography (CT) scans permit the visualization of the brain without significant radiation hazards. Some studies indicate that cerebral hemispheric asymmetries are observable and that the left hemisphere of the brain is somewhat larger than the right among right handers. In contrast, studies showed that left handers have either a reversed asymmetry or no asymmetry. Some reversed asymmetry also has been noted in dyslexics. According to Duane (cited in Kavanagh and Truss, 1988) CT scans are probably not warranted for routine diagnosis, but they are important for future research.

Brain-mapping studies are perhaps more promising. The Brain Electrical Activity Mapping procedures of Duffy (described in Kavanagh and Truss, 1988) allow for more EEG recordings under various activities. MRI and PET scans also may contribute to a better understanding of brain function in normal and atypical learners.

There are, additionally, many new studies of high-risk infants and very-low-birth-weight babies. Such children would once have died, but with the advances in neonatology, many are surviving. Attempts are being made to investigate the effects of smoking, alcohol consumption, drugs, nutrition, and other factors on the fetus. In addition, new types of assessments in the newborn period are being conducted for early detection of later learning disabilities and for early intervention (Als and Duffy, 1989). Some investigators (Adams, 1989) are studying prenatal exposure to teratogenic agents and early postnatal exposure to lead (Bellinger, 1989). All of these studies highlight the complex interaction between the individual and environmental factors. Most studies are done with the hopes of preventing disabilities and future failure (Masland and Masland, 1988).

At the same time, there are many exciting studies of early literacy that emphasize the relationships between oral language, reading, and writing, as well as the relationships between early environmental experiences and later school performance. Families, particularly in lower socioeconomic areas, are being helped to provide the kind of stimulation that will foster later school learning.

There also are new approaches to learning and behavioral assessment (Silver, 1989; Swanson, 1991). In the area of language, reading, and writing, there is much more emphasis on the function of communication, so that evaluations in these areas include more than vocabulary, word lists, spelling tests, and grammar. Rather, the goal is to determine whether the children can use symbols for different purposes. Language is used to convey ideas; for heuristic, interpersonal, and social reasons; to express feelings; and to acquire new information. Writing also is used to aid memory. New intervention programs are directed not to isolated skills but to the broad functions of communication—to the writing process and to reading for various purposes.

In addition, many diagnosticians emphasize curriculum-based assessment rather than standardized tests. In this way, classroom teachers and special educators use the material that children have been taught rather than norm reference tests.

Other psychologists recommend the use of dynamic assessment (Palincsar, Brown, and Campione, 1990), which includes procedures to determine how well a child performs when given assistance. According to the proponents of this approach, dynamic assessment indicates abilities that are in the process of developing. This is in contrast to standardized tests that provide only a single "snapshot" of behavior.

There is growing concern for children with attention-deficit disorders and those with ADD and hyperactivity. The number of such children seems to be increasing in the schools and are of concern to both parents and teachers. According to DSM-III, the criteria include inattention, impulsivity, and hyperactivity. Checklists with specific behaviors are used to make the determination; however, it is essential to observe the child in various settings as well. In the opinion of this writer, studies of children with ADD should include a comprehensive psychoeducational evaluation to determine whether there are specific learning needs. Some ADD children are not underachieving in the traditional sense, but their behavior creates problems for themselves and others in the environment.

Programs for adults with learning disabilities are also expanding (Johnson and Blalock, 1987). Many colleges now offer assistance to individuals with disabilities. Students with known disabilities may ask for accommodations, and in some centers, obtain tutorial help. Often they need emotional support as well. College counselors should be aware of the wide range of learning disabilities and the frustrations students may face. Some become depressed and anxious in highly competitive situations.

Additionally, new efforts are also being made to help handicapped adults with career planning and job maintenance. Individuals with learning disabilities often need guidance to understand their own patterns of strengths and weaknesses.

Summary

The diagnosis of children and adults with learning problems is a process that requires the competencies of many professionals. Because of the complexity of the human organism, the learning process, the symbol systems that must be learned, and the environmental forces, many factors can interfere with performance. Fortunately, most children are quite resilient and can learn from most types of instruction. Our concern is with those who are vulnerable physically, cognitively, and emotionally. With proper multidisciplinary care, many can make significant gains.

Anna-Marit Duve, Ph.D.
Rolf Zachariassen, M.A.
(Adapted by Charles Saltzman, B.A.)

7

The Norwegian Education Assessment Method

his paper describes an approach to the diagnostic evaluation of learning problems developed during the early 1950s by the first author
and reported in the literature many times since (Duve, 1965, 1966,
1969, 1972, 1978, 1980). The procedure known as the AMS Method,
named by some of the children after the initials of the test's author,
blends ideas from psychoanalytic ego psychology and Lewinian Field
Theory with concepts associated with pedagogy, that is, with the kind
of instructional situations found typically in schools. This unique
method of observation is based on the deliberate creation of a setting and

The authors wish to thank Charles Saltzman for adapting their material for this
article.

a progression of tasks that form a close analog of the child's familiar classroom situation. How the child copes with these stimulus demands provides the data for the diagnosis, a method quite similar to the administration of projective tests such as the Rorschach and the TAT, during the course of which the observer notes how the subject responds to the sequence of stimulus demands provided by the cards. The AMS, then, is a method that is positioned between direct observation of the child in his natural setting and the relatively strange and austere setting of the clinician's office.

Initial work on this method began in 1952 when the first author, who had been a teacher of mentally retarded children in the public schools, was invited by child psychiatrist Nic Waal to join the team at her newly founded Child Psychiatric Institute in Oslo, Norway.

The early 1950s was a time when psychodynamic theory held sway in child psychiatry and ego psychology was just beginning to emerge. The psychological terminology in current use included such terms as *ego strength, anxiety, aggression, superego, object relations*, and the various defense mechanisms such as *repression, regression, identification,* and *compensation*. At the Child Psychiatric Institute we were also involved in a medical diagnostic culture that employed such terminology as *diagnosis, symptom, therapy,* and *prognosis*. As an educator dissatisfied with the limitations of educational testing methods that were restricted to measures of ability and achievement, I (Duve) found in this atmosphere new possibilities for professional growth, but also considerable challenges to learn new ways of thinking about and talking about children.

I began to search for methods that would be useful for a teacher in a child guidance clinic. Finding none that suited my needs, I began to develop my own, encouraged in this by Dr. Waal, who herself had been trained in clinics in the United States and who was herself convinced that suitable techniques were lacking.

The challenge involved integrating psychodynamic theory into the work of the educator. That was how the AMS test was created. It is an observational method for teachers working with emotionally disturbed children with learning problems. The AMS is a diagnostic tool, a set of tasks or situations that can be viewed as a projective test, one that provides understanding of the psychodynamics involved in learning problems.

Theoretical Framework

The AMS Method is founded on the psychoanalytic model of personality structure and functioning. Its essential elements were the id, ego, and superego—structural systems described in Freud's tripartite model. Qualities of the mental contents—conscious versus unconscious—were also important distinctions to be made. Clinical work before the 1950s had been preoccupied with the id and with the unconscious. The role of the ego in learning was beginning to be recognized and elaborated. Anna Freud (1948) had stated that "learning is in a high degree a function of the ego." Ego strength was a term in frequent use. Ego psychology, which placed the ego in a central position in the dynamics of personality functioning, moved psychodynamic theory closer to the teacher's frame of reference. Ego strength is involved in perceiving and coping with reality and in the ability to tolerate anxiety, prevent confusion, and maintain the equilibrium of the personality. Ego strength enabled the child to tolerate tension and to delay its discharge (Fenichel, 1945; Hartmann, 1960). Success in learning, a teacher could readily see, depended on the intactness of the ego, the child's ability to control the tensions of anxiety and id impulses. In addition to these Freudian principles of psychodynamics, my work was strongly influenced by several other important writers of the time:

1. Kurt Lewin (1936), in *A Dynamic Theory of Personality Structure*, had introduced the concept of life space, a fascinating idea which seemed to be related to and at times almost identical with the idea of ego. Life space for Lewin seemed to mean that in each individual some representation of the outer world was created, and within that inner-world representation, the individual also actively organized a way of coping with the world. One could imagine that a schoolroom—the outer reality—was represented psychologically in the child's mind as his "educational life space."

2. Heinz Hartmann (1958) introduced the idea of the conflict-free sphere of the ego, an idea that seemed to match the teacher's intuitive understanding that not all problems in learning could be traced to id or libidinal roots.

3. David Rapaport (1952) defined a projective technique as a method, or tool, for mapping "intrapsychic organizing principles." He was referring to principles that work within each individual when challenged by a stimulus, which leads to a response that is characteristic

of the individual's style of processing such stimuli. This definition of projection had some similarity to life space and ego functioning and also seemed relevant to the AMS projective method.

4. Louis B. Murphy (1956) outlined some "inner organizing principles" in play. The personality structure of the child, according to this notion, reveals itself in the child's use of play material. The child tells us about his inner ability to organize: the way he plays is as important as the content of his play. Murphy's idea of controls gave me a fourth building block for the AMS Method. Chaos in play and behavior could be used as an index that reflected chaos in personality structure, that is, lack of control. On the other hand, stereotyped and rigid ways of playing reflected inner rigidity or overcontrol.

The Method

The AMS Method is an investigation of how the child copes with a challenge to his ego, specifically his ability for "control." The test situations provoke anxiety, aggression, and grief, with sufficient precautions to keep these within manageable limits. The instructions and the administration of the method emphasize a calm and nonstressful atmosphere. The AMS Method presents a paradigmatic situation modeled after the school setting, with its special organization, expectations, restrictions, and frustrations. This situation can be examined along several different dimensions. The various elements and the stress they create reveal aspects of the child's ego function. The following thirteen elements were presented in the AMS situation:

1. the schoolroom
2. the teacher
3. the pupil
4. instructions
5. school atmosphere
6. achievement
7. concentration
8. understanding and following instructions
9. endurance
10. planning
11. completing the work

12. earlier learning
13. finishing an obligation

The Seven Schemes of the AMS Test

The AMS Method consists of seven "schemes," the equivalent of the Rorschach ink blots or TAT cards, each of which is designed to elicit information relevant to the four theoretical constructs that undergird the assessment.

1. *The Classroom.* The observation room is equipped so that the child immediately associates it with school and learning and teachers. There is a blackboard, chalk, books, a globe, papers, and the like. We are interested in how the child organizes for himself the life space of the classroom. For some children, the educational life space provokes aggression, for others it is intimidating. The child's behavior, speech, breathing, and body language will tell us something about the child's experience of his "inner world."

2. *Teacher Expectations.* The teacher is the educational superego. He or she leads, organizes, expects, demands, praises, punishes. The child will react to teacher expectations and demands according to his "inner organization" and his own superego. One can observe how a child reacts when meeting a teacher, when he is told to sit down, when it is announced that we are going to read, write or do math.

3. *The Interview (Pedagogical Reality).* A brief interview consisting of sixteen structured questions regarding the child's school situation helps us define the child's construction of the psychological reality of his school situation. The questions cover neutral, pleasurable, unpleasurable, and conflict-charged situations that every child is likely to meet in school. The child is asked his name, age, date of birth, which school he attends, what grade he is in, which other schools he has attended, the subjects he likes, the subjects he dislikes, how well he does in them, and how he feels about those situations in which he is not doing well. Later, his achievement levels will be tested. We can then compare his interview responses to his performance and infer how realistic he is about his situation. The interview allows the observer to note the child's characteristic defenses and the extent to which pressures interfere with his ability to cope with the situation and to learn successfully.

4. *Achievement Demand.* A brief set of standardized measures of reading, writing, and arithmetic is employed. The Goodenough Draw-a-Man and the Bender Gestalt Tests are also used in order to provide information about the child's level of cognitive functioning. The request for the drawings presents something of a surprise insofar as they are not automatically associated with school. Hence, they can tell us how a child deals with situations in life and in school that he cannot anticipate. The observation as a whole also permits us to learn how the child works, what he understands, how well he is able to concentrate, how anxious he is in such situations, and whether or not he is able to ask for help.

5. *Correction and Increased Demands.* How the child copes with increasing demands as the limits of his ability are tested—something every child has to cope with every day in school—is carefully observed. In addition, the child's errors are corrected by the observer. Some children will take this as a challenge and perform better; others will try to correct their mistakes and become confused, sometimes severely; still others will try to correct their mistakes but come to a complete standstill. In between these extremes we find a wide variety of reactions. The purpose of the observation is to determine at what level anxiety becomes disruptive of ego functioning.

6. *Provision of Ego Supports, Reduction of Anxiety.* Supportive help from the teacher-observer and reduction of levels of expectation are introduced in order to observe whether such a change reduces the child's anxiety and increases the capacity for control. We are then able to see to what degree the child's ego structure is resilient and allows the child to profit from supports and reassurance.

7. *Stamina.* The sequence of situations to which the child is exposed in this highly structured assessment procedure tells us something about the child's ego stamina or ego strength. This enables us to make an educational prognosis and to plan interventions.

Organizing and Reporting the AMS Observations

The data of the AMS observational scheme are organized graphically in terms of the seven situations, or schemes, and the child's performance in them along a horizontal axis, which represents optimal ego functioning. Those situations in which the child exhibits deficient ego strength are entered above the axis, the distance from the axis reflecting the extent of the deficit, whereas those situations in which the child reacts with overcontrol or rigid and restrictive functioning are marked below the axis, again quantified according to the extent of the excessive control.

Thus, on a single page, we can summarize graphically a child's pattern of ego functioning in response to the various demands of the school setting. It is a presentation in which the quantification and scaling are admittedly crude, but one that provides for qualitatively rich data.

The AMS test situation permits intensive study of the child's emotional responses to school and the kind of relationship he seeks to establish with the teacher. One can detect at the start the hopes, fear, shame, anger, and demoralization that have been experienced by parents and child as a result of the child's often-protracted series of school difficulties. The family brings to the clinic these negative feelings and often, as well, their high and sometimes unrealistic hopes for a quick and permanent solution to the problem.

In the observation, the child encounters a stranger who holds out the possibility of help. Despite his conflicted feelings, success depends on his ability to be somewhat trusting and to so manage his tension in the situation that he can both protect himself and reveal enough about his difficulty so that something helpful may be offered him. A sensitive clinician recognizes that the very effort to begin a brief relationship under such circumstances is characterized by high emotional drama in the child, as is the swift ending of the relationship that is an inevitable part of the process.

The AMS Method enlarges, in a much-needed way, the scope of child psychiatric evaluations, and introduces into such evaluations the assumptions, aims, and customary activities of the pedagogue. It underscores the treatment potential of appropriate instruction and elevates teaching to full standing as a treatment or intervention available for prescription. Clinical teams in child psychiatric clinics in Norway now consist of a child psychiatrist, a clinical psychologist, a social worker, and an educational therapist familiar with instructional techniques and such assessment procedures as the AMS.

As the second author of this paper, I (Zachariassen) have had many years of experience as an educational therapist employing the AMS. When using it I try to experience and identify not only the child's transference reactions to me but also my countertransference reactions to him. Both are sources of potentially important information. Let me give you two brief clinical examples.

Maja, eight years old, comes to see me for the first time. We had formed a hypothesis that she survives in school only as a result of the tremendous efforts she makes and for her "make believe" attitude. She is in first grade, and the teachers have not yet registered any specific functional lack in her school subjects. At the clinic, however, we are more doubtful with regard to her experience of school success, how she learns, and what her future course of development will be. At this first meeting she greets me with a nice, open, sophisticated look, calling me "Rolfern." Instantly I get the feeling that she wants to reduce me to something I am not—a pal. I start wondering if I am a teacher, if I know everything a trained teacher is supposed to, if I actually have something to give her. For me it is important to think through why this girl manages to make me feel the way I do.

Daniel is ten years old. His parents are worried because he reads poorly. He comes to see me and I find out that he doesn't read very well, but he doesn't read poorly either. Something in between. The same goes for his writing. I try to explain to him that from a teacher's point of view, his reading and writing are not that bad. He is doubtful. He thinks I exaggerate. He thinks I am lying and cheating, and he is not willing to trust my judgment. I begin to wonder if I have been too soft, too kind, as a teacher.

Since the AMS Method allows us to meet the parents, we can learn how they see the problem, what they have tried, what in the family system may have caused or may be sustaining the problem. We can get a sense of what the child and his family can make use of from among the things we can offer. The pedagogical material gained in such assessment also permits me, as a consultant to the child's school, to offer concrete and specific recommendations. As a neutral colleague, this cooperative sharing of information and advice is frequently seen in a positive light and welcomed by the child's teachers. Teachers often feel very much alone and have a strong need to share experiences when working with emotional learning difficulties. At times, however, a consultant viewed as the expert, as one who knows best how to work with the child, can be experienced as threatening.

We hope that this brief description of the AMS Method and examples of its application will acquaint a wider audience with its potential as an integrative diagnostic tool.

Betty B. Osman, Ph.D.

8

Learning Disabilities and Depression in Childhood

i n the past few years, the relationship of learning disabilities and depression has begun to attract interest in the educational as well as the psychiatric literature. Several researchers and clinicians (Colbert, 1982; Livingston, 1985; and others) have found a significant number of children with diagnosed learning disabilities who have a co-occurring or even a primary depressive disorder. This recognition can be attributed, in large measure, to recent advances in the study of depression and the acceptance that it does occur in childhood, and left untreated, may result in life-threatening self-destructive behaviors. The early psychoanalytic view of Freud (1968) and Rie (1966) that children lack the ego structure or superego development necessary for depression has been largely dispelled. So, too, has the argument that children's symptoms of depression are either developmental and/or transitory and, therefore, not diagnosable as a separate syndrome.

Current perspectives on depression in children, regardless of theoretical orientation (biological, analytic, behavioral, cognitive) generally take the position that the problem is diagnosable as well as treatable, even in young children. There is less agreement about diagnostic criteria and clinical manifestations, although in DSM-III-R, the symptoms for children and adults are essentially the same, with only minor differences.

I would like to briefly review the categories of depression listed in the American Psychiatric Association's *Diagnostic and Statistical Manual of Mental Disorders*, Third Edition, Revised (DSM-III-R, 1987), including some of the symptoms that might be observed in children. For a diagnosis of Major Depressive Episode (296.2x), at least five of the symptoms listed must be present for two weeks or more. Without listing all of them, a child might appear sad, lethargic or hyperactive, quarrelsome and irritable, disinterested in activities, unable to sleep, and demonstrate an inability to study or concentrate.

Even more frequently seen in children with learning problems, though, are milder, but more chronic forms of depression. A diagnosis of Dysthymia (300.40) will be made when two of the five criteria in DSM-III-R are present for at least one year. Again, low self-esteem, lethargy, diminished ability to concentrate, and feelings of hopelessness are among those mentioned.

Depression in response to life situations or events, such as learning disabilities, illness, or parents' divorce is known as Adjustment Disorder with Depressed Mood (309.00). In a study of twenty-five children and adolescents with learning disabilities, Cohen (1985) found a low-level chronic depression uniformly present. He claims that depression is frequently an associated response to the experience of being learning disabled, particularly in later latency and adolescence. I also have a colleague who claims he has never seen a child with learning disabilities who is not depressed. He maintains that, typically, depression increases with age as the young person faces more academic and social frustration.

Finally, the classification Depressive Disorder NOS (311.00) is used where symptoms do not meet the criteria for either a specific mood disorder or an adjustment disorder.

Although the criteria in DSM-III-R are necessary for diagnostic classification, it is important for those of us working with children, whether in schools or clinics, not to view the symptoms as fixed. Since

children are more oriented to action than reflection, they are more likely than adults to mask their depression, demonstrating a range of seemingly atypical behaviors. Temper tantrums, hyperactivity, aggression
or delinquency, psychosomatic complaints, and school failure may be
the prominent symptoms displayed, with no apparent dysphoria or
despondency. Children with these manifestations are more likely than
others to be misdiagnosed and go untreated, particularly if their problems are attributed to learning disabilities, behavior disorders, or an
attention deficit.

It seems evident, however, that a depressed child is likely to have
less energy available for learning and a reduced capacity to perform
academic tasks. Not surprisingly, Kashami (1982) found significantly
more reading and arithmetic problems among children with a major
depressive disorder than among those with other diagnoses. Colbert
et al.(1982) found as many as 71 percent of 111 depressed children in
his study to be underachieving, although only 7 percent were diagnosed
as having specific learning disabilities. On the other hand, Brumback
et al.(1980) found that over 60 percent of school-age children referred
to an educational diagnostic center because of learning disabilities met
the criteria for childhood depression.

Although an association between learning disabilities and depression has been demonstrated, the nature of the relationship has not been
established. A bi-directionality can be assumed, though, with the evidence that a depression may induce or exacerbate learning difficulties,
while a learning disability is likely to put a child at risk for depression.
Several factors and characteristics associated with learning disabilities
may account for this reactive depression.

1. Low self-esteem and feelings of worthlessness, well documented in the LD population, have been found to contribute significantly to depression, as well as being a concomitant symptom of the
disorder (Kovacs and Beck, 1977; Stevenson, 1984). Others in the
field (Cohen, 1986) have hypothesized that it is the loss of self, the dis-
parity between what one is and the sense of what one ought to be, that
results in low-grade, chronic depression. Failure to perform in school,
as expected, represents such a loss. To quote Cohen, "Being learning
disabled not only affects the young person's self experience and emotional life, but acts as an organizer of development as well" (p. 289).

2. The anger and rage many youngsters feel in response to their

learning problems may also result in depression if the anger is turned inward. One seven-year-old boy, probably one of the angriest children I have seen in therapy—and also the least able to express his feelings—hits his own head when he is angry, claiming, "I'm dumb and stupid! I have to go back to kindergarten."

3. Poor peer relationships and the social isolation experienced by many young people with learning disabilities have also been associated with depressive disorders. When children have difficulty learning in the classroom and the playground, it is hard to feel happy. I know one youngster who refused to play kickball at recess, claiming, "If you don't play, you can't lose." Of course, the other children never let him play anyway, as I later learned.

4. Seligman (1975) claimed that reactive depression is the consequence of exposure to events outside of one's control. Many learning-disabled children suffer from "learned helplessness," resulting from repeated academic failure and the perception that they have no control over what occurs in their lives. Some do assume responsibility—but only for their failures, while attributing their successes to luck.

5. Rourke (1989), Brumback (1982), and others have speculated that hemispheric differences (i.e., subtypes of learning disabilities) may also predispose some children and adolescents to depression. Rourke, Young, and Leenaars (1989) found youngsters with nonverbal learning disabilities to be more at risk than others for depression and even suicide.

I, too, have suspected that extremely low-performance scores relative to verbal on the WISC-R may be indicative of depression—as well as the visual-spatial deficits suggested by the scores. This is consistent with Brumback's hypothesis (1983) that right-hemisphere learning disabilities may be etiologically related to endogenous depression. In his study, significant Performance Scale deficits on the WISC-R accounted for 34 percent of depressed children as opposed to only 14 percent of the nondepressed.

Not all would agree with Brumback's hypothesis, and depression may not necessarily accompany learning disabilities or other disorders. It would seem evident, though, that a diagnostic evaluation of a child who is experiencing learning difficulties in school should, as a matter of course, include a measure of depression. Reynolds (1985) advocates routine screening for depression in school, just as we do yearly for cognition and achievement. Depression, where present, not only affects the individual, but his or her ability to deal effectively with others.

In the last several years, major advances have been made in assessment techniques for children and adolescents. Although there is still the risk of perceiving only one part of the proverbial elephant so to speak, identification of depression as well as learning disabilities can generally be made on the basis of a comprehensive psychoeducational evaluation in a school or clinic. While it is not the educator's responsibility to diagnose problems, I am convinced that teachers can contribute significantly to the diagnostic process by sharing their observations and insights with other professionals. They should regularly be included as part of the evaluation team. Teachers possess a firsthand knowledge of the student on a day-to-day basis and have an awareness of the child's social and behavioral interactions as well as their academic achievement. In my graduate courses at Sarah Lawrence College, I teach teachers how to screen children and do preliminary evaluations. It is important, particularly with so many children with a variety of problems in mainstreamed classes.

Although a typical evaluation generally includes many of the same instruments and measures, there is ample opportunity for individual preference. I will briefly describe some of the techniques I currently use at the White Plains Hospital Child and Adolescent Service in a problem-solving approach to diagnosis. While most are clinical in nature, informal adaptations may even be applied in the classroom. First, in an intake or initial interview with parents (and child, depending on age and presenting problem), a careful developmental, social, educational, and family history is taken. In addition to the well-known risk factors, there is much evidence to support the familial concordance of both learning disabilities and depression. Social problems are also common to both disorders, but there are likely to be differences. Depressed children may experience fewer negative interactions with peers, but may be involved with fewer interactions overall than LD children—and blame themselves. Learning-disabled children with problems in this area frequently complain of being "picked on" and tend to deny responsibility for their actions, seeing themselves as the innocent victims of others' aggression or mistreatment. During the course of the evaluation, information should also be collected from school personnel, pediatricians, and other specialists involved with the child (of course, with parental permission).

The clinical interview with the child is uniformly used in diagnostic evaluations today, whether structured or unstructured. It is useful to know how children perceive their problems and the circumstances that brought them for the evaluation. Some of the questions I typically ask to elicit clinically useful information from the child include the following:

1. Do you like school?
2. What is your favorite subject or activity at school? What is the "worst"? (The answer to this frequently reflects a child's learning problems.)
3. Do you have friends? A best friend?
4. How do you spend your time after school? With friends or alone?
5. Describe your mother.
6. Describe your father.
7. Is there something about your family that you wish could be changed?
8. Is there anything about you that you wish could be changed?
9. Can you tell about a particularly happy time? A sad time?
10. Do you have any secret worries?
11. Have you ever been so unhappy that you wished you were dead? If yes, did you think of how it could happen? A plan? (This is a relatively new question included in recent years for obvious reasons.)
12. What do you think your problems are? What could help (i.e., solutions)?

In conjunction with the interview, self-report inventories are also especially useful since they tap the child's subjective feelings of sadness, worthlessness, and lack of pleasure in life. The Children's Depression Inventory (CDI) (Kovacs, 1981) and the Reynolds Adolescent Depression Scale (RADS) (Reynolds and Coats, 1985) are two of the measures that assess cognitive, behavioral, and affective signs of depression. The Peer Nomination Inventory of Depression (PNID), while not a self-report test, can also be used in the classroom to indicate children who are depressed.

The mental-status exam, important in the psychoeducational evaluation, can be used qualitatively as well as quantitatively to suggest the presence of depression as well as learning disabilities. Subtest analysis of the Wechsler Intelligence Scale for Children, Revised (WISC-

R) (Wechsler, 1974) can provide a wealth of clinical information as well as normative scores when used sensitively. Although the diversity of diagnostic clues available cannot be discussed in this paper, a few examples will be mentioned. The Comprehension subtest, for example, reflects children's social judgment and the ability to deliberate, control impulses, and draw inferences. Unusually passive, dependent, or personalized references in response to questions can offer insights into the emotional status of the child. "Flatness" of affect and a paucity of language may also suggest a depressed mood. On the other hand, dysfluent or sparse language and/or imprecise definitions on the Vocabulary subtest, in the absence of emotional indicators, are likely to reflect a learning/language disability. In the course of diagnostic assessment, I also use projective techniques (i.e., drawings, storytelling, and the Rorschach for thematic content as well as the quality and use of language).

Direct observation is an invaluable measure of a child's social interaction and overt behavior. During an initial session in my office, I observe a child's exploratory activity (or lack of it) as well as the quality of relating to me. Facial expressions and body language can be at least as revealing as verbal expression. I recently saw a primarily depressed child, for example, who sat passively on the chair in my office, as if waiting for something to happen. There was little eye contact or spontaneous conversation, and my questions were answered succinctly with unelaborated, colorless language.

Another boy of almost seven was referred because of lack of academic progress in first grade. He looked as though he wanted to smile at one point, but almost visibly held it in. When I commented, he said, "I never smile, I don't like to." He told me that both he and his mother felt sad almost all of the time, adding, "I'm the reason (that Mommy is sad)." When I asked him how that could be, he replied, "because I'm bad." He had primary depression, and his mother did too.

A young child with a primary learning disability without depressive symptoms is more likely to look animated and explore the office physically, sometimes feeling objects to get a sense of them rather than just looking. Some children, with poor social perception, will stand too close to me or talk too loudly for my small office. In sum, many indications of depression and/or learning disabilities can be observed clinically with a keen eye and experience with children.

Although no single measure can assess either learning disabilities or depression, the use of multiple sources of information as well as multiple measures can shed light on both disorders by correlating the findings and analyzing the significance, thereby reducing the rate of false negatives or false positives in diagnosis. Difficult as it may be at times to distinguish primary from reactive depression, it is important for teachers and others working with children to be aware of the symptoms of depression and alert to the signs of that disorder in children referred for academic reasons.

I will present two case studies to illustrate the concurrence of learning disabilities and depression: one in which the symptoms were suggestive of a primary learning disability with reactive depression, the other in which a child was diagnosed as having a depression that affected his learning.

Karen

Karen, fifteen years old now, has learning disabilities that were identified in kindergarten. She is, and always was, a beautiful child and an outstanding athlete. She also related well to her peers, but she simply could not sit still or recall letter names or what numbers signified. Even in fourth grade, reading was a slow and laborious process, with spelling and writing particularly poor. Throughout elementary school, Karen had a great deal of academic remediation as well as parental support. In fifth grade, however, she became particularly anxious and fearful following a robbery in the house next door. For several months thereafter, she would not spend the night at friends' homes, and she began playing with younger children, even expressing her wish to be younger. She also worried about her father's safety when he was traveling on business.

In junior high school Karen performed fairly well academically according to her report cards. But she worked exceptionally hard, and she had help at the Learning Center in school. I also saw her for combined educational support and psychotherapy.

In the spring of eighth grade, Karen became overtly depressed and even mildly bulimic. She was often teary in my office and finally acknowledged that she hated the academic pressure of school and would, as she put it, "give anything not to have a learning disability for a whole twenty-four hours." She spoke of her friends knowing more than she "about everything" without studying nearly as hard. Toward the end of the year, Karen became almost school phobic, with headaches and other somatic symptoms that could give her reason to stay home. In part, this reflected her fear of final exams and the grades that she anticipated would be poor.

Dr. S., the psychiatrist in our service, decided to prescribe Prozac for a short time in the attempt to alleviate Karen's symptoms. At the same time, we explored a change of schools. Karen subsequently transferred to a smaller, less competitive school in the area and has also continued in treatment. The results have been very positive. Karen has been successful academically this year and has become a leader in extracurricular activities. She is significantly less depressed and is considering boarding at the school next year rather than commuting.

Although Karen's depression was of great concern, it seemed reactive to her learning disabilities and the pressure she was under in school.

Stephen

Stephen was seven years, eleven months of age when he was referred for a psychoeducational evaluation because of academic as well as behavioral problems in school. His second-grade teacher told me she thought he had a learning disability. Although he seemed to be an intelligent child, his reading and math were not up to par, and his attention span was notably short. He accomplished little work in class and was frequently disruptive, to the annoyance of the other children. Unstructured situations such as recess and lunch were particularly difficult for Stephen. He tended to be aggressive on the playground and at times out of control.

According to his parents' report, Stephen's early history was unremarkable, with developmental milestones within normal limits. His mother had returned to work after two years, confident that he was doing well. She acknowledged that she had also been depressed and hoped that working outside of the home would alleviate her symptoms.

Stephen appeared to adjust well to day care and then to kindergarten. When he began to display behavior problems later that year, they were attributed to his "immaturity." At the end of the year, however, his teacher and his parents recognized that Stephen was not ready for first grade—academically or socially. Consequently, he repeated kindergarten the following year.

In first grade, Stephen continued to have social problems, and his teacher wondered whether he felt too much pressure to achieve. He seemed tense and restless in class, and he tended to give up when challenged. He resisted doing his homework and only wanted to watch television. He had no friends, but did not seem eager for companionship.

Psychoeducational assessment revealed a significantly higher performance IQ than verbal, with a paucity of expressive language and difficulty concentrating on tasks. Stephen's academic skills were also found to be consistently low, with spelling in the 25th percentile and arithmetic only in the 15th on a standardized achievement test. Reading was somewhat better, although Stephen said he hated to read.

Projective material clearly indicated Stephen's negative self-perception and his depressive feelings. For his positive animal choice, he said he would like to be a horse because "it's strong, it's fast, and it can kick away people when it's bothered." He would not want to be a deer: "People hunt for them." Themes on the CAT were replete with stories of hopelessness and distrust. Nothing ever turned out well in Stephen's stories, and he always seemed to anticipate the worst. In my summary I wrote that Stephen seems to be "in a constant state of inner tension and irritability that are suggestive of depression."

Psychotherapy was initiated and we have worked on many issues relating to Stephen's negative outlook and his poor interpersonal relationships. His parents are also being seen in conjunction with his treatment. In the last few months Stephen's academic work as well as his mood have improved significantly.

Although Stephen was initially referred because of concern about his learning, it became apparent that he was a depressed youngster who could not focus his energies on academic activities. A learning disability was ruled out, but Stephen was nonetheless tutored for a brief time to strengthen his academic skills, which contributed to a more positive self-image.

To conclude, it is evident that the link between depression and learning disabilities is a common clinical occurrence. Much work remains to be done to clarify the antecedents, causes, and consequences of this connection. It seems clear, however, that educators need to be informed about the manifestations of depression in children, and mental health professionals must be more fully apprised of learning disabilities. In working with children, we must take into account their affective as well as their cognitive states in our attempt to truly understand their problems and provide appropriate treatment.

Rita Sussman, Ph.D.

9

Differential Diagnosis:

WHAT'S THE MIX BETWEEN LEARNING AND EMOTIONAL FACTORS, AND HOW DO WE UNDERSTAND THE RELATIONSHIP?

a s workers in the field, we frequently find ourselves addressing the question: "Is the child's problem due to a learning disability or are emotional factors the cause?" As varied as our human behavioral repertoire is, it still is true that similar constellations of behaviors may reflect different underlying conditions. Differential diagnosis, then, is our attempt, however faulty and limited, to understand what is happening. What is the child's experience? What are the contributing factors that lead to a particular child's set of behaviors? Our answers, however simple or elaborate, will make the difference in planning interventions, making recommendations, creating a milieu for the child, so that he or she will feel understood and will be able to function more effectively.

I start out with the following assumptions derived from a Piagetian perspective:

1. All behavior is the result of interaction between an organism structured to process stimulation in certain ways and to respond in certain ways, and an environment structured to provide stimulation in specific ways and to respond in other specific ways.

2. When any aspect of this self-regulating cycle of interaction is disturbed, there will be dyssynchrony, or a sense of disequilibrium; therefore, what we observe in children's behavior is their best possible attempt to adapt in order to maintain or to restore this process of self-regulation. Hence the notion that any 'lazy" or "just doesn't apply himself" is unacceptable. I have to know "What's going on?"

3. Any change in this delicately balanced system has far reaching effects not only at a particular moment in time, but as a result of a cumulative process. Hence, as Palombo (1987) suggests, an inability to integrate adequately what one sees with what one hears with what one does, may lead to feelings of fragmentation and problems in developing a sense of a fully cohesive self.* I would hypothesize, as well, that these difficulties with what could be called intersensory integration, inevitably have their effects on children's ability to integrate language with their experience, and to be able to incorporate language, or a "verbal self" as Stern (1985) suggests, into their full experience as people. Without being able to feel like a competent self, a child wonders, "What is wrong with me? Maybe I'm dumb or bad."

If we were to search for one organizer that could help put the issue of differential diagnosis in perspective, it might be the issue of integrative processing and the anxiety that floods in when that process cannot be successfully accomplished. One way of conceptualizing the process is to contrast different kinds of puzzles. We've all experienced the sense of satisfaction that comes from lifting up a portion of a 500-piece interlocking puzzle: many of the pieces still hold together, and certainly if we pushed the table on which they lay, there would be little disruption. Contrast that with trying to align the pieces of a puzzle

* Personal communication, Pearl Rieger, M.A.

such as those found in the WISC-R Object Assembly subtest. The pieces of these puzzles lay side by side; if we accidentally bump the table or push a piece too hard, the pieces shift, leaving gaps among the pieces. Frequently, then, we need to use both hands to align them correctly once more.

For most children the individual aspects of their development coordinate and interlock as nature intended. Even with some environmental pushing and shoving or lifting, the integrative aspects of development proceed, forming character, perhaps, but tending toward a basic sense of stability and competence. For some children, however, each time the table is accidentally bumped or deliberately shoved (i.e., each time there is a crisis at home, a separation, an angry parent, a failure in school), it is as if anxiety floods in the widening spaces, a signal that, indeed, there is vulnerability and danger that cannot be adjusted to easily.

In this context, I'd like to describe Kenneth, a child I recently evaluated, whose case sheds light on the interactive relationship that exists between the need for cognitive integration and the ability to function as a whole person emotionally. Kenneth makes the complementary argument to Rice's plea (1989) that we use projectives in addition to a learning assessment. I would like to suggest that by using the orientation of a learning assessment to disclose weaknesses in auditory processing, visual motor skills and integration, and/or language development, we can begin to understand what is happening when we see dissociative thinking, psychotic process, and elements of a thought disorder in the projectives of a troubled young man whose overall verbal and logical reasoning skills appear to be strong.

As we consider Kenneth, it might be helpful to keep in mind some of the major diagnostic alerts that can be used for considering whether certain neurocognitive deficits (or what we typically call "specific learning disabilities") might be affecting the behavior and personality development of the child or, alternatively, might be signaling the presence of emotionally destabilizing elements.

1. What do funny quirks in language syntax and usage mean? Can children understand inferences, or are they too literal? Is there a poverty of content, a lot of circumstantial reasoning, or a halting or excessive pausing in the formulation of a longer verbal response (i.e., could this signal a language-processing problem or might it connote

the presence of a thought disorder, depression, or inhibiting constriction due to anxiety)?

2. Do you need to repeat directions several times before they understand? Do they have trouble with the first few and then gradually seem to "understand" what is required? Do children confuse certain words or need to repeat questions, or do they repeat the words back to you incorrectly? Could this be distractibility due to anxiety or the symptoms of an attention-deficit hyperactivity disorder, or does the child have trouble with auditory processing or distractibility due to attentional fluctuations and strain on integrative functioning?

3. Even if designs are copied correctly, or blocks arranged correctly, are lines drawn with a paper and pencil wobbly or scrawled? Are blocks handled awkwardly or too deliberately? Are there many erasures or overworked lines? Do children associate fantastical images to them?

4. Are there oscillations in size and shape of designs, letters, names, and numbers? Is the handwriting scrawled or do older youngsters print? Is spelling phonetically accurate but ignorant of rules of spelling or irregularities commonly known? Are we dealing, then, with severe fluctuations in mental stability, a simple dysgraphia, or more complicated, integrative-processing difficulties related to organization of written language?

5. Do children seem unable to talk about Rorschach figures, TAT cards, or pictorial stimuli or have trouble organizing them? Could this be an inability to integrate the visual (pictures) with the oral (language) or to derive adequate meaning from visual stimuli or their own emotional experience? Or are they mentally too constricted, too anxious, too self-critical, or too guarded to respond?

6. Conversely, do children talk about a picture they have drawn while adding more and more detail? This could mean that they cannot fully organize their experience spontaneously, but must instead use language as the organizer. Alternatively, could the drawing "carry" the emotional expression that is stimulated by the language, which then stimulates still more affect that cannot be fully integrated within the expressive process of language alone?

7. To what do we attribute fluctuations in attention, giggling, singing, humming, tapping? Is this emotional anxiety or the strain of having to continue making connections that are hard and that fatigue

the children's ability to exercise cognitive control? What is happening when youngsters have to read a passage over several times before they comprehend what has been read? Could this be accounted for by attentional fluctuations, a dissociative process, or strain due to phonetically sounding out words and then having difficulties with attaching meaning?

8. Why aren't assignments completed or homework that is completed not handed in? Is this oppositionality, passive aggressive withholding, or a conditioned response to the difficulties of writing and fears that one's efforts will be inadequate?

Ten-year-old Kenneth was referred for a diagnostic-evaluation by his school because he was a "puzzle" to his teacher and acted inappropriately in class. He seemed to know more than he could demonstrate on tests; he forgot or lost his papers; he was easily distracted and seemed more interested in his own fantasy; he didn't always catch on quickly to what his teacher was saying. His writing, too, was a problem. Kenneth's parents, both professionals, noted that although he was socially outgoing, there had appeared an angry, defiant, quality to his relationships at home, resulting in emotional outbursts that were alarming in their intensity. Kenneth's developmental and social history included phobias, maternal physical discomfort for several months following birth, multiple arm fractures (his father's arm had been paralyzed briefly during the war), separation and dependency issues for his mother, an alcoholic grandparent, and parental difficulty learning languages and memorizing.

Kenneth was a wonderful, personable boy when I met him: frank, wryly humorous, well mannered, and with an ability to talk about himself and his feelings. How, I wondered, could my impression of such a charming young man be reconciled with the bizarre quality of his productions? When asked to draw a picture of a person, he rapidly drew a naked, "cross-eyed" boy with his hair standing up, "who got hit by lightning." As he talked about his picture, Kenneth kept adding things— a cigarette, police cars, a little person "running, like this, probably a thunderbolt's just hitting him." When asked to write a story about a picture of spacemen, Kenneth's space explorer found a gravestone recording the "death of Rita Sussman," who had taken care of him when his mother died. The vocabulary and sentence structure were much too simple for a boy his age and with his intelligence level, and the handwriting and spelling words were nearly illegible, but the thematic intent was very effectively conveyed through carefully developed parallels and logical reasoning.

A psychoeducational evaluation showed that Kenneth's social insight and verbal problem-solving abilities were superior, at least in more structured situations. However, Kenneth's ability to process auditory stimuli and keep them in mind was weak, especially when he needed to coordinate them with pictures or more conceptual ideas. Having to organize language and to figure out what the word order (syntax) meant, placed language comprehension and language expression at considerable risk for him. He frequently had trouble understanding the directions, either when they were complicated, or when the subtests were complex. He had difficulty figuring out underlying meanings of language or metaphors like "the man drew a gun," and had problems making inferences about situations based upon what people said. He might make reference to something that "gets tooken," or he would give up trying to formulate more complicated sentences using, for instance, "whatever" and "until," querying instead, "Can't I say them separately?"

All of this involves the integration of ideas with meaning, or the coordination of auditory precepts with visual stimuli. As memory becomes involved and the need to concentrate becomes greater, when Kenneth needs to draw upon his own experience to develop concepts and ideas, the strain increases. Kenneth's language begins to get more fragmented as his associational thought processing becomes confused with feelings and impressions that are attached emotionally to these same ideas. Hence, when given a picture and asked to make up a sentence about a simple concept like shoes (that the people are wearing), he says, "All of the people are taking a vacation. They are all wearing shoes. They are putting all their luggage into an ugly car that looks like a shoe."

A similar breakdown in integration and thought processing occurs when Kenneth draws his picture of a person. Because the visual image that Kenneth draws has been revisualized from memory, he needs to refer back to his experience in order to talk about it. The strain of integrating language with the visual precept, then, weakens the more cognitive and structured aspects of his speech, while the planning functions of language get disrupted by the distractions of more emotional associations and the anxiety that swiftly follows. Kenneth becomes overstimulated, his thinking becomes more fluid, and he becomes more impulsive and flooded by terrifying fantasies. Never knowing what will come out, being unable to retrieve it easily from long-term storage, and feeling the strain and fatigue associated with making those efforts, Kenneth may repress or avoid the search for meaningful and accurate information. Or, not fully understanding what people are referring to because of auditory and language processing difficulties that lead to still more holes in his conceptual network, Kenneth may yield to thinking about his more immediate, need-driven preoccupations. In this way, then, integrative difficulties and auditory and language problems pave the way for psychotic functioning and thought disorder.

At this point in his life, Kenneth is a complex youngster who will need skillful psychotherapy in order to build his defenses and also to deal with his underlying anger and terror, much of it identified with school. He will also need sensitive educational therapy to stabilize him and to help him learn processing strategies. If we looked only at his emotional disturbance or just at his intersensory integrative and language difficulties, however, we might miss the intricate interplay of cognition and affect, which leads to the extreme sense of anxiety and disorganization and the impairments in functioning and self-esteem he experiences.

In this presentation I have ignored the pervasive issue of depression, which exists in muted, despairing, or thunder-and-lightning form for almost every child I see. Unable to achieve psychic equilibrium and cognitive competence at age-appropriate levels by himself, Kenneth's depression clearly is a response to the disorganization he experiences and his inability to function effectively.

I believe, therefore, that if Kenneth is to have his chance at feeling whole and cohesive, he will need the benefit of an informed perspective, which forges integrative links from both learning and psychology, in order to work the "puzzle" more precisely.

III

Educational and Therapeutic Interventions

Introduction

Cognizant of the multidetermined nature of learning problems, contributors to this volume describe a variety of treatment approaches, each with a considerable following and with a considerable record of success. No single treatment modality has so far emerged that is universally successful, nor is it likely that any will emerge at any time in the future. Many children, however, benefit from the application of one or more of the interventions described here. Often, simultaneous application or a succession of several treatment modalities succeeds where one alone may have failed. These treatment modalities all seem to rest on an empathic diagnostic process that precedes them. The empathic attitude is at once the diagnostic information-gathering instrument and the affirming stimulating message of care and hope. The intervention techniques, formal and informal, aim to meet and understand children as they experience themselves and to help them develop the competence necessary to achieve whatever successes and satisfactions they seek.

Dorothy Ungerleider, in a discussion that is also a lyrical tribute to the courage of the human spirit, centers the contribution of the educational therapist in an action-oriented role that meets the client in the troublesome context of his life and strengthens him to fare better in it. Ungerleider articulates an eclectic mix of principles that define the role of educational therapist as a variant of the teaching role despite extensive and selective appropriations of psychotherapeutic techniques. She defines the work as a mix of empathically based actions or interventions that engage the client's strengths, weaknesses, and other attributes in some real-life context. It is an ecological perspective that unwaveringly holds in focus the client's embeddedness in some larger milieu—school, work, family. The work of the educational therapist thus requires assessments of performance and ability in relation to real-life tasks rather than the fragmentary, often meaningless or irrelevant measurement typically found in school-based assessments. Goals are set and the means for achieving them agreed to in a continuing dialogue with the client as partner. Her intention is to help the person learn how to learn (metacognitive training) and to enhance the excitement in learning. The process, being meaningful and enhancing of self-esteem, can sustain itself beyond the particulars of the lesson at hand. She is committed to stretching the person's competence beyond the limits already reached, by raising both the level of expectation and the level of stimulation. This too is in direct contrast to the experience of many children in public education, who, having been identified as disabled, are segregated and maintained thereafter in impoverished instructional environments. To achieve her goals, Ungerleider as teacher borrows from the therapist's tool kit whatever she thinks will work—role play, drawing, writing—whatever facilitates access to otherwise inaccessible emotional experience. She, like Oliver Sacks whose work she admires, is continuously aware of the client as a being conducting itself spontaneously in its own natural way, an attitude that suspends all forms of summative assessment and normative judgment.

Marlene Eisen's contribution centers on the role parents play in child development, the manner in which they respond to the disappointment that is inevitable when children do not develop as they had hoped, and how, in the past, educators have intensified the shame, guilt, and anxiety of these parents by holding them responsible not only for the creation of the problem but for its remediation as well. Eisen proposes an empathic, constructive approach that is sensitive to the pain and anguish of the parents as well as the child, one that explores the emotional significance of the child for each parent, and the impact of the child's school difficulties on the family system. She delineates the circumstances in which a diagnosis of specific learning disability can be made and how this often alleviates parents' guilt and rekindles hope of at least partial remediation. At the same time, she cautions that the diagnosis of LD should be used "neither to mask psychodynamic problems nor as a battering ram to beat children into conformity." All the resources at our disposal should be used to help children reach their potential; important among these are the competence, goodwill, and hopeful expectations of parents.

Sydney Eisen describes a multimodal approach to diagnosis and treatment of learning problems practiced by a child psychiatric clinic at a large metropolitan hospital. The children seen here typically have long histories of school difficulties. Many have had multidisciplinary team evaluations and special education placements, yet continue to have problems. Most frequently seen in this center are children whose learning difficulty is complicated by a coexisting conduct disorder, attentional deficit, hyperactivity disorder, or oppositional defiant disorder. Following comprehensive diagnostic assessment, the clinic is prepared to offer treatment recommendations that include simultaneous or sequential use of parent education, family therapy, medication, and individual-psychotherapy of the child, depending on the requirements of the situation and what the family is ready to utilize. These treatment modalities noticeably do not include specific instruction or remediation of school-related skill deficiencies, although such services may be provided concurrently by other professionals in the private sector or by public school personnel who continue to be involved in the child's education.

Colin Webber and Nan Knight-Birnbaum focus on the impact of parent loss and other occasions for mourning that affect the learning process. Interference with learning, temporary or protracted, is almost always evidenced by children following the death of a parent. It is essential that parents and educators understand the nature of the child's effort to cope with the loss and to provide the child with empathic support if he is to resume his normal developmental course in a reasonable period of time. Theirs is a contemporary psychoanalytic perspective which recognizes that young children, even preschoolers, have some capacity to mourn. The impact of the loss varies with the child's developmental status, degree of mastery of earlier developmental tasks, neuropsychological condition, and the environmental supports available. They describe the commonly observed sequence of response stages to the loss—shock, denial, anger, grief, the simultaneously occurring processes of hypercathexis of memories of the relationship and identification with characteristics of the deceased, and the various fluctuations in sequence or intensity of their manifestations. This report assists educators by alerting them to the potential interference with learning that parent loss engenders, allowing them to distinguish this from other causes of learning failure. Educators can assist by offering support, by making tasks manageable (proportionate to the resources the child can muster), and by tolerating the wide fluctuations in behavior that may occur before the child resolves the loss. They conclude with a richly detailed account of the recovery, through psychoanalytic psychotherapy, of a grieving child experiencing learning interference. Edward Kaufman discusses the prospects for the reactivation of learning in late adolescent boys housed in a residential treatment center. In such a setting, the therapeutic milieu is geared to enabling the residents to overcome the disruptions in their development, which include incapacitating definitions of themselves as incompetent or resistant learners because of their histories of repeated school difficulty. The milieu, with its expectations for cooperative problem solving and social interaction inherent in daily life, provides an opportunity for the reactivation of learning. Kaufman demonstrates how the ongoing caring relationships between staff and residents can serve as a medium for revising one's understanding of the world as well as oneself. Learning opportunities in such a setting can be purposefully designed through the milieu and the school program, while others present themselves in the form of unplanned minor incidents, which can be used for the genuine benefit of the residents involved.

Finally, Robert Galatzer-Levy presents a case study involving the psychotherapy, and later psychoanalysis, of a young man with a learning disability. Both treatment modalities are self-psychologically conceived and address large agendas—the emotional problems of living, the consolidation of the self, vocational choice, and competence in living, broadly defined. The treatment effort described here only indirectly is guided by, or linked to, performance in academic subjects or improvement in test scores. The treatments, however, create opportunities for the exploration of the interplay between biological idiosyncrasy, personal experiences, and institutional demands that result in the labeling of some children as "learning disabled." The case illustrates how cognitive modes can shape the experience of self, how they result in the ordering of the world in specific ways, and how they take on symbolic and emotional significance, especially through the environmental responses they evoke. Most important, the case illustrates the benefits that can accrue through psychotherapy and psychoanalysis, treatment modalities that proceed without specific instruction in subject matter or academic skill deficits. These remedial activities may be provided by other professionals trained to do so, professionals who are in most instances, however, not likely to provide the opportunity for the extensive exploration of psychodynamic issues that psychotherapy and psychoanalysis are designed to provide.

Dorothy Ungerleider, M.A., C.E.T.

10

Educational Therapy as Intervention

oday, at this prestigious gathering, the first
international conference of educational therapists to be convened on our continent, I have
been offered the topic most dear to my heart—"Educational Therapy as
an Intervention." Intervention is what we *do,* the coming between to
impart knowledge or skill. It has become clear at this conference, however, that what each of us does in our practices is not always the same
because of the diversity of our training, philosophies, and standards of
practice. Still, education is our domain. We are *teachers*, and I say
that with the utmost pride and respect. But we are *privileged* teachers,
most of us, because we tend to practice our art in the private sector,
most often working in the rose-colored world of one-to-one, free from
bureaucratic abuse and the constraints of school systems. Consequently,
the way in which we decide what must be taught and how it must be
taught is determined not by some district mandate but by the way we *look
at* and *listen to* our clients, trying to see and hear more than is obvious
to the untrained eye or ear.

But educational therapy is not simply a one-to-one luxury. It is a laboratory for determining the most effective techniques and interpersonal attitudes that facilitate learning. The lessons to be learned from individuals can form a theoretical framework applicable to the masses. When we understand the whole child in his whole world, we can plan differently. When we understand the characteristics needed in the helper, we can train people differently. Let me help you see the need for a different kind of training through the example of Randy.

In September of the school year, Randy's teacher requested and received a complete evaluation of him. During three days of testing, he was given eight of the better-known achievement, aptitude, and projective tests. The school psychologist performed her job, observing the mandates of federal and state laws and the rules of her district. Analysis of test scores led her to the following prescriptive plan for the "fixing" of Randy.

Reading:	1. Work on word-attack skills.
	2. Work on phonetic skills.
	3. Work on reading-comprehension skills.
Vocabulary:	1. Increase vocabulary skills through use of pictures.
Spelling:	1. Keep list of reading and vocabulary words.
	2. Work on word-attack skills.
	3. Work on phonetic skills.
Arithmetic:	1. Work on place value, number sentences, decimal points, and rounding numbers.
	2. Work on 3-digit, 3-number addition with carrying, and 3-digit, 3-number subtraction with borrowing.
	3. Work on 1-digit, 1-number multiplication.
Processing areas:	1. work on visual and auditory memory skills.

There was just one problem with this tidy prescription. The real Randy defied the "fixing"—resisted all efforts at implementation—because the real person behind this list had just celebrated his eighteenth birthday. The real Randy would soon be completing the last of three years in a residential treatment facility. Within months of this recommendation, he would be leaving the only place he had called home in his life, with the only caring people he had ever encountered. State funding mandated eighteen as the age for independent living.

In nine months, the real Randy would have to find a job, cook and clean and shop and ride the bus and handle money and make friends and compute his income and expenses and pay the rent and make decisions and solve problems that life didn't rehearse. Phonics and 3-digit math? Word attack and vocabulary building? These would be abstract futilities to a young adult mind so burdened by survival realities and social inadequacies.

If the examiner had only been allowed to make contact with Randy in a different context, she might have heard the goals he articulated so specifically—"to live a decent life, socially and in my employment, and do things correctly"—or his vocational dreams—"to do something in the building trades." Perhaps she would have noticed the magazine he carried, *Popular Mechanics*, its cover worn from frequent readings. Perhaps she might have asked him to read something. From this self-chosen magazine, Randy could read highly technical passages and understand their broad meanings as completely as he would ever need to understand them.

Randy had only nine months remaining to live in a nurturing and academic environment that might still provide relevant interventions for his life needs. Time was in desperately short supply. But the "whole" of Randy had been lost by the nearsighted limitations of standardized, objectivized procedures.

What would an educational therapist *do* with a Randy? What would be the psychoeducational interventions—those interventions that rely on the tools of two disciplines, education and psychotherapy—to foster the acting, thinking, and feeling necessary for learning to take place?

When we borrow someone else's tools to do our fixing, we must always be aware of the boundaries of our ability to use those tools. No one clarifies those boundaries better than Katrina DeHirsch (1977):

> The remedial teacher's goals are educational, and while in the process of learning, the child's inner situation may be modified; she is concerned with . . . the child's ego. Her task is to teach the youngster not only specific skills but to delay immediate gratification, to check unruly drives, to enjoy mastery for its own sake . . . , all of it in the framework of the specific learning situation.

In contrast, the psychotherapist works with disturbed youngsters who may not be available to learning and who, as a result of conflict, (are not able) to give of themselves to educational demands. The psychotherapist directs himself to the child's inner situation, to his unconscious fears, his fantasies, his secret terrors, to those forces that interfere with his investment of psychic energy in tasks unrelated to his drives.

An educational therapist who sees himself as a psychotherapist is bound to fail in both roles. Goals and methods differ. (p. 88–89)

Goals and methods do indeed differ, but in at least three respects, there is a fundamental sameness between these two professions upon which the success of the therapy ultimately depends: (1) psychotherapists and educational therapists cannot succeed without the establishment of a trusting relationship with the client. Ekstein [1969] poetically laid the ground rules: "From having learned to love, children must proceed to love of learning;" (2) educational therapists, like psychotherapists, must develop their Reikian "third ears" and attune their listening skills to hear more than is being said, but for different therapeutic aims; and (3) educational therapists and psychotherapists must feel and demonstrate *respect* for their clients (most clients have little or no self-respect when they enter the therapy, and rarely have they garnered respect from others).

Since the pedagogy of our field, particularly regarding intervention, is still in its infancy, there are no universal standards of practice; however, I will present what I believe are some fundamental principles of psychoeducational intervention.

First and foremost, of course, is a collaborative partnering, at every level and for every goal of the therapy. Even the dreaded testing process can become partnered. I will no longer give a client a test without first asking if he is willing to be tested. The simple act of his granting permission begins a bond and gives some sense of personal power to one who is used to having everything done *to* him instead of *with* him.

But before I ever ask the question, we must first become acquainted. Before testing happens, I must have some idea what *he* thinks he's good at and what *he* wishes he could do better. Before testing happens, I must have told him something about each test itself, what it was designed to show, and at the conclusion, what it seemed to show about him. His opinion of that test interpretation will be solicited and respected. Does he agree with these findings? Do they seem to fit what he knows about himself, his areas of difficulty and strength? At this point,

I often present my Swiss Cheese Theory of intelligence, a theory particularly effective for youngsters from perfectionistic, high-expectation families. The Swiss Cheese Theory compares the concept of intellect to Swiss cheese, with the good, solid representing the stuff we know well, and the holes symbolizing the stuff that's hard for us. No two cheeses ever look alike, of course (I recommend a visit to the cheese section of the market so they can check out my veracity); some have lots of little holes or a few major big ones—but they all have holes! Therefore, one of the jobs of our partnership will be to identify the type of his "cheese" and learn to work around his "holes"—but most important, to accept and embrace those holes for their part in making him such a one-of-a-kind person. The message, of course, is: imperfection is universal, human, acceptable.

Partnering is also crucial to the goal-setting stage. At the end of the initial interview with the parents, goals for the therapy will be solicited, discussed, and jointly determined by client, parents, and educational therapist as a team. The very first remedial intervention, however, (at least in my practice) must always be chosen by my client.

What does he *want* to learn? What is his current source of humiliation? Whether it is short vowels, the War of 1812, the meaning of body language in social relationships, or passing the driver's exam, that request will become the starting point of our work. Using this approach, I have discovered a consistently true phenomenon that I've named the Reciprocal Compromise Principle: Begin by teaching them what they *want* to learn, and they will inevitably allow you to teach them what they *need* to learn.

After determining the "what" of our first intervention, we must consider the "how" of achieving the goals. Again, I share DeHirsch's comment that the goals of education are surely not the amassing of information; rather, they are fundamentally twofold: (1) learning how to learn and (2) getting excitement out of learning. Process-oriented, metacognitive strategy training, the "learning how to learn" approach so popular today has dramatically shortened the duration of my clients' educational therapy. Learning *how* to learn is a principle that transcends all academic, social, and life skills. Many clients are paralyzed by inefficient, counterproductive strategies. For them, "excitement" and "learning" have no connection. They struggle to memorize details, unable to perceive the frameworks underlying all text, lecture, and life-skills information, frameworks within which whose details have meaning.

Interventions must be designed to alter such constricted strategies. For example, I often spend a full hour with a client just studying a textbook's table of contents, never reading a page of text, but having the client speculate what he thinks the subject of this book is all about and how he came to that conclusion. Try this; you will be amazed what you learn about your student's knowledge base, or the lack of it. Can he see the whole point of the topic, the overview? Does he already possess any meanings associated with the vocabulary on that page? Does he have any contextual knowledge to begin to guess what might be coming up inside those pages? This exercise alone would provide a semester's curriculum for educational therapy, because all the related words and concepts unknown by the client would be revealed. Interventions can be most effective if we have one lesson grow out of the unknowns revealed in the lesson before.

One word of caution about metacognitive approaches. Unfortunately, too many schools aren't there yet and too many teachers still perpetuate the myth of memorization as learning. We must always weigh our intervention against the risk of failure in that client's life circumstance, because a major goal must be reversal of failure. Without this reversal, we cannot undo the terrible price of that shame and shattered ego.

With this goal in mind, we have to prioritize our limited time with our clients. If we see a client one or two hours a week, we must carefully determine what strategies can be developed during those hours that will generalize to that client's successful achievement in his working place—the school or the job. We can never forget that school is the child's working place, and whether the "boss" (i.e., the teacher) is in or out of tune with metacognitive theory, that child will be accountable to that boss and the expectations of his classroom.

Now a word about "stretching." Most often, learning-disabled youngsters are not stretched to their potential attainment levels. Too often here in America, learning-disabled children, placed in overcrowded special classes are given a simplified work load and a sense of fraudulent success. They know it is a fraud when their peers are reading fourth-grade novels and they are filling in the blanks in insulting second-grade workbooks. Furthermore, they have been deprived of the language base and information that grows out of content-area discussions occurring in regular classes but usually omitted from special day classes. As guardians for their right to knowledge, educational therapists must demand access to the regular curriculum content for each client. If they cannot read it, it must be read to them. If they do not understand the concepts, then the concepts must be made comprehensible—taken from the most concrete level, in stages, to the abstract. Conceptual input is hierarchical; they *must* have the fundamental concepts to get to the next level.

As far as those tools we borrow from you psychotherapists, let me give some examples of how we use role playing, art, and writing for problem solving and expression of feelings.

First, role playing. Apparently, my ten-year-old student, Michael, had learned to tune out his mother. When Mother complained of this for the third week in a row, I spontaneously asked them to act out the situation for me, but to reverse roles. Mother played Michael brilliantly, mutely playing with a toy and refusing to do homework. But Michael, instead of playing the nagging Mom, was unable to utter a word in that role. I presumed that he had so completely shut out her voice at home, that he had no idea what she might have said. He couldn't play her part. The week's assignment was for him to listen and rehearse for next week's performance. That was the first week that Michael ever heard Mother's instructions.

Feelings are frequently expressed through art and writing forms in educational therapy. The following examples will reveal the ways in which these tools can be psychoeducationally therapeutic for both neurologically impaired and emotionally disturbed clients.

Jack had been in educational therapy for two years for severe visual perceptual and expressive language disabilities. From the very beginning, he frequently mentioned his dog, Troy, and always tried to tell more but could never retrieve the information. As his nervous system matured, however, Jack was able to draw increasingly more recognizable objects. One day he drew a sketch and said, "What is this?" When I said it looked like a table, he said urgently "Yes, but what kind, what kind?" The spiral curve of the table legs he had drawn suggested wrought iron. When I used the words "wrought iron," the memory trigger was released. Out poured the story of his dog, caught in the wrought-iron table, and he and Grandma being sent to the back room so they wouldn't be upset when the firemen came to free the dog. Apparently the dog was so seriously injured that he had to be put to sleep. Jack had carried the horror story, unretrievable, for two years, but that day, we both learned to use sketching as a catalyst for finding lost language. Tom's art work had a whole different meaning. Tom came to me filled with outrage over verbs and participles and the "dumb English teacher" and the incomprehensible textbook. In school Tom had become a "silent screamer" to whom mistakes were intolerable and for whom parts of speech had become a cry for help. I heard him, and we started to work on parts of speech. Then Tom's mother called to say she had found cutouts of female bodies with heads cut off and moved to different bodies, and violent cartoons Tom had created, with a hero called Captain Slaughter, and I heard her too. Tom needed guidance in finding appropriate psychological help. We must be more than remediators—we must be ombudsmen—but that is a topic for another day.

Another fundamental principle of educational therapy is compensatory training. Tim is probably my prime example of a severely dyslexic student who used every compensatory service available to him—note takers, tape recorders, taped textbooks, speeded speech tapes (for speed listening), dictaphones for reports, and secretarial services for typing his papers. He recently graduated from Claremont College with the unique distinction of having listened to every book and dictated every paper. Tim has almost perfect auditory recall, the world's most endearing personality, social leadership skills, and artistic talent (his one-man show in glassblowing sold out every piece of work—a first for Claremont).

But we educational therapists must never forget the toll on these remarkable compensators. When I took Tim to lunch to celebrate his extraordinary achievements, he confided, at age twenty-one, how close he came to suicide during those first semesters at Claremont. Outwardly the world saw a gregarious, kind, dyslexic Wonder Boy. Inside, the scars of self-doubt and confusion of the little boy who was different from all the others left a young man nursing private depression. Our third ears must indeed hear more than is being said.

Flexibility is a fundamental requirement for all educators, but educational therapists must be especially prepared for the unanticipated. By keeping a list of overall goals at the front of each client's file, we can be prepared to adapt the client's need that day to one of those goals, or add a new goal that may have only just surfaced.

Audrey's story will help you understand this principle. I always have such grand plans for gorgeous, scattered, fragile, emotionally battered forty-five-year-old Audrey, plans for strategies that would help her read effectively, write functionally, manage her finances, and gain some independence. But the plans must always be flexible because Audrey goes from crisis to crisis, trying to cover over her very secret but very severe disabilities with some brief performance that will prove her competency to the world of strangers. She has given up trying to prove it to her husband and twenty-year-old daughter, who chronically belittle her in tragic, destructive, psychological abuse. Family therapy is out of the question; husband and daughter are too happy with the status quo.

And so Audrey thrives on an "organic curriculum" that grows out of the week's needs. One week we must work on the reading of multidigit numbers so she won't feel so foolish in reviewing the figures in her aunt's will. Another week she brings a television public-service announcement she has volunteered to write, but, of course, she can't write. So she dictates as I write, and together we edit. Audrey knows when the words need changing. She just needs time, patience, and the belief in her knowing. Homework would be so essential for her overlearning of skills, but I know that there will never be consistent follow-up on assignments, or the kind of time commitment to building the compensations that would give her power over her life. For Audrey, the goal for each session is to take her wherever she is on that day, address whatever her needs are, listen to her, admire her remarkableness, and perhaps provide her the only moments of respect she feels in her week.

Educational therapists must acknowledge their limitations, not only in their own training but in the limiting circumstances of their clients' realities. When I feel frustrated about what I cannot do for and with an Audrey, I remember the gift of these words from one student: "You taught me that I could; I guess the rest is up to me" (Ungerleider, 1985, p. 203).

Audrey's case is a fine transition to the final fundamentals I'd like to discuss here—modeling and cheerleading. We are models in many ways for our clients. At the most basic level, we model how to read with fluency, or how to write and spell and compute with accuracy. But there is so much more. We are models as identification figures, perhaps modeling values, life-problem-solving strategies, language patterns, even personal grooming styles. We model when it is appropriate to laugh or cry, fight or withdraw, argue or concede. We model ego strengths and share our humanness. We listen and moan in empathy at how hard it is to write a paper or study for a test, remembering our own, non-LD struggles with the demands of academia. But then we help them achieve those goals and celebrate with them the feeling of release when it is done, and the feeling of pride when the end product is something of value. If you were a fly on my wall, the word you would hear most often is *Bravo!* My clients must earn their bravos, but they get a bravo for every goal achieved by their own sweat, no matter how small that goal.

Why do I end my talk on intervention with a principle I frivolously call cheerleading? Because it may be the most important sort of intervention of all—the one that builds autonomy. Some interesting research by Borkowski and colleagues in 1986 revealed that students who attributed failure to lack of *effort* rather than lack of *ability* were more likely to persist at efforts to master tasks. How clearly it follows, then, that educational therapists must be cheerleaders for every *effort* our clients exert toward mastery of their goals, whether they be academic, social, or vocational. They must be cheered, even if they fail, to learn that failure itself has a purpose, teaches a lesson. The trick is in understanding the lesson.

Helen, who, at twenty, had never made a decision independently, decided on her own, secretly, to transfer to a different junior college for one summer session. She asked no one, and the transfer turned out to be an educational disaster. When I cheered her move, she looked puzzled until I helped her see that the *decision* was the personal triumph. So what if she lost a semester? She might have lost one at the other school too, if she was so unhappy. But what she gained was a major step toward identity. Helen, young adult person, had a right to make decisions.

I close with a plea: If we are to grow as a profession, we must share our *interventions*, the things we *do* that work. Tests and numbers are not people. We must build a body of effective interventions that our profession can understand and apply with consensus regarding their therapeutic value. Oliver Sacks, in his astounding book *The Man Who*

Mistook His Wife for a Hat (1985) says, "Our 'evaluations' are ridiculously inadequate. They only show us deficits, they do not show us powers; they only show us puzzles and schemata, when we need to see music, narrative, play, a being conducting itself spontaneously in its own natural way" (p. 172). Amen.

Marlene R. Eisen, Ph.D.

11

The Impact of the Learning-Disabled
Child on the Family

n the days before passage of U.S. Public Law
94–142,[1] parents rarely felt any purpose was
served by fighting a system that did not seem to
have any place for their "special children" (Coles, 1987). Furthermore,
they were usually told that their children were "underachievers" or
"troublemakers," daydreamers or easily distracted youngsters. It was
implied, if not stated outright, that if the parents had done a more effective job, the child would not be having problems in school.

The history of special education in the United States is an interesting one. Unlike other changes in educational philosophy and practice—usually the prerogative of theoreticians and educational
practitioners—the growth of special education for children with special
needs was inspired by concerned parents fighting for a fair education for
their children. Schools for the deaf, the blind, and the physically handicapped were established in response to parental pressures. Today's
parents have won the right to (1) be fully informed of the school's

assessment of the child's special needs, (2) take part in decisions made about the child's educational program, and (3) get any necessary help at no extra cost to them (Osman, 1979).

Learning disabilities (LD) was not recognized as a special diagnostic category, however, until fairly recently. Many adults are only now realizing that their difficulties in school were not the result of low IQs or personality deficits, but were caused by endogenous difficulties in cognitive processing, which to the best of our present knowledge, may be genetically determined, or the result of neurological damage.

Some parents find it particularly difficult to confront the problems of their LD children. Their own early cognitive deficits led to school experiences characterized by failure and rejection. Unaware of these deficits or their academic consequences, and accused by teachers and others of failing to set proper standards, their own parents joined the school in berating and punitive behaviors in hopes of improving academic achievements. Now these children, grown to adulthood and parents themselves, are facing the very system that condemned and rejected them, and demanding for their children the support they themselves never received.

One mother says, "Even as I fight for my son to get what I know he needs, I am angry that my parents never did this for me." Another mother reports, "When I go to the IEP[2] meeting, I feel all those eyes on me, all those people sitting around thinking what a terrible mother I am. . . . I feel like such a failure. I get mad at my kid . . . why can't he do better so I won't feel so ashamed? Then I am ashamed of my thoughts . . . and it goes round and round . . ."

The first mother resents the fact that her parents did not recognize her struggle, did not support her when teachers attacked her for poor work in the face of high IQ and achievement test scores. Didn't they see how hard she struggled to understand? Could they possibly believe she enjoyed standing on the sidelines because she could not play the games others found so easy? The second mother says her anger is like a loose cannon, now directed at her child, then at the school, and finally at herself. "My parents only wanted to know I was in school during the day, and what my report card said," she reminisces. "My mother never visited the school until I graduated. That's the way I thought it was supposed to be."

As professionals, teachers, therapists, pediatricians, do we, in our zeal to advocate for children, cast parents into the role of the adversary, objects of pity, inhibitors of growth, or parental misfits? Are we, as the pediatrician Terry Brazelton suggested, in competition with parents for the souls and minds of children (personal communication)? Or can we work together to provide each child with services optimally suited to his or her needs? We must learn to set aside a prevailing belief of the 1940s and 1950s; parents are not malignant forces!

Every parent who holds a new infant for the first time looks at a bundle of potential and dreams of what this child will grow up to be—the smartest, the best, the most beautiful. What happens to those dreams when suddenly, from a kindergarten, or a first- or second-grade teacher comes a dreaded report: "Your child is not measuring up." What has gone wrong? The initial response is to turn on the child. "Why aren't you trying harder? What is the matter with you?" Then the parents turn to the teacher. "Why can't you make my child perform better." And finally, the parent, usually the mother, looks at herself and asks, "Where have I failed?"

Once the child has been officially labeled (after the requisite diagnostic rituals), the parents are left to deal with their grief, with the loss of the dream of that high achiever, that bundle of potential they held as an infant. Parents go through all the traditional stages of mourning: denial, anger, guilt, bargaining, depression, and finally, it is hoped, acceptance (Silver, 1984). In this situation, passive acceptance, the shrugging of shoulders and saying "oh well" is neither desirable nor possible. There is an ongoing issue that must be confronted. This child must be educated, prepared for a useful, independent adult life. In order to play a functional role in this process, the parents will have to work toward acknowledging and accepting their own negative feelings toward the dysfunctional child, without castigating themselves and without acting out their anger and disappointment on their child. Often, parents need help in acquiring insight into their conflicting emotions. A sensitive educational therapist can help parents find ways to work with the school and the child to provide alternative coping strategies to enhance the child's strengths and minimize his deficiencies.

Narcissistic injuries to both child and parent are triggered by learning deficits. For the parents there is also a breakdown in object relations, as the sense of being judged and found wanting leaves the parent vulnerable to the criticism of others. From a self-psychological perspective, the damaged child is a disappointing self-object for parents (Fajardo, 1983), perceived as a reflection or even an extension of the parent, and thus a representation of success or failure of the parental role. As the self-esteem of the parents is threatened, interactions with the child may run the gamut from overprotection to angry rejection.

Normally, school-aged (latency) children derive self-esteem from their accomplishments, as they are rewarded by parental pride, peer acknowledgment, and academic evaluation. The LD child is denied these roads to self-esteem. The child's willingness to attempt to master new skills is based, in large part, on past successes, which have been appropriately rewarded by parental joy. Since failure is such a pervasive part of the LD child's life, he or she hesitates to venture into new arenas. So the child and parent, each narcissistically injured, cannot feed one another emotionally in ways that mutually enhance self-esteem. Narcissistic injuries to child and parent, triggered by learning deficits, create an interactional matrix from which pathology may arise (Garber, 1988).

The parents', and particularly the mothers', affective state determines and modifies the child's affective state, according to Stern (1985). Mothers and fathers may alternate between irrationally high expectations and deep disappointment leading to helpless, hopeless feelings. The child incorporates and recreates these labile parental feeling states, which he then experiences as fluctuations of his own self-esteem. This causes him to withdraw and engage in solitary activity to avoid his painful vulnerability to the moods of significant others. Parents then become angry because the child isolates himself from the family system, and often the shame of having an LD child isolates them from their friends.

Children with learning disabilities have problems not only reading books, but also reading the responses of others. As a result they may be viewed as self-centered, callous, insensitive, and grossly deficient in empathic skills. Fearing criticism so strongly that it is perceived (often wrongly) in every word or look, they become quickly defensive. Afraid of their own vulnerability to emotional shifts, emotional responses are avoided even when appropriate, as in the face of another's pain. The stress of cognitive interactions may lead to withdrawal at socially inappropriate moments. Such behavior makes ongoing object relations problematic, adding to the frustrations of parents and child (Silver, 1984; Shane, 1984).

Given the facts that parents and their learning-dysfunctional children both suffer from problems of low self-esteem, social vulnerability, guilt, and periodic bouts of hopelessness and helplessness, what can we as professionals do that would be most helpful?

In the 1950s and 1960s, the psychoanalytic community believed that all learning difficulties were psychologically based (Garber, 1988) except in children with low IQs. In the last twenty years, however, there has been an increased emphasis on the neurological determinants of LD. As a result, behavior-modification techniques and medications have taken over as the dominant interventions, replacing to a great extent psychotherapeutic interventions (Silver, 1986).

Consistently, through the years there have always been those educators and therapists who agree that psychotherapy has an important contribution to make in understanding and interpreting the emotional impact of learning deficits on children, parents, and the educational community. Furthermore, there are many instances where learning problems are a reflection of family dysfunction, or personality problems. Children struggling with conflicts of separation-individuation may attempt to create distance from parents through passive opposition, using tactics that strike at the parents' greatest area of vulnerability. Parents who put a high premium on education can be most effectively touched by low school achievement (Pollack, 1985).

There is some interesting literature with regard to the differences between maternal and paternal responses to children with special needs in the academic and/or emotional areas (Osman, 1979; Konstantareas and Homatidis, 1981). Fathers tend to respond to initial diagnoses of these problems with anger and denial. "There is nothing wrong with my kid. If the teachers were better or firmer, if my wife didn't spoil the kid, he would be just fine." To the father, a measure of his child's worth, and by extension, a measure of his own worth, are accomplishments valued in the world outside the home. Children often use the strength, success, and achievement of the father to shore up their own fragile self-esteem. (My daddy is taller, smarter, richer, stronger, than your daddy.) The relationship between fathers and their children is often built around what each of them does.

If fathers are underinvolved with their special children, mothers are often overinvolved. Seeing herself as the child's protector and advocate may lead to an enmeshed relationship between mother and child, in which boundaries sometimes become indistinct. Father and other siblings may feel shut out of this dyad. Excluded, father may escape into work, an affair, or a flurry of extracurricular activities to offset his disappointment and loneliness.

In one study comparing parental stress in mothers and fathers of LD children, it was found that fathers were less stressed than mothers. Mothers of boys reported greater stress than mothers of girls (the severity of LD was not a factor). Mothers were more aggravated by social agencies (schools, doctors) because they bear a heavier load vis-à-vis the child. As the primary care giver, they tend to be more knowledgeable, more involved, more preoccupied. Mothers also express more guilt, which is reinforced by fathers and institutions that seem to blame mothers for the failings of their children (Silver, 1984).

Normally, a child's ideals and standards grow from an idealization of the parents' omnipotence and omniscience. Little by little, through a process of "optimal disillusionment," the child takes over more self-care as the parent, necessarily and appropriately, fails him. Thus he replaces the parents' omnipotence with his own developing competence. Functions previously supplied by the parents are gradually internalized to become the ideals, ambitions, and skills of the nuclear self. When the child lacks the necessary skills, or when the parents, fearing the child's lack of capacity, fail to withdraw appropriately, the result is a failure of self-esteem and an unrealistic sense of his strengths and weaknesses (Shane, 1984).

Perhaps the most effective way of remediating behavioral excesses or deficits is to teach the child's first teacher, the parent, to become the child's best teacher. We delimit a valuable resource in understanding and working with these children when we ignore the parents' observations and intuitions about their children's needs and difficulties. Perception of the roles parents of exceptional children have played has shifted throughout the history of the field. They have served alternately as scapegoats, program organizers, political activists, and now, we hope, as participants and partners. As the most frequent and constant observers of their children's behavior, parents can provide important insights by describing the child's interactions and behaviors in the less-structured environment of the home (Coles, 1987).

One way of organizing parental input is the traveling journal, carried back and forth in the child's backpack, with notes from parents to teacher to parents on a daily basis. Scribbled notes telling of a special incident, problem, or accomplishment can fill in for teacher and parent the life of the child in the other setting. I became aware of the importance of feedback years ago when teaching kindergarten. A little boy sat in my class apparently wrapped in his daydreams most of the day. When conference time came, the mother came in full of enthusiasm for all he was learning. Before I had a chance to mention my concerns about his lack of involvement, she showed me pictures and even little stories he had dictated to her about what we were doing in class. Then she spoke of her concern that if he were too active, he would break the very expensive glasses he wore. It became clear that her admonishments to him had been all too effective. I suggested that he be relieved of the constraints she had laid on him, and I would take responsibility for his safety and the safety of his glasses. After that conference Timmy became a much more active class participant.

It is important for therapists and teachers to know what the child represents to the parents, and what his or her special condition means to them within the family structure (Kaslow, 1978). Those of us who work with families with special children have all experienced the situation where the child's deficit serves an important function in the family system. Any threat of amelioration of the child's condition is met with violent, if sometimes masked resistance. One youngster, who was learning how to control his behavior using a simple "magical" ritual, reported being teased by his parents when he was found practicing this ritual, and when it became clear that he was succeeding. When questioned about this, the mother became irate and said it had become inconvenient for her to bring him in any longer, and the child, protesting bitterly, was withdrawn from therapy.

A seven-year-old with troubled teenaged siblings, a father who had just had a heart attack, and a mother fighting obesity, developed academic and behavioral problems. These became the focus of the whole family's attention, allowing them to ignore other, more serious and immediately threatening family issues. When the boy began to show improvement, the parents abruptly pulled him out of therapy. If he were no longer the designated patient, the family would have been impelled to a more realistic appraisal of their dysfunctional system. They simply were not ready for that.

Inviting the parents to come without the child for the initial interview provides an opportunity to get to know their views as individuals, spouses, and parents, and sets the stage for dialogue. This is an opportunity to establish a mind set for cooperation, team action, and mutual respect. Often the mother offers to come, saying father is too busy. It is important to insist on the father's presence if at all possible.

Given the facts that parents and their learning-dysfunctional children both suffer from problems of low self-esteem, social vulnerability, guilt, and periodic bouts of hopelessness and helplessness, what can we as professionals do that would be most helpful? A major problem for professionals at all levels working with these families is a great need to "do something." The focus is on influencing parents and/or children to behave differently without considering what this behavior pattern means within the family system. Teachers set up elaborate tutorial programs, strongly suggesting that if parents care, they will spend hours checking homework and developing systems of rewards and punishments to motivate the child. Because all this plays on the guilt and shame of the parents, who already feel inadequate, it is not possible for them to foresee the prescription for failure inherent in this approach. The most efficacious role of the professional would be to acknowledge the effect of the child's dysfunction on the family system, and to attempt to understand the meaning of this behavior for both parent and child.

If the child's problems are related to a struggle for autonomy, these parental efforts will be met with steely jawed opposition. If it is a real cognitive deficit, the impossibility of complying leads to such frustration and anger on both sides that it becomes grossly counterproductive. The growing parental anxiety is experienced by the child as hostility and rejection, causing the youngster to become more anxious and therefore less functional.

The therapist's first goal should be to deal with anxiety and low self-esteem issues. Only after learning what effect the situation is having on the family as a whole can appropriate interventions be selected. Some questions to ask are

- What were the parents' initial expectations for their child?
- What are the expectations and goals for the child now?
- What is the best thing that can be said about the child?
- What does the child do very well that gives the parents pleasure?
- What is the worst thing the child does?

It is instructive to interview the parents first separately, and then together, to establish a portrait of the child as each parent perceives him or her. Listening carefully as differences emerge concerning perceptions of the child can aid in establishing a sense of the role this child fills in the family system. Focusing on the child's strengths, on his "normal" characteristics, family members can explore ways in which they can interact with the child on the basis of these strengths.

One parent who was very angry with her LD son reported several times how enraged she was when he called her at work. But each time she reported the conversation, I commented on what a delightful sense of humor her son displayed, since he made very creative and funny excuses for his need to make contact with her. Eventually, she began reporting the funny things he said and did in other contexts and to take pride in his developing humor. She encouraged him to take part in more peer activities, which she had avoided in the past for fear of his being rejected, which in turn would make both of them feel awful. Although he still has severe learning disabilities, he has discovered some athletic and musical talents that he can build upon and in pursuit of which he has made friends who do not think of him as impaired, since in these areas he is quite successful. Seeing his successes, his mother has been able to step back and allow him to struggle in his own way with his academic subjects with the help of his special education teachers and a tutor. Both his self-esteem and hers have grown in the process.

We need to identify the healthy, successful aspects of the child and allow a place where these become the basis for the child's interaction with his environment in a conflict-free zone. Giving parents permission to step back and let the child experience the consequences of his limitations and his behavioral choices may be a big step toward a growing sense of autonomy on the part of the child, and increased self-esteem on the part of the parent. The "good enough parent" who is reasonably empathic, helps the child maintain a balance between inhibitions, ideals, and talents, assists when needed and stepping back when it is reasonable for the child to do it alone. Building on this autonomy, the child may feel more comfortable about reaching out and risking more, opening up new doors to potential successes. Thus the child learns to expect success and to tolerate failure (Shane, 1984).

It has been a frequent clinical observation that LD children often exhibit secondary emotional disturbances due to repeated frustrations and experiences of failure. Parent-child tensions, arising as a consequence of the child's academic difficulties, reinforce these disturbances, which in turn exacerbate the learning disability, thus setting up a vicious cycle. I submit that some, if not most, of this tension is iatrogenically created by the educational system's demands on parents, and the rather clear message that the child's failure reflects parental inadequacies or lack of commitment. We need to find a different way to work together—parents, teachers, and therapists—one that addresses the child's needs without negatively impacting not only on the child's self-esteem but that of parents and others who work with the child.

Ironically, in view of our discussion, a diagnosis of learning disability is often perceived as less stigmatizing and seems to be met with less consternation and resistance by parents than such diagnoses as mental retardation or emotional disturbance. It connotes, for some, that no one is to blame or needs to take personal responsibility for the problem. In the public perception, especially among parents of LD children, a diagnosis of learning disability seems to carry with it the idea that the child is inherently capable despite his difficulties in some specific area. There is a degree of optimism that something can be done to ameliorate the problem (Pollack, 1985).

With increased acceptance of *specific learning disability* as a prognostically hopeful and nonstigmatizing term, there is the danger that the formal diagnosis of a learning disability will create premature closure, proving an impediment to the understanding of learning and/or school dysfunction by the family. Parents may even actively seek such a diagnosis, at least partly in the service of obscuring the possibility of more salient dynamics that may be involved.

Illustrative of this point is the case of David, a quiet, withdrawn youngster who had difficulty reading, spelling, and expressing himself in writing. His second-grade teacher feared a learning disability, but was also curious about the child's persistence in drawing pictures, elaborate and detailed, depicting mayhem and death. She suggested to the parents that David be seen by the school psychologist for a diagnostic evaluation. The parents had accepted the teacher's informal LD diagnosis with equanimity, the father reporting that he had always had difficulties with spelling and reading and that his son, was a "chip off the old block." There was, however, considerable discrepancy between the child's test scores and his classroom skills. Finally, with the mother's support, he was tested. No learning disability was found. Instead, there were signs of chronic depression and a pervasive fear of death, particularly the death of his mother. Work with David, utilizing his artistic skills as an avenue of communication, allowed him to confront his fears. His parents learned to pay more attention to his feelings and respond promptly and appropriately to his concerns. His teacher learned to encourage his artistic endeavors and his active imagination, which was more pictorial than verbal. By the end of the school year, David was reading and writing (with illustrations of course) well above grade level. It was important for the therapist to work not only with David but with parents and teacher, in order to effect a satisfactory therapeutic resolution.

Many "false positive" diagnoses of LD represent a child's attempts to assert autonomy in the face of what is perceived as overly restrictive and controlling parenting. The parent-child struggle is played out in the educational sphere through scholastic failure and the child's presentation of himself or herself to others as unprepared, undisciplined, and indifferent (Pollack, 1985). The best a therapist can do in such cases is encourage parents to step back and let their children deal with the academic world in their own way, accepting the consequences that follow. These parents often seem to have great difficulty seeing their children in a realistic and differentiated way. Rather, they see them almost exclusively in terms of their accomplishments or failures in their roles as students and learners. Rigid role assignments are made by these parents, with acceptance and recognition contingent on measures of academic success. Such parents, highly intellectualized and perfectionistic, are not in touch with their children's feelings and personal concerns. Serious communication problems arise between these parents and their children, which transcend academic issues.

As therapists and as teachers, our roles should not be to therapize or unmask the parents, but to view them as natural allies, to enhance their self-esteem rather than attack them for perceived failures. It is generally more useful and more realistic to approach them as mature people in a challenging life situation with an opportunity for growth. The struggle to find solutions to jointly faced problems will have a far more immediate effect on parents, who live with the child, than on the therapist or the teacher.

We need to keep in mind the multidetermined nature of the many learning and motivational problems with which capable children grapple over the years. We need to be aware of the effect of these problems on their self-concept, on their personal concerns and conflicts, and on their relationships with family and peers. Physical deficits in vision and hearing, left undetected, can also have a negative affect on both learning and self-esteem. There are, additionally, normal but inherently stressful transitions in development and in the environment (such as moving) that can effect learning and overall academic achievement at any time. Specifically, according to Jay Haley (1976), the mental-health specialist needs to develop skills in diagnostic interviewing that involve the entire family. When clinical observation, psychoeducational test data, and a review of salient medical and educational history genuinely support the need for a redefinition, it also needs to be explained to the parents that what may appear to them to be exclusively an education-learning problem may be due, in part, to problematic interrelationships within the family.

Except for very severe problems, many disabilities in and of themselves may be remediable and relatively benign in their effect on a person's life. In fact, most of us have learning deficits of one sort or another, which, though annoying, are not crippling. What creates pathology are the ramifications of LD in families where the value of the child is based on academic performance and the success of the parents is based on that same performance. It is the effect of persistent failure, punishment, a sense of hopelessness and helplessness, and pervasive experiences with ostracism that cripple the self-esteem of child and parent alike. Sensitive interventions by members of the psychoeducational community can ameliorate this tragic situation.

The diagnosis of LD should be used neither to mask psychodynamic problems, nor as a battering ram to beat children into conformity to the academic community. Rather, once such a diagnosis is made, we should use all the tools at our disposal to help children reach their optimal potential in all aspects of their lives.

Notes

1. The Education for All Handicapped Children Act, 1975, specified that as of September 1978 all handicapped children must receive a

free and appropriate public education. By September 1980 the law
mandated extending the age limit to twenty-one. Parents have the
right under the bill to (1) be notified before the child is evaluated or
placed in a special program, (2) read any relevant records, (3) obtain
independent evaluations, (4) have an impartial due-process hearing
challenging the child's Individualed Education Program (IEP).
2. Individualed Education Program, a plan proposed by a multidisciplinary team and endorsed by the parents, for the remediation of
the child's educational problem.

Sydney B. Eisen, M.D.

12

Psychotherapy as an Intervention with Children and Adolescents with Learning Problems

ost children with learning disabilities never get to the attention of the psychiatrist. They are handled within the school system, and the child benefits and grows. So who are the children who reach the psychiatrist? When the child hands the teacher a note saying she wants to die, or the child denies there is any learning problem, or he starts being physically abusive in the classroom or on the playground—that is when the teacher may call on the school social worker, who does an evaluation of the child, including conferences with the parents. School psychologists may also be involved at this point. Therapeutic intervention within the school, often in consultation with the child psychiatrist, can be effective in returning the child to his or her developmental line of learning. When these interventions do not produce developmental changes, or where there seems to be a threat to the physical safety of the child or others, then the referral to the child psychiatrist is made.

These are the children in whom the learning disability is either complicated by emotional disorders or children with behavioral disorders whose learning disability is secondary. While attentional difficulties are probably the most common basis for disturbance in learning among children with normal intellectual endowment, the psychiatrist must keep in mind many other types of developmental and emotional difficulties that may impair cognitive processing and school achievement. Anxiety disorders and depressive disorders are common and easier to treat ... Less common and more difficult to treat are childhood psychosis and Tourette Syndrome. In our psychiatric clinic at Childrens Memorial Hospital we most frequently see children whose learning disability is complicated by a coexisting conduct disorder, attention-deficit hyperactivity disorder, or oppositional defiant disorder. It is this group of children that this paper focuses on.

The first step in the treatment of a child or adolescent with a learning disability unresponsive to pedagogical intervention is a careful and thorough evaluation that not only examines the reports of the clinical educator, the school social worker, school psychologist, speech pathologist, pediatrician, audiologist, and neurologist, but also includes an investigation and exploration of current family functioning of both the nuclear family and the family of origin of each parent.

A common question often asked at the outset is this: "My child has a learning disability and behavior problems, so why don't you treat him instead of asking me all these questions?" The answer to this touches on the very basic goals of psychotherapy for the learning-disabled child or adolescent seen in a psychiatric practice.

By the time a youngster is brought to see me, he is usually eight to ten years old, male, bright, but already labeled an "underachiever." Often he is threatened with being thrown out of school because of problems he has on the playground with other children in unstructured social situations. He is sullen and defiant, stating "There is nothing wrong with me!" It is always someone else's fault. The parents are frustrated, angry, perhaps punitive, because they feel his behavior is deliberate and controllable. Mother is often overprotective because father is "overly harsh." Father frequently denies that anything is wrong, sees no problem, or at best says, "I was like that when I was a child. He'll outgrow it."

Some parents show a grim determination to move heaven and earth to solve their child's problem. This kind of attitude is frequently a manifestation of parental inability to grieve over the loss of their image of the child as they wanted him to be. Unless this issue is resolved, it becomes an uphill battle for the psychotherapist, who is trying to help a youngster come to grips with his realistic strengths and weaknesses, when the parents continue to demand performance beyond his capacity.

Other issues that must be explored and confronted with the parents before effective psychotherapy can be done with a child include the following:

1. Parenting skills may be inadequate. The parents may simply not know how to be competent parents, perhaps because they are uninvested or have never experienced good parenting themselves. In these families other children are usually having problems as well.
2. Low self-esteem in other family members stemming from other causes may lead to the child's learning disability, precipitating a depression in a parent, which may then have to be treated concomitantly.
3. The parents may be emotionally unstable themselves, or the family system may be unstable, thus requiring family therapy before individual treatment can be initiated.
4. If the parents have poor self-control regulating mechanisms, they are poor models for teaching the learning-disabled child how to cope with his frustrations.
5. Parents may be more interested in using their child's learning disability as a battleground for latent marital conflicts.
6. The parents may be lacking in insight and/or abstract thinking ability, so that they are unable to convert verbally discussed material into meaningful action in the home (i.e., they have a subtle learning disability themselves).

The next step in the diagnostic process is to determine to what degree the emotional-behavioral elements in the presenting problem are primary or secondary. That is, how much is a secondary response brought on by frustration, lack of self-control, low self-esteem, et cetera.

We are only now coming to recognize that many individuals with clearly defined specific learning disabilities also demonstrate as yet unlabeled disabilities in social awareness and social skills.

We know that learning problems can directly contribute to social problems. The clumsy young child who can't hit the ball when playing T-ball at day camp may withdraw, find himself uninterested in sports, and unable to share social interests with his peers. The adolescent who can't read or play sports or dance may feel himself outside the social sphere, leading to an isolated or delinquent lifestyle. A youngster may seek out much younger children to play with, where his disabilities won't be so noticeable. Thus he gets labeled as immature, and his learning disability may be missed as his parents complain about his "babyish" games.

Some children avoid the stress of failure by withdrawing into themselves, becoming passive, unassertive, unwilling to take risks to achieve mastery because they see the mastery experiences of their peers increasingly outstripping their own achievements. Some develop anxiety over their fear of failure and displace it onto other things—a particular teacher, a bully, a subject area. Some become hypochondriacal, some blame others for their shortcomings consequent to their learning disability, and some develop a clinical depression, or a masked depression manifested by irritability and aggression. Passive-aggressiveness and clowning are still other mechanisms children may use to deal with the stress of "being different."

Treatment for this "different" child involves four components:

1. Environmental adjustments, which include issues such as proper classroom placement, tutoring, and social activities, including youth clubs where the director is aware of the special needs of a youngster for help in dealing with frustrations, poor physical skills, and the like.
2. Medication, if needed, for hyperactivity, depression, or other behavioral deviations.
3. Parental involvement, which might call for group therapy, family therapy, marital therapy, or individual therapy for a parent, and parent counseling, to learn more about appropriate parenting techniques as well as the nature of the disability.
4. Individual psychotherapy of the child, directed toward the goals of (a) an increase in self-control, that is, to help the child develop

a sense of an internal locus of control; (b) an increase in self-esteem; and (c) an increase in frustration tolerance.

As a youngster grows into each developmental phase, the impact of a learning disability is felt anew, and self-esteem, frustration tolerance, and self-control can once again become problems, even though they may have been mastered in the previous phase. This can be extremely demoralizing to both parents and child if it is not anticipated.

First, the parents must play an active role in the child's life throughout all these developmental phases. The therapy hours alone cannot make the difference. Parents must provide a stable, consistent, predictable home environment. They need to learn behavioral therapy techniques of setting expectations and remaining neutral or even detached in the face of failures. They must confront their child as he is, with his disability and with realistic, positive expectations *for* him and *from* him for himself. Behavioral charts can be used by the family to help the child learn to "boss" his own behavior. They should have the faith that he can learn to "stop and think," even though he does have failures.

Next, there is the issue of self-esteem. The therapist must work with both parents and child to clearly identify the youngster's strengths as well as his weaknesses. The child's sense of his parents' pride in him is as important as their support of his efforts to compensate for his disability. While in individual therapy, the child must himself eventually come to grieve for the skills he does not have, accepting that for him there are things that are "hard to do" but that can be done.

Finally, the child must learn increased frustration tolerance. This can be modeled by both parents and therapist. The way the adults handle the repeated temper outbursts from the child can serve as a model, an ego ideal for the child toward which he can strive when dealing with himself when he experiences a failure in performance or in modulating his own feelings.

We come now to the individual psychotherapy of children with learning disabilities. In my experience, when these children reach me they are frequently bright, presentable, often verbally gifted but failing or threatening failure in school and socially on the periphery, usually because of social ineptness and/or a seeming indifference to the feelings of others, which leads to fights with other children and, if adolescent, battles with parents over rules, responsibilities. I don't initiate individual therapy until the other modalities I have described are well underway. In most instances the youngster may have had special education classroom placement, at least part time for several years, and tutoring for at least one year. I institute family therapy and begin working on home life, family conflicts, intellectual clarification of learning disabilities, institution of medication if indicated, and establishment of behavioral regimens to bring about a stable, consistent, predictable environment in the home.

By the time individual therapy has begun, I am aware that I am dealing with a highly narcissistically defended young person. The first months of treatment, despite the preliminary work done with the family, are usually used by the patient to demonstrate to me over and over that he had absolutely no need or use of me. Talking about failing-grade reports are meaningless, or he has an explanation for every one: the teacher was unfair, the test was unfair, he was distracted by others, and on and on. If, however, I am willing to sit passively by, he will be delighted to regale me with tales of his conquests, victories, outsmarting of others, and especially making me look like a fool by playing games with me wherein he changes the rules every time it begins to look as if he might start losing. What stories he does tell me about his daily life clearly define for me his fantasies of omnipotent control, devaluation, splitting, and projective identification. My usefulness to him seems to be only as one more vehicle to defend himself against his feelings of smallness, hunger, and humiliation by telling me over and over, how wonderful he is and, as an afterthought, how worthless I am. He uses me alternately as a mirror to preen in front of, then as a vessel to dump all his rage into. I remember vividly one ten-year-old, screaming at the top of his lungs at me that no adult ever listens to or understands him, so he doesn't even know why he is there talking to me. When I said, "You know, when you shout so loudly it hurts my ears so much I can't concentrate on what you are saying," he gave me an icy stare and, in a cold rage, said, "why in the world would I give a damn about your pain!"

So the major problem encountered during the opening phase of treatment is whether the therapist can tolerate his countertransference feelings of worthlessness, helplessness, irritation, dread of sessions, and the wish to "put the patient in his place." Confronting the youngster with his inner feelings of helplessness and humiliation has to be done slowly and with great tact, being as empathic as possible. The child has come to expect that all the world will be as critical of him as he, in his identification with his parents, is of himself. Only after much testing of the therapist's stability, consistency, and lack of self-aggrandizement does the youngster begin to experience the pain, helplessness, and wishes for dependency that fill him with such fear. If therapy goes well, I expect to see themes of dependency, nurturance, autonomy, and separation begin to enter treatment. The child begins to see me as a useful guy to have around.

I remember one young adolescent patient who, during the first year of treatment, talked about wanting to burn down the slum neighborhoods he could see from my office window. He shared with me all kinds of grandiose schemes for wiping out all the poor, hungry, helpless people in the country. I shuddered at the sadism, but stayed with him through the elaboration of fantasies his liberal parents would have been horrified at. As the months went by and his trust in my objectivity and undemandingness grew, he came to speak of his own sense of worthlessness compared to his brother and sister, who showed no academic defects. If he could not go to Harvard or Stanford, he should be thrown on the trash heap of life. As therapy progressed, his family and school life became better organized, he began to experience more success, became more willing to try, and was less fearful of failure, which created a feedback cycle of success. Near the end of therapy, still clinging to some grandiosity but on the whole more reality oriented, he was talking about how great it was to have a therapist he could try out all his theories of economics on before presenting them in his high school class.

Individual therapy winds down as a youngster gives up his grandiosity, omnipotence, and sense of entitlement to accept satisfactions in the real world, which result in peer relationships he is no longer afraid of, improved academic performance, and within the family, acceptance of him in a realistic fashion, with all of his strengths and weaknesses.

Colin Webber, M.A.
Nan Knight-Birnbaum, M.S.S.A.

13

Childhood Bereavement and the Process of Learning

When a child's parent dies, the focus of her family and the community is upon her adaptation. They eagerly hope that all is well and anxiously guard against any disruptions. School personnel also want to see the child get back in the swing of things quickly. But when the child begins to demonstrate the normal expectable reactions to a loss, many seem alarmed and often, as a result, misdiagnose the problem as a learning disability or attention-deficit disorder.

We have found that the death of a parent usually affects the child's ability to learn, especially during the active phase of mourning. It is our conviction that learning problems for bereaved children occur when the child is actively mourning or when the child's mourning has been derailed. Return to the learning tasks occurs after the child has adequately adapted to the loss.

For example, Bob, age six, was referred to the Barr-Harris Center,* along with his older sister and younger brother, by his mother, who was concerned about their adaptation to the recent death of their father. During the first year following the father's death, the children appeared to be adapting well. Then Bob became more distracted in school. His behavior, although not bad, had become silly and annoying to the teacher. He was not concentrating in class and often appeared to be daydreaming. The teacher thought he may be suffering from an attention-deficit disorder because he had all the symptoms. Although his work was declining, he still was performing above average in his classes. Diagnostic psychological testing was requested, and the results supported the mother's view that Bob did not appear to have ADD, but rather was feeling sad and missing his father. The teacher relaxed but still felt the explanation difficult to believe. Bob continued to test above average. His performance indicated slow but forward developmental progress.

Many children like Bob, whose previous development had been sound, demonstrate moderate declines in learning as a result of the death of a parent. Other children who have preexisting neurocognitive deficits or emotional conflicts or deficits tend to show significant and prolonged regression. Where the death of a parent is due to a violent event or chronic illness, children also have a more difficult time adapting. The most difficult and prolonged adaptation and the poorest prognosis occurs when several of these factors coexist.

Mourning and the Learning Process

To understand the impact of mourning on learning, we will first review the process of mourning in children, the path of average expectable learning, and the factors that interfere with this line of development. Let us begin with a model of mourning, the complex process of integrating the reality of a death. It involves two components: the detachment from the internal image of the lost person, and the process of making identifications with the values, interests, activities, and character traits of the lost person so that versions of those characteristics

* Barr-Harris Center for the Study of Loss and Bereavement, Institute for Psychoanalysis, Chicago.

become part of the survivor. An individual's initial reaction to the death usually consists of shock, denial/disavowal, and disbelief. The individual cannot integrate the new reality and is temporarily over-whelmed with a variety of feelings. This is particularly true if the death has been unanticipated. Shortly, grief sets in along with partial recognition of the reality of the death. Grief includes feelings of sadness, lone-liness, yearning, and anger.

The bereaved individual initially hypercathects the memories of the deceased person and the relationship they shared. Gradually there is a detachment of investment in the internal representation of that lost object. As identifications are made with aspects of the personality of the deceased person, the individual's self-representation is reshaped and partially modified in the image of the lost person. Identification provides an adaptive potential that enriches the personality of the survivor and preserves aspects of the object representation.

If mourning proceeds, ambivalent memories too are reexperienced, and with their resolution mourning begins to come to a close. The object representation is preserved in memories, the emotional investment is withdrawn, and energy becomes available for new relationships.

The work of mourning is never entirely completed. Aspects of the attachment remain, with some residual investment. Mourning is some-times partially revived in reactions to significant events that present conscious reminders of the deceased. These include such develop-mentally significant landmarks in the life cycle as graduations, marriage, birth of a child, and career achievements.

Adults demonstrate considerable variation in the capacity to mourn and in the degree of resolution of mourning achieved. A complete detachment from a lost object may not occur, but some form of reorganization of the attachment usually does. Mourning is dependent on the individual's attainment of certain developmental capacities and levels of object relations rather than on chronological age. In considering the pattern of childhood bereavement studied at the Barr-Harris Center, we have shifted from asking the question, "Can children mourn?" to "Can children adapt to the death of a parent without significant impairment and if so, under what circumstances or with what assistance can they do so?" Garber (1981) and Pollock (1978) describe a continuum of responses to the death of a parent. At one end of the continuum are those responses of a group of children identified by the Furmans (E.

Furman, 1974; R. Furman, 1964a, 1964b) who possess the necessary skills as well as the cognitive and emotional capacities to engage in an intense, sequential mourning process resembling that observed in healthier adults. In many instances the mourning is facilitated by the children being engaged in a psychotherapeutic or psychoanalytic treatment process. At the other end of the continuum are responses of a group of children who seem incapable of engaging in a sequential, step-by-step mourning experience. Such children have been described in the literature by Wolfenstein (1966) and others. In the middle of the continuum are responses of a group of children who appear to be neither avoiding nor massively defending against the loss. They demonstrate an intense attachment to the image and the memory of the dead parent and yet do not appear to be engaged in a predictable, adultlike mourning process. Their memories and feelings are intense but are not yet integrated. Instead, they experience the grief-related feelings over and over in an attempt at completion or closure, which is never quite accomplished. At best they reach an uneasy equilibrium.

Garber and Pollack postulate that there is a developmental line for the capacity to mourn. Components of that capacity mature and become available to the child sequentially. Mourning in childhood thus is a process that goes on over a long period of time with reworkings at each developmental phase. The work of adaptation may stop at a certain point, only to resume later when new capacities mature. A new phase of mourning can be stimulated by the challenge of developmental tasks that entail further individuation, such as the remarriage of a surviving parent, which offers the potential for new object relationships.

In addition, the parental death often leads to the loss of specific functions provided by the parent. These include care giving and buffering for developmental traumas, supporting self-esteem, and supporting the other parent (who now may be involved in his own mourning).

When we think about a prototype of an "average expectable reaction" to a death, the picture develops as follows. At the time of the loss, the child goes through the phases of mourning previously described in a bit-by-bit manner. We see progression and regression continuously over several years. Moods will fluctuate and significant relationships will become more and less important over time. When the child is in the midst of mourning, she will invest in the memories of the deceased parent and may be emotionally more distant from the surviving parent. As the child distances herself from the internal representation, she becomes more invested in her contemporary relationships. For some children the loss is traumatic.

Defenses are penetrated, and the child feels flooded by defects, and regresses in an attempt to maintain control over (and lessen) the pain. The regression may affect many ego functions including reality testing, sense of reality, object constancy, decision making, synthesis, defenses, object relations, and affect. The child's ability to concentrate, regulate tension, and make decisions may all be impacted. Under these circumstances we cannot expect the child to be able to integrate new learning. With the support of the surviving parent, the child is likely to reconstitute her defenses, and learning and development will resume.

The developmental stage attained by the child when the parental death occurs determines which ego functions are likely to be affected. For example, very early losses in the first year can affect sensory-motor skills, the development of object representations, and evocative memory. When the loss occurs within the first three years of life, language problems and related learning inhibitions may ensue. The process of learning can become disrupted along the developmental line at any point. The line is disrupted because of the trauma and also by the child's struggle to find appropriate defenses to cope with the loss.

Potential Interferences with Learning

Children with neurocognitive impairments have specific difficulties in their ability to process the death of a parent and to adapt to the loss over time. These difficulties are influenced by this impairment, distorting the child's understanding of the loss.

Although all losses are painful, there are those that appear fairly consistently to be traumatizing. Deaths that are violent or the result of chronic illness have a great potential for protracted interference with the child's development. Cases at the Barr-Harris Center include instances of murder, suicide, sudden illness, chronic illness, and severely pathological mourning of the surviving parent. What is evoked for the child in these extreme situations is fear and anxiety. No single pattern of symptomatology seems to be present following a parent loss. All of the children, however, exhibited school problems that varied with age, sex, and proximity to time of death. Altschul (1988) and Furman (1986) delineate the criteria for assessing whether a loss is traumatic. Furman believes that a clinician may not be able to differentiate the existence of trauma until a treatment process with a child is underway.

During the traumatic episode, the child is overwhelmed by an excess of excitation, as ego functions collapse and the defensive organization that provided protection fails. Thinking is diminished and physical responses predominate. These vegetative reactions include frantic motor activity and bodily distress (abdominal discomfort, nausea, urgency to urinate or defecate).

When the protective shield is moderately breached rather than totally overwhelmed, the reparative effort begins immediately with an attempt to drain off or reduce the overstimulation. These defensive responses manifest themselves in states of shock, paralysis of action, numbness of feeling, apathy, and in forms of depersonalization. Traumatic states may last for minutes, hours, days, months, or years, (Furman, 1986). It can be hard to differentiate these states from other disturbances especially in younger children, since the states can be transient and the child and others may not notice them or may misinterpret their meaning. A child experiencing a traumatic state is clearly not able to learn.

The reparative process of reestablishing the defenses and binding the excitation can itself temporarily interfere with learning. The process takes the form of repetition-compulsion as the stimuli are mastered (Furman, 1986). Some of the manifestations of the repetition-compulsion include repetitive play, which entails making active those events that had been experienced passively. It also includes repetitive dreams and nightmares (Furman, 1986). Activities driven by the need for mastery through repetition can exercise a preemptive role in the child's life so that she does not invest in her usual interests or in learning.

There are a number of signs that indicate that reparative progress is occurring. First is the recurrence of brief episodes of the traumatic state, preceded and followed by longer periods of normal functioning. The second entails repeating an experience with variations suitable for its assimilation, such as turning a passive experience into an active one (Furman, 1986). A third indicator is that the child manifests various forms of signal anxiety, then swiftly institutes defenses against this anxiety. A further measure of recuperation is that the anxiety occurs in an increasingly narrow set of circumstances. The child experiences the traumatic state in specific situations that carry reminders of the original trauma, and eventually only in the context of psychotherapy and transference reactions with the therapist.

Although the majority of children seen at the Center respond to loss with learning inhibitions, a few manifest the opposite: a hypercathexis of learning. This intense involvement with learning is often unstable, since it also serves as a defense against the mourning process.

It is important for adults to remember that traumatic states are temporary. They need not be alarmed by a child's regressions. Interventions that are of an ego-supportive nature include clear structure, reliable scheduling, and emotional accessibility. Learning tasks should be broken down to a scale small enough for the child to be able to integrate.

Traumatic states can be reactivated at various times throughout the mourning process—when litigation is completed, when the estate is settled, or when anniversaries of the death occur. These events tend to disrupt the forward progress of the child, but they may be brief in duration. During these episodes, the child may need additional support.

Let us consider the situation in which a parent's death came after a prolonged illness. (Death following lengthy illness occurred among 30 percent of the families seen at the Barr-Harris Center.) Family life was organized around care of the chronically ill parent. The child's personality development had often been pervasively affected by the altered relationships and familial anxiety. The experiences formed a prelude to the actual loss. Cumulative strain contributed to the surviving parent's emotional exhaustion. Delay in the unfolding of mourning was common under these circumstances.

A child's understanding of the parent's illness affects the meaning the child attributes to the illness and the kinds of defenses he chooses to adapt to this reality. Notable among these are conflicts and inhibitions about competition and self-assertion. The child is more likely to develop inhibitions about aggressive impulses. The amount of help offered in understanding such experiences, through verbalization and dialogue, varies considerably in these strained families. Verbalization is a major facilitator of ego development and a means of mastery over experiences that evoke anxiety. When verbalization about the parent's illness was limited, the child was often left with a generalized sense of danger and anxiety, which impaired curiosity and learning. In some families, the unintegrated experience had to do with an earlier phase of the parent's illness and remained unnoticed until it presented itself in psychotherapy.

Another contributor to learning inhibitions may be identification with aspects of the parent's illness or with the parent's defenses in coping with the illness, which may leave the child feeling disabled or defective. When such identifications had been made, learning could be seen by the child as something that threatened separation from, or even abandonment of, the parent by the child.

Chronic, severe illness in a parent can also affect a child's learning by its subtle influence on parent-child interactions that affect self-esteem. Parental preoccupation and anxiety casts a shadow over the child's experience of being mirrored, in Kohut's sense, by the ill parent, thereby making it more difficult for him to internalize feelings of being valued and affirmed, which are the spurs to academic achievement.

Clinical Example

The effects of the death of a parent on a child's learning pattern are illustrated in clinical work with Emma, an eight-year-old girl seen in psychotherapy a year after her father's death from a rare degenerative disease. The effects of lengthy parental illness, traumatic reactions, and regression in disrupting learning are evident in this child's experience.

Emma was seen in intensive psychotherapy following an evaluation, which indicated that she was traumatized by her father's death and was significantly depressed. Emma was a slim girl with long, brown hair, who seemed emotionally burdened. She was waiflike and forlorn. Her expression was often tense; she seemed alert to the mood changes of adults. When she became animated, especially when she gave a hint of mischievous and feisty feelings, she was appealing.

Emma's mother was exhausted from the long, painful course of her husband's illness. Despite her grief and anxiety over raising her family alone, mother offered Emma a nurturing and stable relationship. She sought help because of Emma's intense separation anxiety, sleep difficulties, self-criticisms, regression to soiling, and learning problems.

Her father's illness had been diagnosed when Emma was four years old. Sleep difficulties, general fearfulness, as well as episodic soiling began shortly after his diagnosis. When Emma was seven, her father had a cardiac infarction at home late one night. Emma witnessed the medical care administered by paramedics and then accompanied mother to the hospital, where her father subsequently died.

Vulnerabilities and developmental problems were evident before father's death and made the task of mourning and integrating this loss particularly difficult. Emma's reactions to witnessing her father's heart attack also contributed to fantasies and fears, which persisted through a prolonged period of regression. This occurred in spite of the fact that mother was recovering from the deepest phase of mourning and was providing good care. It was apparent that the loss presented a developmental interference in many areas of Emma's functioning, including learning. While Emma had experienced some initial grief, she had been too frightened of the meanings she attached to father's death, and fantasies about her role in it, to undertake mourning.

Prior to her father's death, Emma had always engaged school and the challenges of learning with anxiety. Nonetheless, she succeeded in doing work appropriate to her grade level but took little pleasure in these activities and productions. After her father's death, Emma's academic work markedly deteriorated. She produced little work, could not finish assignments, and was increasingly anxious and fearful of undertaking new work. She seemed to soothe herself by involving herself even more intensely than usual in conversations with her best girl-friend. Initially, the school interpreted this academic regression as a sign of a primary learning difficulty and did psychological testing to determine whether a neurocognitive learning disability existed. None was found; the testing indicated that intense feelings of anxiety and depression contributed to Emma's learning difficulties.

Emma's third-grade teacher liked her and understood intuitively her need for a slower pace of learning while Emma struggled with her fears. She sought to engage Emma and made herself emotionally available in many ways through the school day. Her teacher remembered that at the beginning of the year Emma was cautious and wary of group situations. She observed from the sidelines before joining in. Emma initially kept her distance from the teacher, as if she anticipated criticism and intrusiveness. Their relationship grew warmer over the course of the year.

Emma's emotional investment in learning was erratic. Occasionally, she could concentrate and retain what she had learned; more frequently, she seemed disinterested and apathetic. She feared making mistakes and avoided new work.

As the treatment alliance with her psychotherapist deepened, an initial reduction in anxiety led to a period in which Emma began producing in school, but this was followed by a period in which she stopped working and withdrew. A pattern of producing and then withholding was repeated throughout treatment, and in the pattern of occurrences of soiling at home. It was repeatedly reenacted in the transference in terms of conflicts over producing words and play. Emma evoked anxiety, frustration, and disappointment in her teacher and her mother.

As we attempt to understand Emma's learning problems and their relation to the mourning process, we should first consider the dynamics related to the period of her father's illness. The cumulative strain on both parents made it difficult for them to admire and encourage Emma. They had difficulty affirming her and helping her learn to regulate tension. Both capacities are prerequisites for learning. During the illness, Emma became frightened of any activity that entailed curiosity. It was difficult for her parents to explain her father's deteriorating condition and his inability to play with or care for the children. While his prognosis was terminal, the course of his illness was unpredictable. This was extremely anxiety provoking for him and his wife. He felt quite helpless and increasingly, depressed. He was often angry at his wife for her good health and her future with the children. He worked and maintained interest in hobbies for as long as he could. He demanded good performances from the children, and Emma strove to please him and idealized him.

After her father's death, the family spoke little of his illness and of the night of his death. Emma observed a great deal, but was not helped to verbalize her thoughts and feelings and ask questions in order to understand the experience. She viewed her father's illness as a terribly dangerous event that had threatened him and now threatened the rest of the family in some ill-defined way.

Emma's learning inhibitions were also related to the meanings she attached to father's death, as these were shaped by current developmental concerns. The loss also became an organizer for earlier deficits and developmental conflicts. Fantasies about his illness and death contributed to inhibition that directly interfered with Emma's learning. She was afraid that her angry, aggressive feelings were like uncontrollable bowel movements that were dangerous to those she loved. These fears led to Emma's erecting a series of defenses that compromised curiosity and self-assertion.

Father's death occurred during a phase of Emma's development in which she was struggling with jealous, competitive feelings and with intense anger (related to earlier arrests and the particular configuration of oedipal issues). These conflicts became associated with fantasies that she had contributed in some way to her father's death. She imagined that her soiling had poisoned her father: her destructive wishes had taken concrete form. This sense of responsibility seemed related not only to Emma's developmental fantasies, but to her regressively intensified feelings of grandiosity and omnipotence.

Emma believed that she needed to be passively compliant, harmlessly forlorn, and nonaggressive in order to protect against calamity. She could not experience herself as a person who, for her own reasons, wanted to learn things and was capable of doing so. This fantasy was expressed in a series of nightmares Emma discussed after a year and a half of treatment.

In the first dream, a girl wishes to be initiated into a gang and must enter a cemetery or a morgue as part of the initiation. Dead people rise out of their coffins, surround her, and kill her. This dream was followed by a second dream in which a group of six children, three boys and three girls, enter a house, where they find swords on the floor. The girls are menaced and finally decapitated by the boys, who wield the swords. The boys cannot escape from the house. They eventually escape and seek help from a man and a woman, who refuse to assist them. A sheriff finally finds the bodies.

The dreams followed Emma's expression of angry feelings toward her envied brother, as well as anger at me. These dreams introduced new material and signaled a deepening of the alliance. The nightmares represented a stage of recuperation from the trauma. Emma had gained a degree of mastery that permitted transformation of the anxieties into phase-related anxieties as well as transference fears that were not yet part of the treatment process. The elaborated themes about mutilation, death, and murderous feelings were part of the maternal transference that had to do with her fears of her mother's unavailability and, in parallel fashion, of my unavailability.

Other fantasies emerged in the transference—that things inside her, feelings and thoughts, like her feces, were dangerous. One variation of this was a fear that her therapist might develop a terrible illness. Emma watched the state of her therapist's health, worrying that it might be fragile. Competitive feelings were dangerous. She feared her therapist would be humiliated if she were victorious at games, or that she might poison her therapist if she soiled during a session. Similarly, Emma had to test her therapist's reaction to her wishes and interests by bringing them up in indirect forms for many months before she could talk about them forthrightly. A similar testing process occurred at school with her teacher. Emma practiced a skill privately before demonstrating it to her teacher. In the therapy, Emma withheld her words and thoughts until overexcitement about some wish caused a torrent of speech, which later frightened and shamed her. For Emma, in a symbolic parallel to her encopresis, her "flood" of words seemed dangerous to both of us. Similarly, a spurt in learning was followed by a depressive retreat.

A final aspect of Emma's learning problem was connected to her fear of thinking about her father's absence. The defense erected against "thinking about" and "knowing about" her soiling was connected to fear of mourning her father. Emma could not think about bowel control, or lack of it, for fear of thinking about losing something and thus being reminded of losing her father. This anxiety generalized to "knowing" academic subjects and to exercising control over other aspects of her mental life that affected learning. These included anticipation, planning, and diligent application.

As the defenses against mourning were altered, Emma entered a period of intense grieving. Tremendous rage at father emerged. She felt abandoned as he grew physically weaker and could no longer play. The idealization of her father, which served as a defense against disappointment and depression in the relationship with her mother, came into clearer focus. The long work of treatment addressed both aspects of the idealization. Emma became deeply sad about her father's absence from her life. As the mourning work proceeded, Emma's learning again slowed dramatically, but this time as a consequence of the diversion of energies. Gradually, she resumed learning with genuine autonomy and consistency.

This phase of treatment dealt with Emma's initial attempts to master certain traumatic aspects of her father's death. It also dealt with the deficits caused by not having a mirroring parent whose presence was sufficiently under her control. Later work involved an attempt to understand the fantasy of responsibility for her father's death. The ego regressions and inhibitions evident in Emma's reaction to the loss were at the heart of her learning difficulties. As Emma was gradually able to really mourn, these ego capacities were more available to her, and contributed to a resumption of learning.

In summary, the death of a parent is a disruptive event in a child's life, with potential for interfering with many developmental tasks, especially that of learning. In this paper, we reviewed the points at which the developmental lines of learning and mourning intersect. Impasses in learning are likely at these intersections. The impact of the loss on a particular child depends on many factors, including the child's unique developmental experiences, the intactness of neurocognitive capacities, the degree of trauma associated with the loss, the capacity to mourn, and the availability of support from family, teachers, and, in some instances, therapists.

Edward P. Kaufman, M.S.W.

14

Reactivation of Learning in Residential Treatment

would like to begin by recounting a vignette described by Elizabeth Young-Bruehl in her biography of Anna Freud. While listening to a case presentation in which the therapist announced he was going to discuss the case of a thirteen-year-old girl with "hysterical aphonia manifested by expressive aphasia as a conversion symptom," Anna Freud asked, "Why don't you simply say that this is a thirteen-year-old who developed an inability to speak?" I will try to heed that good advice by keeping this presentation down-to-earth and straightforward.

The purpose of this presentation is to examine and explore integrative approaches in dealing with learning problems within a residential treatment center. Within the context of residential treatment, we are always reconsidering issues concerning emotions and learning. In theory, an examination of these issues can be empirically explored, because a therapeutic milieu allows for maximum management of the educational and emotional attitudes of the staff serving the residents.

The material I am about to present covers a nine-year period when I was the administrative director of a transitional group home for adolescent boys. During that period of time, the program served fifty-one residents. The home was established for adolescent boys, ages seventeen to twenty-one, who were unable to live either in their own homes or independently in the community. They needed a therapeutic milieu that focused on the task of preparation for independent living. The length of residence was designed to be one year in duration. For those boys who needed longer placements, extensions were granted up to two years. Thus the average length of stay became fifteen months. In addition, those boys who completed the program were offered a year of post-placement, after-care service including ongoing psychotherapy and educational/vocational planning services.

The population included adolescents whose inability to live at home covered a wide range of circumstances from family breakdown to a variety of psychopathologies of the boys. The admissions policy excluded the developmentally disabled and youngsters with diagnosed neurologically based learning disabilities; therefore, those adolescents who were admitted evidenced learning problems arising out of emotional issues. These learning problems were referred to as "learning difficulties" by our staff so as to be distinguished from neurologically based "learning disabilities." The agency's school, designed for students with primary problems of emotional disturbance, was not geared toward developmental and learning disabilities. Also excluded were adolescents with histories of severe, violent acting-out behavior, which precluded their living in a small group home located with open access to the community. The facility itself was a split-level single-family home with a capacity for seven boys, located in a middle-class residential neighborhood and within walking distance to stores, transportation, and other community resources.

All admissions were predicated on the boys' willingness to enter the program voluntarily. Their problems and backgrounds were diverse, ranging from inner-city ghetto life to suburban backgrounds. Their pathology ran the gamut from severe neurotic to borderline, schizoid, and other characterological disorders. The vast majority had either academic or behavioral difficulties in school. Most of them felt educationally inadequate, and associated school with a sense of failure and/or frustration. Learning was associated with pain. More important, they considered themselves uneducable. For the few who were doing well academically, their behavioral problems overshadowed and interfered with their school performance. Two of the boys had a positive attitude toward school, which was their only stable, predictable, and easily comprehensible environment. Central to the residential program's structure was the requirement that the boys attend school, work, or do both. It was vital that they learn basic self-care skills to develop the ability for self-management. As such, the structure of the program often ran counter to the defenses that these boys had erected to protect themselves against their anxiety vis-à-vis the educational experience.

The manifest structure of the program focused on the skill building that was requisite for them to be able to manage their lives in the community. They needed to develop academic and vocational goals, learn how to cook, manage a budget, do laundry, care for their personal property (which included themselves), accept responsibility for making and keeping medical and dental appointments, and learn to dress properly for the never-ending weather changes of Chicago. In the main, these boys shared one thing in common, which first baffled and later amused the staff: on vocational testing, the results for almost all of them indicated a desire to be a pipe fitter as either a primary or a secondary goal. It naturally followed that we included birth-control information!

The agency operated a full-time special education school housed in its own building in close proximity to the group home. A close working relationship with the school was an essential part of the program. Because we were caring for the total child on a twenty-four-hour basis, philosophically we felt that the treatment modality was an ongoing process and should not be compartmentalized into group home, school, work, et cetera. Since it was a continuous and contiguous process, it was vital that all significant people in the child's life be in open communication with one another. There was never a hesitation for group-home staff and school personnel (either by phone or in person) to share significant information about a resident. As Bettleheim (1980) has noted, when a child is under severe stress, the energy that he has available for learning and experiencing school as meaningful is greatly diminished. It was therefore essential that the school personnel be aware of the stress factors impacting on the student as he began each school day. Conversely, it was equally important for the group-home treatment team to be apprised of problems or difficulties that arose during the resident's school day. In addition, educational planning was individualized to meet the needs of each of the residents. For example, some students attended the special education school on a full-time basis; those who were able would split their day between our self-contained special education program and public school; others attended trade or vocational high schools; some (of particular importance for seniors) attended either regular or special education classes in their high school of origin. Work-study programs and GED classes were also available to those students where indicated.

The basic process of getting a child to school and mastering the transition from the inner to the outer world often involved creative and innovative techniques in just handling the morning wake-up period. Some residents needed to be awakened and simply left alone, whereas others (in a more regressed state of being) required a more prolonged welcome greeting of the new day, fortified with orange juice at bedside. Some just needed the aroma of freshly brewed coffee. One boy, who suffered a transitory phobia related to separation issues, needed the comforting presence of a child-care worker to sit through two weeks of classes with him. Another, who was experiencing a deep, almost immobilizing depression, had homebound classes taught to him both by school and child-care personnel. In not a few instances, the mere task of being in the school required the optimum effort of the resident's ego. This was understood and accepted by school personnel. Demands for classroom attendance were reduced until the resident began to feel comfortable within the physical building. Just being there was the object of the day. For some, it was the object of the half-day. In those instances, a child-care worker would help the boys to return home with some prescribed lesson plan in hand. When school strikes occasionally occurred in Chicago, the teaching staff provided lesson plans to the child-care staff, who then functioned as their teachers at the group home. Thus, there was continuity in their education and concrete evidence that despite circumstances that precluded their teacher's availability, the educators' concern for them was genuine.

In addition to the need for learning about the world and how to function independently within it vis-à-vis school, work, and self-management skills, it was essential for each of the residents to become more acquainted with his inner psychological and emotional self, so they were all in individual treatment with the group-home social worker. In addition, where the residents had significant relationships with community therapists, they were encouraged to retain those alliances. The basic orientation was psychoanalytic, but in attempting to make contact with the these boys, sometimes their idiosyncrasies demanded the creation of unusual settings for the therapy to take place. For example, the therapist had to talk to one boy while he was perched in a tree; sessions were sometimes held around a pool table or through an open window when a boy insisted he was more comfortable sitting on the adjacent rooftop, and once, to a disembodied voice under a blanket. Additionally, interpersonal issues between the residents were dealt with in weekly group meetings with the entire staff. If a resident needed a short-term hospitalization, arrangements were made with the receiving hospital for the resident to continue his treatment with his therapist as well as have regular visits from child-care staff. The school provided ongoing assignments so that the availability of educational material was accessible to him, so the integrity and continuity of the educational and therapeutic aspects of the residential program was maintained even though the resident was temporarily absent. The boy was thus assured, both tacitly and verbally, that the group home remained as a welcome residence for him following the interlude of hospitalization. Often it was the knowledge that he had a "home" to which he could return that helped expedite a successful course of hospital treatment.

As previously stated, a common element for all the boys was their difficulty with learning and, in particular, their negative attitudes about formal, structured schooling. Despite a wide variety of psychodynamics that influenced their individual learning difficulties, phenomenologically, most of the boys felt that school had little or no meaning to them, and they saw themselves as uneducable and not as smart as their peers. In order to coalesce the various programmatic aspects of the treatment milieu, we needed to find ways to make the learning experience meaningful and to stimulate their imagination.

Toward that end, we addressed the educational philosophies and psychoanalytic clinical principles to best assess and implement appropriate interventions to reactivate the learning process for these boys. The aims of education, according to Whitehead, are to translate abstract bodies of knowledge into meaningful concepts that have a relevancy to life. In his book, *The Aims of Education* (1967), he cites an example of taking trigonometry students on land surveying field trips to demonstrate the practical uses of trigonometric concepts. This educational point of view was best exemplified by the field theory of teaching, popular some twenty-odd years ago. This theory essentially attempted to translate the educational experience into immediate everyday life application. Regrettably, its misapplication led many of its critics to decry its use as making the educational experience simply a toolbox for success in the external world. Nonetheless, its basic *intent* was an attempt to vitalize the educational experience and to stimulate and support an individual's innate curiosity and desire to learn about himself and the world in which he lives.

Frequently, youngsters served in residential treatment facilities have had educational experiences in which they have been tested to see how well they have learned their lesson but not how much knowledge they have acquired. The results are often discouraging and the resultant self-image is that they are uneducable and, even worse, dumb. This negative self-perception reinforces preexisting negative self-precepts caused by intrapsychic, familial, and environmental difficulties.

In order to support the vital balance required by the ego for learning to occur, Sperling (1967) notes that there must be a minimizing of internal or external stressors so that the ego can move from a strictly beleaguered, defensive position to a more adaptive, exploratory one. Bettleheim, in his article "Education and the Reality Principle" (1980), stresses, "We must all start where the child *is* and guide him to where he should *be*." In this process, Bettleheim recommends a series of recognizable responses to the child within the child's frame of reference as a way of additionally supporting the ego and making modifications within the ego-ideal. Thus, the ego is ultimately supported by the superego as well as the environment. In consulting with a group of inner-city teachers who were burdened with limited resources and supplies, Bettelheim suggested that the teachers abandon their concern about waste of material and, instead, support the creative excitement that their students had in the learning process per se.

To develop meaningful communication with the boys, we used Freud's method of taking an active, receptive, observing position as well as utilizing therapeutic interventions through demonstrable interpretation. The type and quality of interpretive work varied according to the staff positions and functions. The child-care workers limited their interpretations to life-space interviewing, focusing on the here and now. The social worker used more traditionally understood forms of interpretation, from surface to depth. The administrator used a combination of these approaches. Following Aichorn's (1964) concept of libidinal economy, we felt it was important to demonstrate that the learning experience could be fun, and through this, we could engage the boys' natural curiosity, creativity, and talents.

The kitchen frequently became the arena in which this was explored. Each boy was responsible for menu planning and preparation. As length of stay progressed, the meals went from prepackaged (frozen, canned) to "from scratch." Or, as the boys put it, "Simon and Garfunkeled with parsley, sage, rosemary, and thyme!" Our erstwhile chefs were unburdened by cleanup and followed the dictum of Samuel Johnson, who proclaimed, "My kitchen is chaos!" The kitchen became a culinary laboratory. One resident excitedly discovered that garlic was the same as wolfsbane and used it con gusto. During mealtimes, its magical and flavorful qualities made the house safe from any Transylvanian predator who might have been lurking in the nearby environs. The residents had to employ their reading skills to follow directions or recipes and their mathematical skills to measure quantities, manage a budget, and ensure second helpings. Sometimes these adventures in the culinary arts had unusual results. Irving, whose high school diploma had been hard won, prided himself on his reading skills. He laboriously reviewed the heating instructions for the fish sticks, Tater Tots, and frozen-spinach dinner he was planning for the evening's meal. The child-care worker on duty was momentarily called out of the room and upon his return, Irving proudly announced that dinner was cooking. Moments later the smoke detector alarmingly sounded. The directions did not state "remove wrapping," and the fish sticks were silently smoldering in their box in the oven! With aplomb, the child-care worker congratulated Irving on his initiative for starting dinner and calmly taught him to "magically" prepare tartar sauce to complement the smoked fish sticks. He explained to Irving that, in general, food needs to be removed from the container before heating, strongly emphasizing, however, that it was an omission in the directions that caused the problem, not a deficit in Irving's reading skills.

From the outset, we were frequently confronted by a resident unable to acknowledge, or at times even recognize, that he had learned information and had skills at his disposal. Johnny, another resident, felt that all relationships would end in disappointment despite his conscious wishes and hopes. From his point of view, it was easy to see why he was an avid Chicago Cubs baseball fan—the perennial bridesmaids of baseball! He calculated voluminous statistics on that team's fateful history. Despite his sophisticated mathematical skills, which were played out on his Wrigley Field of Dreams, he complained that he could not figure out how to make monetary change. He was absolutely insistent that he could not add, subtract, multiply, or divide. The staff was duly impressed with his ability to calculate daily batting averages, earned run averages, and other wondrous measurements of his heroes' successes. They used his baseball metaphor to help him discover that he had mathematical skills, and once he comprehended that, they were able to help him apply these skills in his everyday life. Concurrently, Johnny worked on these issues in therapy. What evolved was his eventual understanding that he was displacing his feelings of being shortchanged in life onto the area of learning. Phenomenologically, learning was taking place within him. The acknowledgment of learning, however, was an affirmation of his own painful history. In this situation, the difficulty in learning differs from the classical understanding of a learning block in which one does not take in or learn the material because the material is unconsciously associated with or symbolizes conflictual ideas. Johnny's inability to recognize that he was learning was a defensive maneuver connected to the need to deny the reality of his own life.

Parenthetically, another example of this clinical phenomenon occurred with an eight-year-old girl, Molly (an outpatient), who tested at an early first-grade reading level. She was extremely fascinated with my books on "Pischiatry" and had a particular fondness for volumes that she called "The Psychoantics of the Sturdy Child!" Both Johnny and Molly showed ego capabilities that they were either unaware of or needed to deny. This display of actual learning, which is not recognized and integrated into the conscious ego, can be metaphorically and colorfully described as a window in the wall of repression. It has been suggested to me by Giovacchini (1989) that the ego mechanism involved might be a split rather than repression. Regardless of its etiology, the technique we found useful was to observe these displays of unacknowledged learning, which afforded us opportunities to share with our patients our own curiosities about this paradox they presented to us.

Our curiosity and interest often reactivates the child's innate curiosity about himself. The freedom to explore in one's mind the movement, as Ekstein (1969) puts it, "from playing with toys to playing with ideas," and from this, as Winnicott (1965) describes it, "to playing with words"—this is the milieu we wish to create in residential treatment from an educational as well as a psychotherapeutic point of view.

Basch (1980) suggests that one of the goals of psychotherapy is to help a patient understand his perceptual set and then to help him expand his perceptual framework, thereby breaking out of a self-limiting mold. The perception these boys had of themselves, as mentioned before, was that they were either uneducated or uneducable, and thus they saw themselves as helpless victims with no control over their destiny and no hope for the future. Those who tended to act out would react by doing it to destiny first! When they were able to feel that they could learn, there was a change in their perspective that allowed them to have hope for the future. Within the group home, we established an atmosphere and an attitude that would support and emphasize learning. These boys had previously felt many restrictions and frustrations in the formal learning situation. The emphasis, therefore, was on learning per se rather than formal education. Developmentally, the latter can only evolve through the process of sublimation, which was a much higher level of ego achievement than most of these adolescents had attained. They generally assumed a posture of defiance toward traditional education.

Significantly, when most of the residents began to feel the desire to write, it usually took the form of poetry rather than prose. In retrospect, I believe this was because poetry is a vehicle that travels on the "royal road to the unconscious" and uses many of the elements of dream formation: representation, displacement, condensation, and symbolization. We had an open log in which the boys were welcome to make entries as well as review the staff notations. One classic poem that was entered and became evidence of a sublimatory process read as follows: "If I had the wings of an eagle / and the balls of a buffalo, / I would fly to the top of the highest mountain / and piss on the world below!" Needless to say, there was a marked diminution of his acting-out behavior and an increase in his academic performance. Thus he moved from the use of action to the use of words to express his inner feelings.

Although the resident population was not supposed to include adolescents with known learning disabilities, several did get admitted.

Matthew, despite intense effort, had the greatest difficulty in achieving academically. Psychodynamically, there did not appear to be an intrapsychic conflict to support his school failure. During one of his therapy sessions, he expressed his frustration by complaining to his therapist about the "lousy bugs" outside the office window. She observed that those bugs were butterflies, a kind called monarch, and from her point of view they were rather attractive. Matthew retained his initial perception, exclaiming they were just annoying bugs all the same. In response to his therapist's query, he began to explain what was really "bugging" him—his frustration and sense of incompetence at his lack of success in school.

Around this time Dorothy Ungerleider, an educational therapist from California and author of *Reading, Writing, and Rage*, happened to be visiting Chicago and we had him evaluated by her. She diagnosed his learning disability and offered recommendations, which the teaching staff was able to employ. Matthew was greatly relieved to learn that there was a palpable reason for his school failure. Several months after the evaluation, he initiated his therapy session by asking, "Doesn't monarch also mean king?" His therapist confirmed this, and he reflected that maybe the king butterflies were kind of pretty after all. The therapist helped him understand that he was at last feeling like a king, in control of his own destiny! She further pointed out the parallel between the metamorphosis of the caterpillar to the butterfly and that of his perception of himself from incompetence to mastery. It should be noted that this young man's current achievement includes full-time employment and attendance at a trade school, where he is learning to become a skilled craftsman.

Such a metamorphosis was not so easily achieved with two other residents who discovered they had learning disabilities. Both responded paradoxically to the new information. They had presumed, defensively, that they couldn't learn because they didn't want to. The idea that their learning problem was not based on "they couldn't because they wouldn't" made them feel absolutely impotent. Before remediation could be useful to them, their reactivated sense of castration had to be dealt with clinically. In essence, when dealing with adolescents with learning problems, regardless of their etiology, metaphorically the staff had to deal continuously with the process of metamorphosis with regard to the boys' self-concept. They didn't all develop into butterflies, but we had a fair number of "margarine-flies!"

I would like to share some statistics concerning the fifty-one residents with regard to their educational progress while in the boys' transitional group-home program. The study covers a nine-year period. Of the fifty-one residents, five were discharged to psychiatric hospitals because they required a closed residential setting. Two others were excluded from the program because they were unable and unwilling to work within the parameters of the program (which is a fancy way of saying they used drugs extensively). The remaining forty-four residents (or 86 percent) of the total group under consideration successfully completed the program. Specifically, forty-two of the forty-four young men in the group had not completed high school at the time of their admission to the group home. As part of the successful completion of their placement, thirty-five graduated high school, and an additional three graduated from a technical or vocational high school and/or trade school, making a total of thirty-eight graduates.

Statistically, this translates into 91 percent of the forty-two residents eligible for high school diplomas. In addition, one resident successfully attended and completed a vocational workshop program, which enabled him to find employment in the open community. Of those who received their high school diplomas, thirteen went on to postsecondary educational and/or vocational training. Six (or 16 percent) continued their education in trade schools, and seven (or 19 percent) entered college following their graduation. Two have received bachelor's degrees, two have received associate degrees, and one student entered college on a part-time basis when he became a resident in the program. The combined total of students involved in post-high school education was thirteen (or 34 percent).

In conclusion I would like to refer to the preface of Dorothy Ungerleider's book (1985) *Reading, Writing, and Rage.* In it she notes that whenever her mother, Florence Fink (whom I had the pleasure of knowing), traveled on a bus, her seat companion would quickly engage her in conversation, confiding his or her life's history in response to Mrs. Fink's unarticulated but very warm and active receptivity. Mrs. Fink was an exquisite listener and her advice was always delightful. Similarly, our staff related to the boys by actively listening and thus enabling the boys to share their intersubjective experiences. They were then able to identify with our interest in them, gradually take a second look at themselves, and recognize their capacities to learn and change as well as to develop a new perspective on object relations.

Ekstein (1969) noted that in normal development, children progressively move from learning for love to the love of learning. Inherent in the learning process as in psychotherapy, the relationship between the child and the significant others in their world becomes the medium through which growth and change can take place. In the residential program, the total therapeutic milieu was geared toward enabling the residents to overcome the disruptions in their development. The relationship, the most essential ingredient for the reactivation of the learning process, was important because, on the most elemental level, it restored trust in oneself and in the world in which one lived. The therapeutic and educational staff thus worked in concert with one another to enhance and strengthen the individual assets of each adolescent.

In thinking of these children and this conference, Robert Frost's poem "The Road Not Taken" comes to mind: "Two roads diverged in a wood, and I—I / took the road less traveled by, / and that has made all the difference." Children and adolescents with learning difficulties, not by choice, take the road less traveled by . . . and that makes all the difference. Through our various efforts and interventions, we offer them the option to travel on the road they have not taken . . . and that can make all the difference. For each of us, the coming together to learn from one another brings these two roads closer together for us . . . and that *will* make all the difference!

Robert M. Galatzer-Levy, M.D.

15

When You're Stupid and
Things Don't Work Right:
NOTES FROM THE ANALYSIS OF AN

ADOLESCENT BOY WITH A

LEARNING DISABILITY

his paper explores the experiences called "learning disability" for an adolescent boy. For him, like for most people so labeled, this experience has two interrelated aspects. Failing to perform at expectable school tasks had symbolic and narcissistic meanings that interdigitate with his unconscious conflicts and self-experience (Schwartz, 1989; Rothstein, Crosby, and Eisenstadt, 1988). At the same time, the probably biologically based variation in the learning-disabled way he experienced the world seemed to affect many dimensions of his organization of experience, including his experience of self and others (Garber, 1989;   Rourke, 1989;   Silver and Hagan, 1990).   Although the shifts in cognitive organization associated with learning disabilities have been widely explored regarding their effects on intellectual function, their effects on subjectivity, emotional life, self-experience, and relations with other people have not been adequately explored.

The case under study illustrates how cognitive modes can shape the experience of self, how they result in the ordering of the world in specific ways, and how they take on symbolic and emotional significance, especially through the environmental responses they evoke.

In exploring these issues, an enlarged self psychology formulation is useful. Self psychology is a point of view in psychoanalysis that takes the cohesiveness and vigor of the self as central to psychological well being. Its central finding is that other people function as self objects, supports of and aspects of the emerging and mature self (Kohut, 1971;   Wolf, 1988).   In recent years the self-object concept has been extended by several researchers who have explored more mature forms of self-object functioning and the way self-object function is integrated with the other meanings and functions of others in psychological life (Bacal and Newman, 1990;   Cohler and Galatzer-Levy, 1990;   Lachmann and Beebe, 1990;   Galatzer-Levy and Cohler, in press).   The psychological significance of learning disabilities may be formulated from a self psychology standpoint as how self-object functions are affected by cognitive organization through the course of life.

Psychological function in people with learning disabilities can be studied in depth using psychoanalysis, psychoanalytic psychotherapy, and psychoanalytically informed observation.   No single case history is typical of learning disabilities.   The following material does, however, raise a spectrum of issues important in thinking about learning-disabled youngsters.

Background and History

Johnny, aged sixteen, was a big, athletic-looking youngster. He dressed in baggy black or khaki clothing. A rhinestone earring decorated his left ear. Johnny's multicolored hair was cut in a zigzag on one side. Bangs covered half his forehead and left eye, while the right half of his head was covered with Marine short hair. The style was not quite punk nor anything else Johnny or I had ever seen. It was, he said, "the way I like it, or maybe it was a mistake." Johnny's manner was that of a polite, depressed middle-class youth. His fluent verbal expressivity contrasted with a working-class "dese and dose" accent.

Johnny's parents met and courted as teenagers in the farm community they had grown up in. Mother went to college and professional school, eventually becoming a respected professional. Father, who always did badly in school, failed his first college semester and entered the military, where, I learned much later, he had an adventurous and distinguished four years. Back in civilian life, he trained in a skilled trade and had a successful career. He eventually attained a supervisory position, which he liked far less than his trade. Even so, the prestige and income of his work was below mother's.

Johnny first came to see me after a traumatic surgical operation. The surgery was intended to correct a deformity that troubled him not at all. The doctors said "the deformity might produce functional problems in middle age," an utterly meaningless concept to Johnny. Mother believed the surgery was important, and Johnny, in rather typical fashion, gave in after mild protests. The surgery was far more complicated than anticipated. Johnny was hospitalized for three months, during which he was immobilized. He became severely depressed and he had episodes of intense rage followed by disorientation, confusion, and profound desperation.

One thing kept him sane through these horrifying experiences and a growing sense of helplessness, rage, and worthlessness—the daily visits of his girl friend, Janet. The daughter of a chronic alcoholic, Janet seemed dedicated to the care of distressed young men, of whom Johnny was the third in a series.

After he left the hospital, though he found her less attractive than other girls, Johnny felt bound to Janet for two reasons. He felt guilty about not wanting to continue a relationship with a girl who had been so kind when he needed her. His needs continued in a specific way. Johnny found it essentially impossible to learn from written material, although he understood and remembered virtually anything he heard. Janet, who took many of the same classes as Johnny, read the texts to him or summarized them in her own words. The two breakfasted together to study and be reassured of the other's availability.

Johnny's memories of difficulties and depression went back to first grade. Although he attended a first-rate, progressive private school, his recollection was of his first-grade teacher calling him "stupid" and humiliating him. His great difficulty in learning reading led him to agree with her. Johnny's mother hoped and planned that he would enter her profession, but Johnny was convinced that he was too dumb for it.

During the first school years, some of Johnny's teachers noted that in addition to the learning problems, he was depressed. After several years of prodding by the school, Johnny was taken to a child psychiatrist at age ten. Analysis was recommended, but Johnny's parents viewed his problems as relatively slight, so he was seen in weekly psychotherapy. Johnny remembered little about the treatment, except that he felt liked, a feeling he got nowhere else. After a few months of treatment, Johnny's mother became interested in the idea that Johnny had a learning disability and had him evaluated. Testing revealed he had an IQ above 140 and a "specific dyslexia." Mother took these results to mean that Johnny's emotional problems resulted exclusively from shame over academic performance. She interrupted his therapy in favor of tutoring designed to improve his school work.[1]

Psychotherapy

Initial therapeutic work with Johnny centered on his traumatizing surgery, particularly Johnny's feeling of helpless passivity. As his acute reaction to the trauma was worked through, Johnny focused on his sense that mother dominated his life. He felt he had to conform to her fantasies about him, no matter how damaging or unreasonable. Undergoing what he viewed as unnecessary surgery at her demand was merely the most dramatic of many similar episodes. It was pointless to stand up to her—she always got her way anyway. She always "knew best." Furthermore, Johnny was never sure that she was not right.

Although I agreed that Johnny's mother was a formidable character and that his henpecked father provided no model to deal with her, I said I thought there was something more that made it difficult for him to assert his opinions with her. I observed that when problems arose between us because changes in his schedule made appointments inconvenient, he failed to mention the difficulty until rescheduling was impossible. As we explored this question, Johnny realized that he often felt "something was wrong," but he could not focus sharply on what it was. Often, he literally did not know what he wanted, not only about emotional matters or complex conflictual situations, but about concrete ordinary things, like scheduling sessions.

Very tentatively, Johnny began to tell me about the one aspect of school he enjoyed: plastics shop. There he made what he called "things," objects that just pleased him. One day he brought in one of his "things," a striking, small, abstract sculpture. I was astonished by its beauty. Johnny deprecated it, but he was clearly pleased by my spontaneous delight. He began to talk—always fearing that I would think him silly—of aesthetic experiences ranging from decorating his room with stolen street signs when he was fourteen to staring into bare light bulbs to produce intense visual images as a child of six or seven. This tentative foray into the private, devalued world of Johnny's aesthetic productions was short-lived; he guarded it carefully most of the time.

Johnny's school difficulties were at the surface of his low self-opinion. Since first grade, he had thought of himself as "stupid," unable to live up to ordinary standards. Nothing about him worked right. His discovery, at the beginning of high school, that he could learn material very well aurally did not help his self-esteem. It did, however, increase his pleasure in school because he liked learning things. Some of his teachers respected his different way of learning and believed him when he said he remembered things better when he did not take notes. Attempts to take notes left him confused and feeling incompetent. Other teachers insisted that he take notes and stop "goofing off," which invariably led to poor grades. Johnny began courses listening in his own way. When teachers asked him to take notes, he tersely said he learned better without them—a response many teachers took as indifference or defiance. If his statement was not accepted immediately, Johnny complied with the teacher's demands and did poorly.

Janet played a central role in Johnny's academic life. She read material aloud, which he could then easily master. Although he found this useful, he felt even more shamed and angry being tied to Janet by his need and gratitude.

As Johnny came to feel that I understood his painful struggle between his need for Janet's help and his shame about it, he told me of another aspect of Janet's hospital visits. She had regularly masturbated him and performed fellatio on him. This was not important primarily because of the pleasure it gave; rather, he felt it kept him sane. It was the only thing he felt he could control in the hospital.

In addition, he felt sexually inadequate. Johnny was convinced that his penis was "tiny." This concern went far beyond the worries about penile size common among neurotic patients. As we discussed this issue it became clear that not only in terms of his genitals, but generally, Johnny had extraordinary difficulty forming an image of his body. His girl friend reassured him of his normality. He did not particularly enjoy sex with her compared with other girls, but felt it necessary to have a predictable, appreciative partner. Regarding his sexual life, he also identified with his father, who had committed himself to a relationship with Johnny's mother at age seventeen. Father's youthful sexual naivete and inadequacy were the subject of "humorous" family stories—like the time he drove into a ditch while trying to kiss Johnny's mother. Johnny found his situation with regard to his father captured in the movie *Back to the Future*, in which an adolescent boy remakes his own life by traveling back in time and making his father a more adequate and assertive adolescent.

Johnny strenuously avoided masturbating himself, as he had since age ten. His parents were "liberal" about masturbation (though not about other sexual activity). Johnny observed that neither parent reprimanded his younger brothers when they fondled themselves, but he regarded masturbation as disgustingly stupid and tormented his brothers about it. Gradually he realized that although he did not experience his parents as prohibiting masturbation, he believed his mother thought it contemptible, an activity engaged in by boys and men reflecting their sexual incontinence and generally second rateness. They were all silly little boys with silly little penises.

Johnny's psychotherapy was interrupted after a year when he graduated from high school. He wanted to go to a local college so he could see his girl friend, continue treatment, and stay at home. But his mother thought it essential that he attend a school with a learning-disabilities program. In addition, Johnny, I believe accurately, assessed the school his mother chose as academically and socially inadequate to his needs. More important, he found the idea of being again labeled as learning disabled and being tutored utterly repugnant. He saw himself once more sent off to a "school for stupids," but he felt incapable of doing anything about it. Both Johnny and I knew he would be distressed and have a hard time at school, although neither of us anticipated how bad it would be.

A look at Johnny's college record suggest things went well—it shows mostly grades of B's, no drops, no failures. These inflated grades only added to Johnny's sense that he was not going to a real college, since he attended few classes, showing up only for exams, which he found easy. The only class he went to regularly was photography. He felt bad about himself—that he was labeled for life and that he had accepted the label and attending the college.

For the first time, he drank heavily. By the middle of the academic year he regularly consumed a quart of vodka each afternoon. This made him anesthetic to his depression, although it left him surprisingly coherent. His erotic life involved enormous degrees of passivity. Girls seemed to come into his room and "do things" to him. He was so drunk during most of these episodes that he was uncertain what had happened. He became involved with a severely depressed girl who had made several suicide attempts and threatened to kill herself if he left her. He felt guilty both about wanting to be rid of her and for his unfaithfulness to his girl friend. Although he used no drugs except alcohol, he spent most of his time with delinquent, drug-using students. In retrospect, he said, "I felt so bad, so stupid, so hopeless all I wanted was to stop everything."

Toward the end of the academic year, one of the boys Johnny was involved with decided to steal some computer equipment from the college in order to buy drugs. He recruited Johnny as an accomplice. It "didn't matter enough" to Johnny not to go along. Incriminated after the theft, Johnny readily admitted his guilt and, out of depression, failed to protect himself from the resulting legal and academic consequences. His return to treatment followed an urgent call from his parents after his arrest.

I had always thought that Johnny should be seen intensively, and though I anticipated their support might wane with the acute emergency, went along with their wish that I see Johnny four times a week as I had recommended two years before.

The Analysis

Johnny saw me principally as someone who thought well of him and liked him. Very early in our work he brought in some of his photographs from the college course. The work was interesting and original. He wondered about becoming a photographer. Somewhat less impressed with this work than with the wonderful plastic sculptures he had shown me two years earlier, and thinking his vocational idea was but one of many career plans he periodically spun out, my own response was rather tepid, although my words were positive and encouraging. He asked whether I would like to have the photographs. Not wanting to seem greedy, I chose one I particularly liked. After the session, I passed a wastebasket in the hall and found the remaining pictures there. I retrieved them from the garbage.[2] In the next session, I asked him about throwing out the pictures. Sadly, he said that even if I didn't like his pictures, they weren't worth anything. They were like everything else about him—second-rate and stupid.

Johnny often missed sessions, offering seemingly flimsy excuses of demands by his girl friend, friends, or mere acquaintances for his time. At first I interpreted this as resistance to an intensifying transference and understood his need to protect himself from knowing about my importance to him. Although we explored the idea in depth, it carried little conviction for either of us. Johnny knew and avoided thinking about how important I was to him. Furthermore, exploration of this avowal as compliance or an admission intended to avoid further exploration was unrewarding.

Missing sessions seemed instead to reflect Johnny's enormous difficulty in attending to what mattered to him. Immediate demands were almost always more important than his ongoing interests. As we explored this phenomenon we discovered how hard it was for Johnny to order his wishes. His characterological passivity was consistent with an underlying difficulty in attending to what mattered to him. We readily understood the defensive operations in denying his own wishes, how it was consistent with his pervasive depression, and how it fit well with his overbearingly opinionated mother.[3] At the same time, there seemed to be something more—as if all these motives and their history flowered in a matrix in which the ordering of goals and attention was almost impossible for any extended period of time. Johnny seemed to have a primary deficit in ordering experience, which was exacerbated by an environment that chronically used confusion—and the implication that one was mad for not collaborating in that confusion—to maintain control. Johnny valued being alone. He often escaped into his basement bedroom and just sat. Being alone was especially valuable because it allowed him to "think" without being confused.

As the topic of being unable to think about and act on his own wishes in an orderly way was explored, a central transference emerged, along with a group of fantasies that were repeatedly enacted. In the transference, I was seen as a nice man, rather like the patient, understanding of his difficulties but entirely ineffective in changing anything. My disorderly office symbolized my lovable, bumbling, and ineffectual nature. My wife must pester me to be tidier. When I got haircuts, it must be because of her nagging. He patiently tolerated my inquires about why he chose to interpret these things in this way, saying that he knew I had to imply that I was not henpecked to avoid my wife's anger.

When we talked about sexual matters, it was as boys hiding our dirty secrets from women. I was seen, in other words, as the father who enjoyed and appreciated his son's accomplishments, but who himself was so diminished that his mirroring responses were of small value. Kohut once commented that for the mirroring self object to function well, it must be idealized to some extent. He said, "You can't be mirrored by a garbage man" (Kohut, personal communication, 1975).

At the same time that this transference emerged clearly, Johnny began to talk more of wishes to be a fireman or a policeman. During the summers he worked as a lifeguard, an activity he at first talked little about. It turned out that he loved rescuing people and, by choice, worked at a beach where he had ample opportunity to do so. In contrast to the passive, dreamy youngster he presented himself as, he evidently was vigorous and athletic in rescuing people. At one point he described carrying an unconscious 270-pound man out of the water. I commented that that must have been hard, and he responded that, on the contrary, when saving someone, he never even noticed the physical exertion. In his mind, being a policeman or fireman only consisted of rescuing needy people through one's competence and physical prowess. In other words, he made himself into the father he needed, the person who rescued the helpless child immersed in swirling confusion.

The repeated reworking of these themes gradually lead to the emergence of new ideas and new ways of doing things. As the thought grew that he might be able to survive without his girl friend's support, Johnny became more critical of her and more reluctant to put up with her dominance. For years she nagged him to stop smoking. He invariably responded to her nagging by feeling angry and smoking a cigarette to calm down. As we analyzed his response to her demands, it became clear that he equated smoking with masturbation. His girl friend was, in effect, insisting he not masturbate, and he was asserting his right to do so. The struggle between, on the one hand, smoking (masturbation) and not giving in to women's demands and, on the other, tolerating the tension of not smoking (intercourse and submission to women) became the arena in which mother's internalized denigrations were reworked. This paralleled Johnny's struggles with his cognitive style. He recognized that his cognitive organization produced substantial difficulties for his formal education. It also involved unusual and valuable capacities. What it did *not* mean was that his desires and opinions were valueless.

As he came to value his own capacities, opinions, and wishes, the difficulties became less centrally important. In particular, his long-depreciated father became an important source for reawakened identification. Increasingly, Johnny's vocational ideas shifted from fantasies of rescuing people caught up in a swirling destructive abyss to ideas that combine his native artistic talents with father's craft. Rather than seeing himself as a failed professional, Johnny increasingly saw himself as a valuable artisan. Father, who probably had a very similar learning disability to Johnny, slowly emerged as an idealizable self object with whom processes of nontraumatic deidealization were also occurring.

For several years I continued to serve as a mirroring self object for Johnny, whose steadfast interest and good opinion helped him think well of himself and maintain a coherent self-image. He found my recollections of what he said and did in the past particularly important, as it helped him develop a sense of his own continuity and stability over time. This was a new and highly valuable experience for Johnny, who gradually developed the capacity to use verbal memories to provide himself with an increased sense of coherence and continuity.

Termination provided a particularly important opportunity to use and extend this capacity. His new capacity to use language for *his* purposes allowed a new kind of organization that made him less dependent on archaic self-objects. At the same time, he could employ a wider range of more age-appropriate self-objects—male friends, his father, a mentor in his field, and a girl friend from whom he continues to seek mirroring but whose responses are not essential to his sense of bodily and psychic integrity.

Conclusion

Johnny's analysis illustrates several themes that recur in the psychology of people diagnosed with learning disabilities. First there may be primary variations in the organization of experience. These variations range from the construction of body image to the sequencing of ideas, which may be extraordinary in ways that may be evaluated as maladaptive or creative or both. Johnny's difficulties with sequencing and ordering are not only manifest in his dyslexia but in the ordering of values and time sequences. His unusual perception of form shows itself in his artistic work and his profound difficulties forming a consistent view of his own body, as well as his difficulties with the written word. Thus, distinctive variations in the ordering of experience are commonly associated with learning disabilities.

These primary variations in experience take on added personal meaning as the person finds it difficult to negotiate a world largely designed for people whose cognitive organization differs from his own. Depending on the environment's response, the variation is commonly experienced as a defect and may come to symbolize other feelings of defectiveness, incompleteness, or vulnerability.

This is especially true if the people who perform self-object functioning are inadequate, because the affected person's different organization of experience can lead to inaccurate empathy from people who could easily empathize with psychological organizations more like their own. Johnny's mother had her own motives for "misunderstanding" him, but Johnny often left her genuinely perplexed and uncomprehending. If, as is common, the child's difficulties stimulate parents' feelings of defect and inadequacy, the child may be confronted with even more inadequate self-object function as the parent defensively protects himself against this experience. Parents and their advisers often oversimplify the complex situation of learning disabilities by addressing only deficits in academic settings, in the attempt to protect parents from the painful complexity of the actual situation. In the long run, these defensive operations intensify the child's difficulties by making much-needed assistance less available. In Johnny's case, his parents' need to protect themselves from the depth of Johnny's difficulties deprived the boy of psychotherapy throughout his childhood.

It has long been recognized that characterological defenses can be difficult in terms of cognitive operation (Rosen, 1977). These defenses work best when they are consistent with the native cognitive style native to the person. Johnny avoided the conflicts and pain of knowing his own opinions by keeping them muddled and ill-focused, but this seemed very much of a piece with his difficulties with sequential organization in general. Similarly, the mother's confusing communicative style took on special force for this boy, who had so much trouble ordering sequential experience and whose sense of self was so tenuous that it was particularly difficult for him to identify and resist her pseudorational impositions on him.

Johnny's psychoanalysis centered around the development of a stable mirror transference and its vicissitudes. Earlier failures of adequate mirroring arose from a confluence of Johnny's unusual psychology, which demanded a particularly wide empathic capacity to be understood, his parents' depression and need to defend themselves against Johnny's psychological reality, his mother's negative attitudes toward the sexuality of boys and men, and teachers' failures to appreciate those capacities that Johnny did have and placing too strong an emphasis on his disabilities. Each of these factors was exacerbated by Johnny's emotional withdrawal, which provided potential mirroring self objects with even less information than they might have had about his internal states and psychological needs.

The self grows and is shaped by the ever-interacting native talents, history, and self-object environment of the individual. Each of these elements affects and gives meaning to the others. It is clear that there is wide biological variation in people's cognitive endowments. As analysts, our task is to explore how these variations affect the overall development of the self in all its complexity.

Notes

1. Dichotomous thinking, learning disability vs. psychogenic distress, was a recurrent theme in mother's thinking about Johnny. Mother repeatedly used the idea of a learning disability to avoid confronting Johnny's chronic depression. It is easy, with twenty-twenty hindsight, to blame her for several unwise discussions about Johnny and her other dyslexic children. On one level Johnny's mother, like many other people, finds the idea of learning disability less shameful and more manageable than that of psychological disorder, defending herself against her feelings about her son's psychological distress by falsely dichotomizing cognitive and emotional problems and seeking a panacea in cognitive training. Over the years this mother received much support for her thinking from various educators who gave lip service to psychological issues, but always recommended primarily cognitive interventions. Her experience, unfortunately, is not atypical.

2. Many analysts would object to my accepting Johnny's picture and retrieving others from the garbage. I do not regard either action as unanalytic. Rather, they are part of the ordinary courtesy and respect with which analytic patients of all ages should be treated to avoid iatrogenic confusion of the transference and so allow the patient's central concerns to emerge within the transference (Galatzer-Levy, 1991; Lipton, 1977, 1979; Wolf, 1988).

3. My own interactions with mother made it clear how her maintaining control interfered with the boy's capacity to note and attend to his wishes. In telephone conversations with me and occasional office interviews, she spoke rationally and we seemed to solve problems together. But as we said goodby, or at the door, there was often an abrupt change in attitude and ambiance. Johnny's mother would make a decisive statement negating all that had gone before. I had several tastes of the patient's experience, which included not only frustration at having gotten nowhere but, perhaps more important, feelings of being somewhat insane, as if I had misunderstood the whole of what had preceded out of some defect in myself.

Training, Supervision, and Consultation

Introduction

educators at all levels and in all fields of educational therapy and psychotherapy, and scholars concerned with issues of human development, affect, and cognition are involved, at least to some degree, in issues of training, supervision, and consultation. The group of papers assembled in this section focus on these issues. A careful reader, however, might recognize that these papers could easily have been placed in other sections of the book.

Kay Field argues that recent prescriptions for educational reform such as those embodied in the 1986 Carnegie Report, "A Nation Prepared: Teachers for the 21st Century," rest on an unrealistic vision of today's youth and classroom life. This depersonalized, decontextualized view of teaching has its conceptual roots in the philosophy of technical rationality that Donald Schon and others have criticized as being outmoded as a serviceable model for training professionals in many fields, including education. Field contrasts this deeply entrenched perspective with one that is humanistic, context-particular, and subjectively based, arguing for the advantages inherent in such a view. She then describes the Teacher Education Program at the Chicago Institute for Psychoanalysis, a program she founded, based on contemporary psychoanalytic and psychodynamic understandings of the educational process, together with prescriptions for reform of essential aspects of the education of teachers: supervision, field work, evaluation, and post-graduate education.

Charles Saltzman argues that educational reform should primarily be aimed at addressing the developmental needs of children. His contribution evolves as a manifesto for an empathic approach to education. Among the elements essential to this task, he chooses to emphasize three—theory, technique, and self—and discusses these within a framework based on the ideas of Kohut and his followers. Self psychology, which has thus far served primarily as an explanatory system for the study of clinical interactions in psychoanalysis and psychotherapy, is employed here to illuminate the patterns of interaction within the social system of the school, particularly the interactions between teachers and students. Saltzman calls for more vigorous recruitment of young men and women possessed of broad empathic range and offers a method for the further enhancement of empathic responsiveness in these prospective teachers through the study of the writings of gifted teachers of exceptional children. These autobiographical accounts, often reporting the work of the teacher with a small group of children over the course of one year, are, in Saltzman's view, a means of access to theory, technique, and self, which, in addition to subject matter competence, are essential elements in the repertoire of teachers.

Linda Cozzarelli adapts the model of intersubjectivity developed by Stolorow and Atwood as a conceptual framework for studying psychotherapeutic interactions to the dialogue between supervisor and supervisee in the teaching and learning of psychotherapy. Examining the interplay between the subjective worlds of supervisor and supervisee provides potential benefits, not only for the parties directly involved in the dialogue, but also for the absent third party, namely, the patient being treated by the therapist. The model rests on some familiar assumptions: that later learning involves recapitulation of earlier learning experiences and that relationships vary over time, expressed in this context as an expectation that intersubjective conjunction (congruence of subjective meaning) is not consistently sustainable but is followed by expressions of intersubjective dysfunction. The capacity of the participants for decentered self-awareness, introspection, and empathy permits the examination and exploitation of these oscillations in the relationship for learning and growth. Cozzarelli cogently points out that professional and personal self-esteem are less differentiated for those in the helping professions because the instrument of practice is the self. Even though the theoretical exposition and the richly detailed case illustrations are drawn from the realm of supervision of psychotherapy, the model clearly has widespread applicability. The discussion highlights the narcissistic vulnerabilities and consequent defensiveness that are inherent in any encounter between teacher and learner, and indicates how the success of the endeavor ultimately rests on the ability of the participants to negotiate the differences between their intersubjective worlds of thinking and feeling.

Edward Kaufman focuses on the state of "beleaguerment," a frequently recognized component of teacher burnout, dysphoria, and dysfunction, leading in some instances to the decision to abandon teaching in pursuit of another profession. Kaufman proposes, as both a remedy and a preventive, understanding the dynamics that create the feeling state of beleaguerment. This understanding leads to self-empathy for the teacher and that, in turn, restores the teacher's capacity to empathize with his students. Kaufman states that beleaguerment is a regularly occurring experience and is ubiquitous throughout the teaching profession. Using some films as a visual textbook to serve as documentation, he shows that the state of beleaguerment is a normally occurring part of the educator's subjective experience. The very fact that such films are made, he points out, dramatizes the cultural recognition of the universality of this phenomenon. Thus, when the individual educator recognizes this universality, it helps to overcome his sense of aloneness that contributes to paralysis and the further ebbing of morale and hopefulness. Kaufman illustrates an approach to interpretation of film from a psychoanalytic perspective. At the center of focus is the interaction of teacher and pupil, each with his own set of needs and vulnerabilities, as well as the student's resistances to involvement in the relationship or in the subject matter. The resistant learner who succeeds in thwarting himself and the teacher can have a profoundly demoralizing effect on a teacher who is inclined to accept a disproportionate share of the responsibility for the educational failure. Kaufman recommends the formation of peer, professional study groups to provide support to educators in a trusting, collegial atmosphere. Within these groups, teachers can refortify themselves and gain additional perspectives regarding their students' learning resistances and problems. When they feel they are not entirely alone, teachers are better able to face their daunting tasks.

Kay Field, M.A.

16

Re-Forming Teacher Education:

TWO VISIONS

The transition from a paradigm in crisis to a new one from which a new
tradition of normal science can emerge is far from a cumulative
process, one achieved by an articulation or extension of the old paradigm. Rather it is a reconstruction of the field from new fundamentals, a reconstruction that changes some of the field's most
elementary theoretical generalizations as well as many of its paradigm methods and applications. Thomas Kuhn

eachers, second only to parents are surely
among the most extolled—and denigrated—
professionals in our society. They are seen
through the hazy screen of private memories and public images, real or
unreal, and so teachers are ever available, made-to-order targets for
displacement. Their training, in turn, has reflected and usually reinforced the stereotypes and contradictions of their public image. Given
the ambivalence and ambiguity surrounding our images of teachers

and teaching, theirs is a profession in a class by itself. Its status and standards of practice are subject to the judgments, ideologies, and constraints imposed by persons outside the profession who usually have little firsthand knowledge of the realities of classroom life yet have strong convictions about what it ought to be. No other established profession is so externally defined and so arbitrarily regulated by those it is designed to serve. Indeed the prevailing vision of the teaching profession originates in the minds of observers stationed outside the classroom door, where the voices of teachers and students are muted and unheard and the drama of life within—its tensions, its conflicts, its uncertainties, its triumphs and disappointments—are either ignored or dismissed as a form of classroom static, evidence of teacher mismanagement.

Let's open the classroom door for a moment, and observe the scene through the eyes and sensibilities of those teaching as well as those taught. Recently, a college graduate who was seriously considering a career in teaching wrote a former, highly respected teacher for advice. Here is an excerpt from her letter.

> I am told that I didn't have to go to Brown University to become a teacher. I am told that teaching is a "wonderful" thing to do until you decide what you really want to do with your life! I am told that it's nice to be a teacher. Why does it seem that the decision to teach in our society is analogous with the decision to stunt one's growth, to opt out intellectually in favor of long summers off?

Here are excerpts from her teacher's reply:

> I admire your courage to consider teaching. Your friends and relatives are not alone in their negative opinion about teaching. I am sure you read the claim in the President's Commission on Education, that education is a national disgrace—at least four blue ribbon studies have concluded that teacher education is inadequate, that the pay is the lowest of all professions, that schools have deplorable management, and that the job is full of meaningless paperwork. . . . To most people I am just a teacher! But this is the outside reality.
>   The interior world of the teacher is quite different. Although you have to come to terms with the outward flatness of the career, I want to assure you that teachers change and grow. So little research has been done on stage development of teachers that the literature recognizes only three categories: intern, novice and veteran. This is laughingly oversimplified. There is life after the *1st* year . . .

Britzman (1980) gives this picture of the "interior [subjective] world" of a teacher:

> [Being a teacher involves] the difficult process of making sense of and acting within self-doubt, uncertainty and the unexpected, while assuming a role which requires confidence, certainty and stability. It is a painful experience, often carried out in a state of disequilibrium.

And speaking from the other side of the teacher's desk, Freud (remembering his teachers) wrote about his student days in an essay prepared for the fiftieth anniversary of his own school:

> We courted them or turned our backs on them, we imagined sympathies and antipathies in them which probably had no existence, we studied their characters and on theirs we formed or mis-formed our own. They called up our fiercest opposition and forced us to complete submission; we peered into their little weaknesses, and took pride in their excellences, their knowledge and their justice. At bottom we felt a great affection for them if they gave us any ground for it, though I cannot tell how many of them were aware of this. But it cannot be denied that our position in regard to them was a quite remarkable one, and one which may very well have had its inconveniences for those concerned. We were from the very first equally inclined to love and to hate them, to criticize and respect them. Psychoanalysis has given the name of "ambivalence" to this readiness to contradictory attitudes, and it has no such difficulty in pointing to the source of ambivalent feeling, of such kind.

Listening to teachers and students talk about their experiences in the classroom and school, leads one to the conclusion that all teaching and learning are organized around complex, emotion-charged human interactions under the strong influence of ever changing human contexts. Philip Jackson (1991), in his recent book on *The Practice of Teaching,* wondered, "why is teaching so often described in simplistic terms, when careful observation reveals it as an extremely complex activity." Teaching and learning are never simple, never solely objective or rational, certainly never ordinary, yet we keep trying to make them so.

What emerges from the anecdotes above is a vision of the classroom drama as it is perceived, experienced and enacted by the very people who are its actors and producers—teachers and students. They call our attention to the subjective underside of classroom events, and remind us of the complexity and multidimensionality of teachers' work. Clues to the functional significance of this subjectively experienced and contextually-based vision of teaching are contained in the reflections of another teacher:

> When I think of myself as a teacher, the word "middleness" comes to mind. I believe that what I do as a teacher lies appropriately between therapy, with its inward orientation and emphasis on personality growth, and on vocational growth, with its external orientation and emphasis on the content and standards of the subject matter disciplines. I see myself standing at the midpoint of that continuum and thus feel compelled to keep both ends in sight and in balance. (Howard, 1989)

This teacher conceptualized a space at the borders of pedagogy and therapy within which to define what she sees as her dual pedagogue/therapist role. The emerging field of educational therapy is based on the concept of "middleness" so clearly portrayed in her reflections. It provides a frame of reference on teaching-learning that is wider than the specific learning task or activity, in that it views learning as an interpretive rather than a reproductive process. Educational therapy emphasizes *personal meaning*—the lived reality and subjective experience—of learning for both teacher and taught. Zimiles (1987) captured the complexity and multi-dimensionality of the educational situation encompassed in the humanistic, developmental vision of educational therapy:

> *I came to view all education . . . not as a means of implanting specific skills and pockets of knowledge, but as a form of profound, multifaceted psychological intervention in the lives of children.* [Emphasis added] After having been trained to view children through peepholes defined by the atomistic one-variable-at-a-time research fashion of the day it was eye-opening to conceive of the classroom and the school as a psychological field, as a broad stage on which the full range of the drama and intricacy of psychological development is being enacted. The opportunity to deal with real children, each one obviously distinctive, once looked at for more than a moment, and to bear in mind the full spectrum of their developmental needs during a school career that spans more than a decade, plunges the psychologist [the educator, as well] into a level of complexity and compelling reality that is at first staggering. It is a complexity that can only begin to be ordered and understood, at least from my experience, by viewing it through the lens of dynamic psychology.

Not only has Zimiles sharply delineated the contrasting visions of the educative process, which we aim to address, he also calls attention to the important role that theory plays, (psychodynamic-developmental theories, in particular), in the preparation of teachers.

There are several fundamental differences which distinguish the educational vision embodied in the theory and practice of educational therapy from the prevailing vision of teaching and teacher training in the reform movements of the 1980s and 1990s (and those before them as well). Educational therapy is attuned to the voices, sensibilities and subjective experiences of both those teaching and those taught and thereby introduces new data and new avenues of inquiry. It takes cognizance of the untidy, messy, emotion-laden nature of teaching and looks for the patterns and meaning behind the inchoateness of surface events; and it directs attention to the spontaneous, experientially-based, situationally-particular, person-specific contexts of the educational enterprise.

In 1962 and 1986 Sarason et al. examined the problems of teacher preparation and both times came to the conclusion that the teaching task was "psychologically unknown," which is to say that its clinical aspects have been ignored:

> There is nothing in the selection and preparation of teachers that sensitizes them to and refines their grasp of the obligations and dilemmas of their clinical roles. . . . the training of teachers . . . ill prepared them for the realities of the classroom . . . . What was going unstudied . . . was the relevance of their preparation to the kinds of problems that they had to understand and manage. (1986)

This conclusion is born out by teachers themselves. Among both new and veteran teachers, who may disagree on many other matters, there is an overwhelming consensus that their training "ill prepared" them for the everyday predicaments they face in their classrooms.

The topic of teacher education is too broad, too complex, too fraught with controversy and ideology to be encompassed in the short space of a single chapter. What I hope to present here is an elaboration of a point of view about teacher education which has been in the process of evolving in my mind for nearly three decades. During those years I have been educating teachers, working with both novice and veteran teachers and allied special service personnel in an unorthodox training program located in the largely unexplored space at the borders of two disciplinary cultures: education and psychoanalysis.

What made this teacher education program (TEP) unusual was, in part, that the impetus for its development originated at the grass roots level with practitioners (classroom teachers) who were looking for help with the predicaments encountered in their classrooms, but also for their turning for assistance to the Institute for Psychoanalysis, an educational institution known for its clinical focus and clearly outside the mainstream of teacher training institutions. The teachers who founded this program, like those who pioneered the development of educational therapy (Caspari, Barrett, Duve, Ungerleider etc.—see Chapter 1, this volume) during roughly the same time in the 60s, had been seeking the clinical skills needed in their work but were not taught earlier.

The major thesis of this chapter is that the humanistic and integrative vision of the educative process exemplified in the theory and practice of education therapy complements, in a significant way, the dominant, depersonalized, decontextualized vision of teaching and teacher education embodied in the various reform proposals. We have based our position on teacher training on close to three decades of experience in the TEP of the Institute for Psychoanalysis in Chicago. The program offers a design and a curriculum that has as one of its principal aims an understanding of how we learn from a subjective perspective. This is to say that students (in this case, practicing teachers) would not only learn about learning ("learning," in its broad sense) but would come to understand in an immediate and personal way what that experience is like for themselves and for others.

It has been said that a person living at the borders of a province is better able to decide which peaks inside are the highest than an observer living amidst the peaks themselves. If this be true, and my experience tends to confirm it, then what we have observed in our work with teachers may point with constructive specificity to some of the missing elements in the prevailing vision and practice of teacher education.

Rather than devote this essay to an exposition of the TEP model of training, I will try to convey instead its defining vision and paradigmatic features via a comparative commentary on the prevailing vision as embodied and articulated in the educational debates and proposals for school reform. The prevailing vision of teaching and teacher education is, in our view, most fully delineated in the report of the Carnegie Forum on "Teachers for the 21st Century: A Nation Prepared," published in 1986. My reasons for selecting this report over the many others that have been debated are twofold. In its explicit focus on the issue of enhancing teacher professionalism and its concrete proposals for achieving this much desired goal, the Carnegie report opens up some critical questions unique to teacher education and, therefore, of enormous consequence for the direction and content of educational reform in the 1990s and beyond. Inasmuch as current educational policy, teacher certification and evaluation standards, in addition to the requirements for training, already bear the imprint of the Carnegie reform proposals, a second look at its informing vision, this time from the vantage point of practicing teachers, may offer a useful balancing perspective.

Five years ago, the publication of the Carnegie report provoked a responding white paper from a task force consisting of members of the TEP faculty, its students, and alumni (all were practicing educators and representatives from other educational institutions in the Chicago area). The commentary to follow is a considerably expanded version of our response to the vision of teaching and education in the 1986 Carnegie report. It was prepared by members of the TEP faculty, alumni and representatives of the educational community.[1]

The Prevailing Vision

The educational vision portrayed in the Carnegie Report appears in the section of the report entitled: "Schools for the 21st Century—A Scenario."[2] The classroom there envisioned reflects both the focus and the kinds of reform the authors advocate. What is most powerful in the Carnegie scenario is the ethos of this imagined school. The school described is intended to represent a typical high school in a midwestern city serving children in a low-income community. The students are presented as highly motivated, purposeful, actively engaged in problem solving, eagerly collaborating with each other and with their teacher. This school is replete with rich technical resources; there are secretaries to do the paperwork, freeing teachers for instruction; there is an atmosphere of mutual involvement with ready collaboration between students, teachers and administrators. Students are intellectually curious, eager to acquire new learning skills and, apparently, unfazed by taking examinations. In fact, what is presented is an abstraction, a romanticized, utopian image of an ideal high-school classroom.

This image, unfortunately, does not correspond to the existing reality of adolescents and schools anywhere in modern society, let alone those in a low income, urban neighborhoods. All uncomfortable and discrepant aspects of present-day life and schooling are cleansed from this picture. The emotional turmoil of adolescence is implicitly disavowed. The burgeoning sexual and aggressive feelings commonly manifested in the behavior of teenagers are unnoticed. The unruly or nonconforming student has been removed from the lecture hall and is silent. The hungry pupil, the frightened one, and the confused and depressed youngster are conspicuous by their absence. There appears to be nothing unpleasant to divert students and teachers from the appointed tasks of learning. This is a classroom as an adult wishes it to be; all troublesome feelings and attitudes have been expunged. This vision of a high-school classroom anywhere is flawed because it totally denies the existence of those human experiences which inevitably complicate learning and teaching and interfere with the acquisition of knowledge. Acceptance of this vision by the teacher not only falsifies classroom reality and invalidates her perception of the problems she faces, it also precludes the teacher's use of one of her most powerful educative tools—her sensitive understanding of the behavior and experience of the young people she needs to reach and engage them in the process of learning how to learn.

The exclusive focus on the cognitive mode in this vision leads to the conclusion that both teacher and students manage to check their emotional baggage at the classroom door. The acquisition of knowledge cannot be so compartmentalized, however; it undergoes an integration of affect and cognition if it is to have personal meaning for the learner. It is in facilitating this personally meaningful integration of knowledge that the teacher exercises her professionalism and her competence as an educator. The teacher's self-understanding and awareness of her own past and current experiences as a learner enables her to better understand and empathize with her students' efforts to learn how to learn.

Let us look now at the classroom situation familiar to the majority of teachers today. In this scenario, the teacher, immediately upon entering the classroom in this urban high school, also in a working-class neighborhood, confronts thirty girls and boys, some eager and attentive, some apathetic and withdrawn, some restless and inattentive, some anxious, some depressed, some angry and provocative, some quiet, some noisy, some comfortable and selfassured, some tense and self-doubting, some there to learn, some to socialize, and some to thwart the teacher's every effort to provide a climate for learning. In addition, it is sure to be a culturally and racially diverse group of young people, bringing with them different languages, attitudes, values and family backgrounds. Let us assume this is a science teacher with many years of experience and a solid background of knowledge in her subject and no stranger to the myriad needs presented by such a group of young people. Her mandate is to transfer a predetermined body of scientific knowledge to each and every student in that class. She knows, however, that no matter what material she presents, some will get it and some will not. This is to say that some will readily integrate this new knowledge; some will memorize, regurgitate it for the test, and soon forget it; some will be so depleted by malnutrition, physical illness, developmental deficits, and/or emotional problems as to be unable to concentrate on the task. Some, afraid of another failure, will be threatened by the new material and be unable to process it. Some will ignore it out of disinterest, and some will reject it because of a compelling inner need to reject whatever the teacher/authority presents. Some will be suffering from primary learning disorders. Many will enter the class below grade level. The teacher also knows that some students will be coming to class under the influence of alcohol or drugs, or overwhelming sexual stimulation or burdened by family turmoil, illness, divorce and separation. Given these realities, how is she to fulfill her instructional mandate?

If her students are to learn science and tolerate the anxiety inherent in learning anything new, the teacher must first engage with each student and with the group as a whole in an ongoing, mutually trusting, mutually respectful, and mutually hopeful relationship. With some students this kind of relationship with the teacher will form naturally and quickly without conscious effort on the part of the teacher; with others, the teacher will have to work very hard and long to encourage such a trusting relationship; with some others she will fail. Inevitably, there will be some students in every class who are unable to enter into a learning alliance; consequently, these individuals are likely to fail.

Our experienced teacher, knowing herself, also is aware that she will be tempted to gravitate toward the highly motivated, successful students, and to shy away from the more problematic students. The emotional impact of students on their teacher is undeniably as much a part of the classroom reality as is the impact of the teacher on the student. Recent research has sensitized educators to the fact that reciprocal processes of influence operate between students and teachers, exploding the myth that influence flows in one direction from teacher to student. Or, as Miriam Elson (1989) has put it, the teacher may be viewed as a learner and the learner as a teacher.

The teacher's capacity for self-awareness, self-reflection, and empathy should enable her to overcome, at least in part, her reluctance to work with the more difficult, learning-resistant students. However, teachers cannot be expected to acquire all the necessary insights and understanding for negotiating such complex, high-stress interactions which are inherent in their work, independently and unaided. Nor can they ever be fully prepared for them by their preservice training. What all teachers require is a form of ongoing staff development[3] aimed at enabling them to initiate school-based dialogues with colleagues which focus on their everyday classroom experiences and concerns, and permit them to have a voice in setting their own agendas for learning. Such an ongoing, participatory approach to professional learning is in sharp contrast to the existing models of staff development in most public schools, which are typically one-time, single-session, didactic presentations by "experts," most of whom present generalized teaching methods and techniques intended more for controlling behavior than for facilitating learning. While such programs have their place, they overlook the emotional realities—the subjective side of being a teacher and a learner. A school-based forum designed to raise the muted voices of teachers, notably the repositories of their subjective experiences with students in their classrooms, is an essential component in the continuing education and professionalization of teachers. Typically, schools offer no such forum.

That city schools today have become the hub of an array of services heretofore provided by families, religious institutions and community agencies is readily apparent to everyone. The days of the intact family are long since past and that convenient, if simplistic, division of labor that once separated child-rearing and teaching, no longer exists. Schools in working-class or disadvantaged areas, indeed even in the affluent suburbs, are fast becoming the primary, if not the only, source of a broad range of human services to young people and their parents. Emphasis is shifting to a view of the school as a complex ecological system, in which members of different disciplines engage in a process of collaborative learning.

As a consequence of these present-day school realities and expanded service mandates, it follows that teachers require a responsive support system if they are to be effective in meeting the diverse educational needs of such heterogeneous student populations. All teachers need to have ready access to collaboration with principals, counselors, educational specialists, colleagues, social workers, psychologists, psychiatrists and physicians, as well as time for self-reflection and dialogue.

Since problematic children come from problematic families, it is clear that the schools must provide a range of educational and social services to parents as well. It is not enough to simply inform parents that their youngster is in trouble. The teacher together with appropriate members of the school's professional staff need to actively engage parents in an ongoing, mutual effort aimed at helping that youngster and his/her parents as well. Here, too, teachers are at a disadvantage because this is an aspect of their professional function that receives little more than didactic attention in their training. Teachers' anxiety about working with parents is matched only by parents' anxiety about their meetings with teachers.

We have presented a highly condensed portrait of a modern high-school classroom which differs significantly from the utopian scenario presented in the Carnegie report. Our scenario calls attention to the influence of contextual factors and subjective experience on the teacher's work. The social-psychological realities of classroom life today refute the validity of an approach that focuses almost exclusively on what the teacher knows or ought to know about her subject. Necessary as this is, it is of little avail if the teacher does not understand the impact of psychodynamic and developmental factors on the learning process. As we have argued, what must be taken into account in teacher education is not only the heterogeneity of school populations, but also the inherent ambiguities, uncertainties, and complexities of the teacher's task, and the multiplicity of human variables that shape and direct all educational activities. We contend that while these elements constitute the essence of teacher professionalism, they have been, and remain, largely ignored and unstudied in their preservice and postservice training.

History tells us that educational reform, like learning, cannot succeed by piecemeal methods; it must be ongoing, comprehensive, coordinated and integrated. Accordingly, it must start at the very beginning of a youngster's school career. The lasting benefits of high quality early childhood educational experience have been widely recognized. With this in mind we turn now to a second scenario, this one from either a Head Start program, a day-care program or a nursery school classroom.

In this instance, the teacher is an experienced, early childhood educator. What will she confront when she meets her class? In this group of three- to four-year-olds, some will be bright, energetic, curious, eager to learn, ready to separate from their parents and engage with the teacher in exploring a whole new world; others will be subdued, apprehensive and inhibited; some will look and act more like two year olds and display regressive behavior; some will battle with peers and ignore the teacher; some will be impulsive, inattentive and hyperactive; some will be withdrawn and unreachable. This teacher has the responsibility and the challenge of starting all these children on the path to learning. What happens in her classroom will profoundly affect each child's subsequent view of learning and of himself as a learner. Here is where one sees the scope of the teacher's dual educational and clinical role writ large in all its complexity. This teacher, too, is expected to emphasize cognitive functioning and the transmission of appropriate factual knowledge. But, as we have argued, she can only do this in the context of ongoing, trusting relationships with each of these children and with their parents, as well. In the words of Stern (1985):

> An implicit assumption of modern psychological thought, is that the individual is constantly in transaction with his environment and that both are subject to change as a result of these transactions. The setting is at least as important as the actor, and both must be analyzed together as a single functional system if the act itself is to be made intelligible.

The preschool teacher may be in even greater need of a framework of theory, a professional support system, ongoing staff development, clinical supervision, consultation, and built-in opportunity for multidisciplinary collaboration than is the case with the aforementioned secondary schoolteacher.

We have emphasized that, to be effective, the educative process must be not only multifaceted and multimodal, but also integrative. It requires attention to both the predetermined formal curriculum (typically a major focus of teacher training) and to the rapidly expanding body of contemporary knowledge and theory about human development and learning, and to the less tangible, but powerful relational, subjective and affective dimensions of the teaching-learning process. We have seen how the traditional boundaries separating the tasks of teachers and clinicians are shifting and moving closer. Indeed, as Sarason (1985) explained:

> The role of the teacher is quintessentially clinical in that she deals with the problems of individuals, problems requiring special knowledge, "insight and sympathy" (Flexner's words) and interpersonal skills geared to remediation, secondary and primary prevention. (p. 64)

In our two scenarios we have tried to show the complex situations teachers face in their classrooms every day. What kind of professional training can best prepare a teacher for such tasks? It is a given that a competent teacher needs to be expert in the subject she teaches. But it is also apparent that what makes for an effective teacher goes beyond subject matter. There is no known research that shows an invariant relationship between knowledge of subject matter and teaching effectiveness, yet the twin thrusts of curriculum and method continue to dominate teacher education. This is not to deny the importance of knowing one's subject. But, like love, this is not enough. The key to effective teaching lies in the teacher's capacity to catalyze, facilitate, and extend student learning through a complex process of intersubjective (as well as cognitive-verbal) communication and empathic interaction with students as total persons. Sarason, Davidson, and Blatt (1986) remind us that

> The teacher must be viewed as a kind of psychological observer and tactician in a learning situation structured so that children are able to absorb and utilize knowledge and skills in an increasingly independent, curiosity-satisfying, productive attack on the world of ideas and problems. To the extent that the teacher perceives her role as primarily concerned with the transmission of knowledge, ignoring the more covert, emotional communications, she is performing as a technician. (p. 73)

It is also apparent that the personal qualities of the teacher are no less important than her cognitive and verbal skills and knowledge of her subject. A competent teacher must have what Greene calls "a passion for learning" and be able to inspire like passion in her students; she must have the ability to connect with young people and guide them in their struggles to learn; she must understand the psychological forces that motivate learning or interfere with it; she must be able to balance the needs of the individual and the needs of the group; she must have achieved that inner personal equilibrium necessary to sustain her in the inevitable moments of uncertainty, ambiguity, frustration, and injured narcissism that are the lot of every teacher. She must have a capacity for "reflection-in-action" (Schon, 1973) and introspection as well as an understanding of the inherent reciprocity and complementarity of the teaching-learning relationship so that she can correctly interpret the behavior and communications of her students. In the words of Lawrence Kubie (1958):

> Educators must be able to study not only the variables in the students to be educated, and the variables in the methods used, but also the variables which occur in themselves as teachers and as learners. (p. 19)

A Design for Teacher Education

How would one design a program of education for teachers which not only ensures subject matter expertise but which also promotes their ongoing professional growth and development, one that encompasses both the personal attributes and skills we have mentioned and the areas of epistemic knowledge indicated above? We propose that the design of such a program must encompass: pre-entry level (baccalaureate) education, graduate study, field work experience, clinical supervision, and ongoing professional development.

Let us consider first, the body of pedagogic and clinical knowledge teachers must integrate in order to function competently in the modern classroom. Teachers need to be as aware of the subjective aspects of the curriculum as of the cognitive. For example, they must appreciate that the meaning of a given text varies with each reader, and that part of effective teaching is ascertaining the personal meaning for the student of the subject studied. Here is where teachers and students together construct the curriculum and learn from each other. Second, they need to understand those individual differences in their students which cannot be measured by objective tests. These are the differences determined by sociocultural factors, genetic factors, the influences of early family experience on subsequent capacity for learning, personality differences—in short, all of the factors determining the individual's psychological readiness and capacity for learning at any given time in his development. Third, they must know how to observe and apprehend the meaning conveyed by children's nonverbal as well as verbal communications. Fourth, they must understand the psychodynamics of the teaching-learning process; the meaning of the interactions between individual pupils with each other, with the group as a whole and with the teacher. Fifth, they need both theoretical knowledge and clinical skills if they are to establish an effective working alliance with parents. Sixth, the teacher must understand the complex internal forces and subjective experiences that motivate children to learn or fail to learn. Seventh, they must be familiar with the range and nature of psychological as well as neurological problems which can interfere with learning. And they must develop a repertoire of psychological as well as pedagogical modes of intervention which makes integrated learning possible.

We are in accord with the goal of enhancing the professionalism of teachers. Toward this end it has been proposed that professional training be deferred to graduate study. Nominally, this is to strengthen undergraduate education in the liberal arts and sciences. There can be no quarrel with extending the liberal arts background of teachers. However, we think it is crucial that the study of liberal arts be integrated from the beginning with the multifaceted, rich, and complex process of developing a professional identity. Accordingly, we strongly propose that professional development begin in the baccalaureate years. If the professions of law, medicine, business and science begin their preparation at the undergraduate level, so should the teaching profession.

There are many advantages to having the undergraduate years integrated with graduate education. First and foremost, it would provide an opportunity to introduce prospective teachers to the human sciences—personality development, psychology, anthropology, and family dynamics. What better place and time to introduce teachers to the essential elements in learning and teaching, to understanding children and themselves, than during those college years when they themselves are exploring their own identities, personally and professionally. These studies would provide a foundation for advanced studies on the graduate level.

Traditionally, graduate studies in education emphasize methods of teaching different subjects. But this emphasis was outmoded for the teaching profession as it is for the medical profession. Noting that medical schools have been moving away from the Flexner model, Silberman (1970) wrote:

> There is at least as much ferment over what should be taught in medical school as over how it should be taught. "The primary purpose of medical education in the past was to impart a closed body of knowledge or identifiable content requisite for a physician's education," Dr. Charles G. Child III and Dr. Ralph J. Wedgewood write. "This is no longer true." It simply is not possible for doctors, any more than teachers, to learn in professional school more than a fraction of what they will need to know for careers that will extend into the twenty-first century . . .
>
> What medical schools lack and must now develop, the Millis Commission argued, in terms remarkably evocative of the literature on teacher education, is "an intellectual framework into which the lessons of practical experience can be fitted."

The foundations of contemporary teacher education must be brought into alignment with what is known about the complex task of teaching a psychologically and culturally diverse student population. How the prospective teacher experiences, being taught will influence her eventual mode of teaching others. Irrespective of whether she likes them or not, as with her own elementary and secondary school teachers, her instructors now will provide the model for behaving and interacting with students. In other words, how teachers experience their interactions with their instructors, with individual students and with each other in the college classroom, how they perceive their use of the curriculum, will be a far more powerful and enduring lesson to them than any of the subject matter assigned for study. Only when these heretofore unexamined processes are scrutinized and understood and the teacher's own subjective experiences taken into account, will the teacher acquire some basic knowledge of what it means to teach and be taught. Sarason, Davidson, and Blatt (1973) described this aspect of the learning process as follows:

> Educational psychology (as the psychology of learning) is viewed as something which has to do with how children learn and not with how teachers learn. The student in the process of becoming a teacher is not

made acutely aware of how he is learning, that is to use himself as a
source of understanding of the nature of the learning process. . . . of the
major reasons so many teachers are dissatisfied with themselves in their
work is that their training did not illuminate the nature of their learning
processes and how this relates to and effects the learning process of their
pupils. They teach, but in the process they tend neither to give expression to their own experiences as a learner nor to perceive the identity
between themselves and their pupils. As a result, the teacher tends to function as a technician who applies rules which are contradicted by her own
learning experiences and her pupils' unproductive learning. (p. 118)

To facilitate this reflective, subjectively and contextually based
mode of learning, we propose that ongoing, intensive individual and
group supervision be incorporated in the graduate training period. In
supervision, the prospective teacher is enabled, with the expert guidance
of the supervisor, to reflect on her own subjective reactions to learning
and being taught and to study their effects on her interventions and her
students' reactions to them. This perspective on the self of the teacher,
has been largely ignored in professional education. In our experience,
teachers point to supervision as the crucial element in their training
which enables them to transfer and apply their graduate education to their
work with children, individually and collectively.

In designing the ideal graduate education program, the questions
Sarason raised are most pertinent: What kind of person do we want
the teacher to be? How do we help the prospective teacher become such
a person? By putting persons in all their complexity and diversity at
the center of the educational process our proposal for graduate preparation of teachers is in striking contrast to the Carnegie reform vision
and blueprint for educational change. Implicit in the reforms proposed
is an assumption that learning and teaching are subject-matter specific,
mainly cognitive operations which yield outcomes that can be assessed
by means of objective measures. We start from the assumption that
human learning is a purposive process which involves an interlocking
of cognitive, affective, social and psychological forces that engage the
whole self or person of the learner, not his cognitive faculties alone.

We need a point of view about teacher preparation that puts persons (teachers and students) ahead of subject matter, for, in the final
analysis, it is teacher and students together who construct and give
meaning to the curriculum. There needs to be systematic conceptual-
izations of the impact of adult development on teaching and learning,

which, in turn, would provide the necessary guidance for establishing educational goals, curriculum, methods, and assessment. Human developmental concepts provide the guidelines for planning the following: sequence of studies, thematic content of the curriculum, methods of instruction, teacher-student relations, decisions about interventions, understanding group process. Developmental factors represent the ultimate yardstick for performance evaluation.

Areas of knowledge important in the graduate teacher education curriculum—assuming these build on an undergraduate foundation—include:

- In-depth knowledge of human development from infancy through adulthood.
- Knowledge of the nature of the learning process across development, in both its normative and pathological constellations.
- Knowledge that provides for contextual competence (interpersonal skills, communication skills, cross cultural differences).
- Knowledge of family and group processes.
- Knowledge of the manifest and covert meanings of the curriculum.
- Knowledge of human motivational systems.
- Knowledge about different kinds and levels of pupil assessment.
- Most important, the teacher must have knowledge of herself, her vulnerabilities and her strengths.

Supervision

We need to ask how an educational program can foster the teacher's capacity for reflective teaching. This is not a quality that can be acquired from textbooks. Learning about the self can only be achieved in the context of relationships with other people. This means that the teachers of teachers must exemplify in their teaching the reflective mode in action. Teachers always convey more than subject matter—they also "teach themselves." Of the two, the latter is the most powerful and enduring achievement. We have found that the most effective tool for fostering reflective teaching is the supervisory relationship. Supervision, as we define it, is an individualized form of education, not unlike coaching or mentoring. It focuses on the interactional and experiential dimensions of learning and teaching, and helps to bridge the gulf between theory, research, and practice. This form of supervision is to be distinguished from the model of supervision in which the principal aim is teacher evaluation. This latter evaluation model is the most common in educational settings. The former model, known as clinical supervision, is essentially an educational tool aimed at the integration of the objective and subjective dimensions of the teaching-learning process, conducted within an individualized format. Ideally, supervision should accompany classroom learning as well as fieldwork over the entire course of graduate training. It might be offered in the form of an ongoing small group seminar or, if resources permit, in individualized sessions supervised by a member of the faculty.

Fieldwork Experience

In addition to ongoing supervision, we propose that prospective teachers have the opportunity for a rich and varied fieldwork experience. First, considering the diversity of students attending our urban schools, teachers should be exposed to students of different ages, abilities, and family and ethnic backgrounds. A high-school teacher needs to understand the learning of young children, just as the teacher of young children needs to have an understanding of subsequent developmental stages to prepare her to recognize and adapt to the different developmental levels in her students. Such an experience would expose the prospective teacher to instructors with different teaching styles and to different school cultures as well. Second, fieldwork should also offer participation in parent conferences, if this essential component of teaching is to be better understood and more effectively managed. Finally, fieldwork should also acquaint prospective teachers with the professional perspectives and contributions of the many different specialists who are typically a part of the modern urban school (psychologists, social workers, language therapists and the like). In this way teachers learn to function as active, integral members of the multidisciplinary school team in a relationship of mutuality and reciprocity, learning with, and from, the allied professions. Toward this end we propose that supervised fieldwork accompany the didactic work from the beginning of the graduate program to the end. This would provide the time necessary for the prospective teacher to work through her own problems with learning, to integrate the multiplicity of variables involved in teaching and learning to begin to establish a stable professional identity.

Evaluation

The consequences of the two contrasting visions of teaching and teacher education presented in this chapter emerge most clearly in the evaluation process. It is here that we must confront the relation between the stated aims of the training program and its outcomes. If the transmission of factual knowledge from teacher to student (the jug-mug model of teaching and learning) is its central aim, then the evaluation of outcomes can be reduced to measurement. Those aspects of the training program that are amenable to objective assessment will be measured, while those difficult to evaluate are likely to be disregarded or underrated. Reliance on tests, in turn, becomes a "lesson" of their training that teachers internalize and tend to reproduce in their own practice. When tests become the chief instrument of evaluation, they not only tend to dictate which subjects in the curriculum should be emphasized, but also how teaching should occur. In this way, the technology designed to improve education paradoxically becomes its constraint.

It is axiomatic that teachers instruct their students as they themselves have been taught, not alone in the context of their professional training but throughout their own student years. Training for teaching predates the period of a teacher's formal training—it starts when she enters school for the first time.

To effect a change in the way teachers have come to define themselves and their role in relation to their students, to change such deeply ingrained, taken-for-granted, attitudes and values, to put teachers in touch with their feelings about learning and about themselves as teachers, to sensitize them to the feelings and concerns of students and parents, to foster creativity, flexibility, commitment to persons, for uncertainty, ambiguity and complexity—qualities we look for in teachers—all this takes more than intellectual knowing. It will require more than simple didacticism, subject matter expertise, and management skills, all of which are hallmarks of the prevailing rationalistic, technocratic, depersonalized, decontextualized vision of teaching and teacher education. This vision entails a transformative rather than a reproductive task, one that engages the whole self of the student-teacher. Sarason's (Sarason, Davidson, and Blatt, 1986) question, "How do we determine whether the teacher we have trained is the kind of teacher we intended?" is especially pertinent here. Implicit in this question is his focus on the inherent mutuality and reciprocity in the teacher-student relationship, the teacher learning as she teaches, the student teaching as she learns (Elson, 1989). Teaching faculty serve as models for the teacher-to-be, they teach themselves as much as they teach their subject matter. Learning how to teach, like learning how to learn, is a process that cannot be learned from books alone. The qualities we want in a teacher can only be acquired in a dialogic process which provides the context in which teachers learn how to learn, grow in self knowledge, acquire a capacity for "reflection-in-action" (Schon, 1973) and empathic communication with others. Whether we call these skills pedagogic or clinical, is unimportant because they are as necessary in the educational situation as they are in the therapeutic. The medium in which this aspect of professional learning or personal growth takes place is the supervisory situation, be it in the context of a one-to-one relationship or small group supervision or both. Evaluation, from this perspective, turns out to be multimodal, multifaceted and multidisciplinary, because we are dealing with human diversity and complexity. The prevailing vision of teacher evaluation, by focusing mainly on measurement and intellectual modes of knowing, grossly oversimplifies the teacher's task, and, in so doing, distorts the realities that teachers will face in the classroom. It is not enough to present facts and information. It must be done in a way that the learner hears it as intended. This is a difficult skill to acquire since a person gets meaning for what she sees and hears from behind her eyes and ears rather than in front of them.

Professional Development

The teacher, having graduated, is ready to enter the crucible of the classroom on her own. Now she is fully responsible for a group of children and is confronting problems she could not have anticipated from her professional preparation. This naturally propels her into the next phase of her professional education. Whether or not she continues learning in this phase will depend on what conditions the school provides to facilitate her learning, namely, support, opportunity for regular supervision, dialogue with colleagues, freedom to learn from her inevitable mistakes, and the availability of postgraduate seminars relevant to her ongoing needs and problems. All of these are necessary to facilitate the transition between graduate study and on-the-job training. This is the way teachers develop motivation for lifelong learning and a commitment to advancing their professional competence throughout their careers.

What we have been describing for teacher education is no different in kind from what we think of as the ideal education for children: all learning takes place over time in the context of a human relationship, with the goal of continued self-learning. The question is not what or how much has been learned, but rather, how has learning taken place and how has that contributed to a love of learning?

Summary and Conclusions

In this chapter we have presented two contrasting visions of teaching and teacher training, one representing the deeply entrenched perspective that has dominated educational discourse and practice for most of this century; the other, that of the emerging, more theoretically and clinically informed paradigm of educational therapy. By virtue of its humanistic, context-particular, person-specific, subjectively based view of the teaching-learning process, the latter vision effectively reverses figure and ground in our conception of the educational endeavor and opens up new avenues for exploration.

The educational reform movements of recent decades have proposed changes in the structure and content of the educational enterprise which not only reinforce the prevailing vision, but in our opinion, also tend to reify many of its essential features, namely, its rationalistic, depersonalized, decontextualized view of the teaching-learning process. It has been our contention that improving the quality and effectiveness of teaching and teacher education is not likely to occur in any significant way as long as this unrealistic vision holds sway. Merely raising standards for teacher certification, augmenting teachers' knowledge of their subject matter and methods of teaching it, extending the period of professional preparation, insisting on more scholarly rigor and professional accountability, or providing teachers higher salaries and more opportunities for professional advancement (all of which are, to be sure, desirable changes)—none are likely to accomplish the desired outcomes, because these do not address the current realities depicted here earlier that teachers face every day in their classrooms. It is our contention that the prevailing vision may actually contribute to the demoralization of teachers and lead an increasing number to leave teaching, a trend that, as mentioned, parallels the growing alienation among students and their disquieting drop-out rate.

Our aim in this chapter has been to propose a design for teacher preparation that is grounded in the realities of classroom life as these are perceived and understood by practicing teachers and allied professionals who know from direct experience the immediacy, uncertainty, and ambiguity, the personal tensions and disappointments, as well as the joys and gratifications, that every teacher experiences in her work with children and their parents.

Theory informs only a small portion of most teacher training. As a result, teachers are forced to fall back on a grab-bag of techniques designed to help them control student behaviors which they are unable to explain:

> Most theory about teaching—and, in consequence, much policy, too—is at best simply the rational application of means to given ends. In this light, all the ambiguity, irrationality and conflict that teachers feel in their bones, if not used to talking about are simply evidence of teacher failure. (MacDonald, 1986)

We have argued that the clinical theories of contemporary psychoanalysis and developmental research provide the theoretical frameworks that best explain the subjective experience of teaching and being taught. "The phenomena of educational practice," according to Schon (1973), "involve complexity, uncertainty, instability, uniqueness and value conflict," all of which are rendered invisible if not inactive under the prevailing model of "technical rationality." To demonstrate the utility of psychoanalytic perspectives we have drawn upon a psychoanalytically informed Teacher Education Program, now in its twenty-sixth year. The emphasis in this program is on helping teachers understand how we learn from a subjective perspective. It looks to the influence of meaning and intent on student perceptions and response to the materials of instruction. Our students not only learn about learning (learning in its broadest sense) but also come to understand, in an immediate and personal way what the learning experience is like for themselves and for others. Knowledge does not reside between the covers of a textbook, or inside the minds of teachers; nor is it finite or unchanging. It is partly the product of student perceptions, needs, concerns and aspirations, and teachers' and students' interpretations of them. What this Teacher Education Program seeks to accomplish is twofold: to highlight the hidden landscapes of learning in education which come into view when observed through a psychoanalytic lens, and to call attention to the new directions in psychoanalytic inquiry and developmental research which invite cross-disciplinary dialogue and collaboration.

The psychodynamic vision of the teaching-learning interaction is contrary to the implicit assumption in education that the student's response to the teacher, as expressed in his overt behavior, academic performance, and manifest attitudes, constitutes the major focus of educational concern. Overlooked is the equally present, however repressed dynamic of the teacher response to a particular child, or a student group, or the class as a whole. Each teacher and student is mutually caught up in a highly affect-laden process in which each one is highly vulnerable to the intentions of the other; each one guessing, assuming, inferring, believing, trusting, or suspecting; each generally satisfied or dissatisfied. The much-vaunted shield of teacher objectivity and neutrality falls away once we recognize the force of these subjective processes, and realize that there can be no objectivity without subjectivity. It is not the teacher's ability to function as an impartial, objective observer that makes for effective teaching. Rather, it is her capacity to tune in on the subjective experiences of students, to reflect on her own subjective reactions to individual students and the group as a whole that confers the badge of true professionalism and guides her interventions.

We believe that to be effective educational reform must reach deeper and include the emotional as well as the cognitive determinants of the educational process, long ignored and neglected. It must observe more directly the complexities of life in classrooms and study the experiences of teachers and learners in order to understand how best to engage them in the process of change.

We have suggested that educational therapy provides a new par-

adigm for the study of the teaching-learning process, one that complements and deepens but does not replace the existing, if flawed and
incomplete, educational paradigm, which currently appears to be suffering what Kuhn calls "a paradigm-in-crisis." We hold with Kuhn,
however, that it will require "a reconstruction of the field [of educa-
tion] from new fundamentals, a reconstruction that changes some of
the field's most elementary theoretical generalizations as well as many
of its paradigm methods and applications." We are also acutely aware
that the present climate in teacher education is reflective of the dominant rationalistic, technocratic disposition and values held by our society, making the kind of reconstruction I am proposing highly unlikely
at this time. I am comforted by the fact, however, that growing numbers of educators and clinicians are also railing against this trend and are
working for more humanistic approaches to the crisis in education.

Notes

1. [A response to the 1986 Carnegie Report: "A Nation Prepared:
   Teachers for the 21st Century."] The authors based this white paper
   on the work of a study committee, appointed in 1986 by the Teacher
   Education Program of the Institute for Psychoanalysis, consisting
   of the following members: Andrew Boxer, Ph.D., Bertram Cohler,
   Ph.D., Kay Field M.A., Dorothy Freedman, M.S.T., Dren Geer, Jr.,
   M.A., Nancy Marks, M.S.W., Dennis McCaughan, Ph.D., Jerry
   Olson, Ph.D., Charles Saltzman, B.S., Marilyn Silin, M.A., Glorye
   Wool, M.D., Mary Alice Deneen, M.A.
2. An earlier version of this section was written with Glorye Wool,
   M.D. It reflects the thinking and contributions of the Task Force.
3. Data obtained from a staff development project (1983–84) conceived as an action research project, sponsored by the Teacher Education Program of the Institute for Psychoanalysis of Chicago, and
   conducted and reported by Andrew Boxer, Ph.D., was the basis of
   this finding.

Charles Saltzman, B.S.

17

The Education of Teachers and

the Education of Children:

ELEMENTS OF AN EMPATHIC APPROACH

n recent years a confluence of social, economic, and political forces has focused international attention on the schools and their relative efficacy in advancing national interests and in improving the quality of life for the emergent generation. As part of this wider trend, heightened concern has been expressed for the many children whose learning goes awry and whose emotions and behavior in school settings limit not only their own success but that of their peers as well.

The programs established as remedial interventions for this substantial subset of the school-age population invariably involve diagnosis (often merely classification) and specific (categorical) interventive programs. Whatever terms are employed, most educators are inclined to define a problem (i.e., think diagnostically) before trying to solve it (i.e., intervene), and regardless of how the intervention is characterized or how the professional who implements it is identified, the activity inevitably draws on the cumulative wisdom and technology of both pedagogy—with its characteristic focus on instructed learning and normal functioning—and clinical psychology—with its encompassing concern for affect and behavior—in addition to learning and its attention to deviant or abnormal functioning.

The fundamental decision in all of this, however, is whether the approach we adopt is inherently empathic or nonempathic; that is, whether it takes as its central concern the developmental needs of the young (if not exclusively, at least in large measure), or whether we create systems in which the developmental needs of the young are substantially subordinated to national, state, and local bureaucratic interests and shaped by economic, political, and social interests of the adults who run them.

This discussion begins with the premise that schools exist primarily to promote the quality of life for all children by enabling them to acquire knowledge about the world, to understand and solve problems, to express themselves verbally and in writing, to develop skills necessary to lead productive lives, to appreciate beauty, and to live peaceably with themselves and their neighbors. That we fail with a sizable minority of them makes it urgent that we reexamine our educational practices at all levels. When so many do not complete high school (dropouts number 30 to 40 percent in many urban centers in America), when so many others graduate unable to read or compute well enough to manage their personal affairs or to find employment in a highly technological economy, when many succumb to drugs and become socially alienated or habitually criminal, we indeed have cause to be concerned. Yet this segment of the population, about which we hear so many cries of alarm and consequent criticism of the schools—including the charge that we have lowered academic standards, diluted the curriculum, and tolerated substandard teaching—is not the only segment we must be concerned about. We have, at the other extreme, the repeated public spectacle of young men of considerable academic accomplishment, graduates of the finest preparatory schools and of the most distinguished universities, who have been caught up in private and public scandals. They too must be recognized as a societal, if not an educational, failure, where intellectual attainment, though unimpeded, is harnessed to corrupt values. (Surely the remedy for this group is not tougher academic standards.) In defining the problem, and in designing solutions for these contrasting concerns, more care than has heretofore been evident must be taken to assign to schools an appropriate share of responsibility. The declining influence of social institutions, shifting social mores, the deterioration of the urban infrastructure, the proliferation of single-parent families, widening use of drugs, and concentration of the poor in the inner cities have placed many children at risk long before they enter school.

How then shall we define the purposes of schooling and structure the schools to serve those ends? Sizer (1989) offers this simple and exquisite double-entendre: the purpose of schooling should be the development of "thoughtful" adults, the term hinting simultaneously at intellectual competence and empathic sensitivity. Both ends are desirable and both are attainable. Both are facilitated, it is argued here, by a stance that is essentially empathic with the developmental needs of the young, needs that include, significantly, a quest for competence and a quest for connection.

If we so define the aims of education and the preferred means for attaining these ends as empathic responsiveness, how can we proceed to recruit and train individuals to staff these schools? What, in addition to subject matter competence, would we require in their personal repertoires so that they will effectively educate thoughtful citizens? I would like to stipulate three essential elements—theory, technique and self—examine their constituents and relevance, and then describe a method for enhancing these characteristics during professional education.

Theory

Everyone, in all situations, operates with theories about the world. Theories are the cognitive maps, the meanings and patterns we detect in the otherwise chaotic and random stream of events we find ourselves in. They insure our safety. Some of our theories are explicit and testable, whereas others tend to be implicit and therefore insufficiently available for empirical validation. Theories are patterns of expectations regarding the structure and organization of the world, how we affect it, and how it, in turn, affects us. Teachers and therapists operate with theories of human development and interaction, theories of the individual child as they encounter him, and theories of the group and larger social systems. They require, as well, theories of themselves, their motivation, and how they realize their intentions—instructional, inspirational, supportive—in relation to their students. Theories permit us to ride on "automatic pilot," as Friedman (1987) put it. They carry us through the uncertainty that exists at the start of every new relationship, and as well through the later, inevitable uncertainties and problems that occur. Theories provide us with a set of ready-made categories or hypotheses into which the subsequent data will fit, more or less. They allow us to coast in confidence before our convictions are confirmed or refuted by the facts.

The complexity of human behavior has thus far eluded the grasp of individual theories (e.g., Freudian, Skinnerian), schools of thought (e.g., psychoanalytic, humanistic), or broad perspectives (e.g., psychological, sociological). Measured against extant theory, complex phenomena like "educational development" are grossly underdetermined, any theory by itself accounting for but a small portion of what is already known.

How is one to choose, assuming that one indeed has the choice? Time, place, and circumstance impose real limits on the opportunity to study thoroughly the complete array of extant theory. Educators of many different persuasions tend to agree, however, that instructed human learning cannot be sufficiently understood by the tenets of any modern learning theory or any of the models provided by cognitive science. Neglected in one way or another by these is the role of affect, interest, and human relationship. Among these educators, there are many also who by temperament, life experience, and personal philosophy favor instructional approaches based on an empathic, deeply respectful regard for the individual person, and who have found that psychoanalytic theories, as a group, provide a comprehensive framework for their professional efforts, a framework that not only provides useful insights into the motives and meanings defining their own behavior and that of others, but one with a long and rich tradition and substantial empirical support as well.

Psychoanalytic ideas promulgated by Freud and his followers today comprise a library unto themselves. Readable summaries of Freud's metapsychology can be found in Brenner (1973), Holzman

(1970), and Rapaport (1967). These ideas were applied in various ways to the field of education by Aichhorn (1948), Bettelheim (1950, 1955), Bettelheim and Zelan (1981), Redl (1966), Redl and Wattenberg (1959), and Ekstein and Motto (1969), among others. Further elaborations of the central framework of psychoanalysis were cast in the form of "object relations" theory, which describes the nature and origins of interpersonal relations and the nature and origins of intrapsychic structure deriving from the internalization of experiences with others (Kernberg, 1976). The predominant and central paradigm of this combined body of theory was the idea of intrapsychic conflict, the view that the mind evolved through a sequence of predetermined crises, and that the degree of resolution of these conflicts determined the shape of the adult personality.

Still more recently, psychoanalytic theory has been augmented, and perhaps enduringly altered, by the emergence of a new paradigm of human development promulgated by Kohut (1971, 1977, and 1984), Tolpin and Kohut (1980), and Basch (1983a, 1983b, 1984), ideas collectively known as self psychology, the psychology of the self, or the self object theory of motivation. With the centrality given the concept of empathy as the basic information-gathering instrument, self psychology is among the most serviceable of theories for professionals committed to a student-centered approach to education. Since relatively few educators have had a chance to become familiar with self psychology, and since, in addition, this discussion will attempt to demonstrate the applicability of these concepts to education, some brief exposition is in order.

Self psychology supplements the classical (conflict) model of psychoanalysis with a model focusing on deficits in the structure, cohesiveness, vitality, and harmony of the self, now viewed as the basic constituent of the psyche (Kohut, 1977). The self, which is experienced as the center of initiative and experience, is a product of genetic endowment and relationships with care givers who serve as "self objects" (i.e., experienced as part of the self) whose functions are later internalized as enduring structures of the self. The developmental line of self-object functioning and self-object relations is distinct from that of libidinal objects described by classical theory. The fully structured self is bipolar: one pole being the source of ambitions stimulated originally by the mirroring and affirmation of parents, and the second (the seat of guiding ideals) the residue of experiences with accessible ide-alizable, competent care givers. Talents and skills are drawn into the service of realizing ambitions, guided by ideals. Self psychology de-emphasizes the significance of drive and energy concepts. Drives are viewed as normally embedded in larger wholes in most human inter-actions. Self psychology emphasizes the importance of the regulation of self-esteem, the maintenance of self-cohesion, the accomplishment of life goals, and the role self objects, throughout life, play in these functions.

The psychology of the self as a model of human development forcefully underscores the active participation of parents and other care givers in the formation of the self of the child. There are two basic psychological needs of the child to which the self object must respond in order to allow the child to achieve a strong, cohesive, and enduring self. One is the need for the self object's mirroring, affirming delight in the child's proud display of himself; the second is for the self object's capacity to serve as an image of calm strength and limitless power into which he can merge when his equilibrium is disturbed (Tolpin and Kohut 1980).

Let us briefly consider what such a system suggests about the process of education and, in particular, the process of schooling. These extrapolations are offered as conjectures, since Kohut himself did not write directly about the problems of education.

Kohut's work suggests that schooling must first be responsive to the developmental needs of children, by providing the support and stim-ulation necessary for children to complete their development. It must recognize, in particular, that the child of nursery school age and the child of the primary grades is far from having consolidated a firm sense of self. The social system of the school, the human psychological envi-ronment, is a network of self-object relationships with potential for sus-taining or retarding the consolidation of the child's sense of self. The teacher's role as successor to the parent in performing self-object func-tions for the child—mirroring his grandiosity, providing soothing and calm, comforting strength, wisdom, and competence, and in turn accept-ing his admiring idealization—is crucial. Members of the peer group may also serve as structure-building or structure-supporting "twinship" or "alter ego" self objects.

Neither Freud nor any of the object-relations theorists, Kohut included, provides a comprehensive and explicit theory of human cognition and learning. To compensate for the insufficiency of psychoanalysis as a theory of cognition, psychoanalysts have looked with increasing favor at Vygotsky's work (1962, 1978), plugging it into the larger theory as a module, if not fully integrating it with their system. All of the psychoanalytic theories emphasize the crucial role of object relations in human learning. In Kohut the absence or diminished significance of drive and energy concepts, however, brings the theory into alignment with recent data from the direct observations of children. Contrary to Freud's view, and in accord with Piaget's and Vygotsky's, Kohut's theories represent the baby as an active, assertive learner from the start.

Kohut's theory allows us to represent the hundreds of thousands of children who arrive in our schools with insufficiently consolidated selves, children who were never able to kindle a gleam in a parent's eye and who were never adequately soothed and protected by parents whom they could idealize. Such children require completion of their development, in this case the consolidation of the self, more urgently than they need to learn to read.

Technique

Teachers and therapists employ techniques to implement their aims. Methods courses comprise a sizable proportion of the courses in the undergraduate curriculum of aspiring teachers. Techniques are also stressed in the training of psychotherapists: techniques for history taking, for making interpretations, for dealing with transferences, and for handling resistances. Therapists trained in other modalities (family, group, systems) or in other theoretical frameworks (behavioral, humanistic) will be instructed in the techniques indigenous to those systems. In recent years, particularly in education, we have witnessed a strong reaction (often well taken, in my view) against a strong emphasis on technique. It is argued that the attention paid to technique must come at the expense of time devoted to substance, to knowledge of subject matter. That achievement test scores of this nation's children show alarming deficiencies in subject-matter competence is a fact often cited by these critics.

Techniques prove to be highly perishable commodities. They do not transfer well from one situation to another or from one person to another. What works with one child or class may not work with the next. Without a thorough understanding of the ecology or context, which is always complex in the realm of human learning, gross applications of technique often bring disappointing results. These and other considerations have led some psychoanalytic educators to de-emphasize attention to technique per se and to trust that a dedicated novice, having thoroughly analyzed an unsuccessful encounter, will discover a different and better way to proceed the next time. The talented novice learns through reflecting upon his or her own successes and failures, and in the context of empathic supervision improves his or her performance.

Technical competence, as I will attempt to illustrate, can also be enhanced by careful study of the writings of gifted teachers of exceptional children, whose descriptive narratives, unselfconsciously and without theoretical jargon, reveal their spontaneously enacted techniques in real-life situations. By attending to what they said and did, and noticing what followed, we can discern whether the technique failed or succeeded, and by bringing theory to bear, we may in many instances come to understand why. In this way is technique rendered transferable and teachable. Something of the unique (never to be exactly duplicated) successes of these extraordinary teachers can be acquired by each of us. Much as theory—by influencing what it is that we notice and regard as important and universal—expands our capacity for empathy, so too does the attention to successful technique beneficially influence our capacity to respond empathically.

Self

The psychoanalytic community, beginning with Freud, recognized that the success of the therapeutic enterprise rested primarily on the personality of the therapist. The self of the therapist *is* his instrument. His ability to comprehend his own motivation, master his own anxiety, and maintain empathic contact with the analysand foretells in large measure the success of the enterprise. This holds true as well for the success of the educator in the schools, although there is no clear consensus in the educational community on this point, even in early childhood education, where the need is critical. Whereas theory and technique are fairly effectively taught, university training programs are not likely to noticeably alter fundamental deficits of the self. Universities can and must recruit more aggressively those talented young people whose capacities for empathic responsiveness to children make them particularly suited for careers in teaching.

Teacher training programs typically enroll students who present themselves on the basis of high school grades and achievement test scores, with little or no attention to capacity for or range of empathic responsiveness to children. The claim is either that this consideration is irrelevant or that such judgments are highly subjective, altogether lacking in empirical validation, and their use consequently indefensible.

In addition to a capacity for empathic responsiveness, other aspects of the self implicated in teaching are a capacity for self-awareness and aspects of character such as integrity and steadfastness of commitment. These dimensions of self play a role in all human relationships, but in work with very young children, with alienated or severely emotionally disturbed or otherwise disabled students, aspects of self equal and often transcend in importance subject matter or technical competence. Again, the autobiographical narratives of gifted teachers make this abundantly clear. The possession of a mature self, arrived at through fortunate life circumstance, genetic endowment, successful resolution of the problems of living, or facilitated by personal psychoanalysis or psychotherapy, is decisive in working with the young, in benefiting from supervision, in managing crises, and in growing professionally. Individuals possessing mature, cohesive selves are capable of substantially regulating their own self-esteem through productive endeavors and involving themselves with appropriate self objects, that is, with individuals and organizations that will sustain them. They are likely to be recognized for their wisdom and sense of humor as well. By means of introspection, they remain in reasonable empathic contact with themselves and with others.

An empathic stance requires the possession of a mature self and the maintenance of a theoretical perspective that comprehends the meaning, motivation, and affective experience of others through vicarious introspection, that is, from the vantage point of the observed. It is this that allows one to respond appropriately, tactfully, and constructively with interventions aimed at enhancing competence and self-esteem or regulating tension. To respond empathically does not mean indulging in maudlin sentimentality, failing to hold students to high standards of performance, or providing a constant supply of infantile gratification. It does, however, allow (even prompts) extraordinary responses to emergencies and considerate, tactful, respectful behavior in normal situations.

It goes without saying that multiple obligations create real limits on a teacher's capacity for empathic responsiveness. The needs of one child may not be in harmony with those of the six, ten, or thirty other children she must relate to. The question, with whom or with what shall we be empathic presents itself in many forms. Shall we empathize with the child, with his parents, with the principal, or with society, when there is evident conflict among them? The teacher's obligation to teach a predetermined curriculum also imposes a continuing restraint on her freedom of response. On the other hand, relative to the analyst and psychotherapist, the range of response accorded her is considerably wider.

To what particular aspect of a child's behavior or experience shall we respond? (Kohut reminds us that the analytic field is defined by "complex mental states.") This question, too, admits of no easy answer, save that it is better to respond to something that is at the moment salient, strong, and accessible. While behavioral and other so-called objective stances—and the interventions that flow from them—are often successful and often empathic as well, they are only coincidentally empathic, by definition.

Autobiographical Accounts of Gifted Teachers: A Neglected Resource

During the past twenty years or so, there has accumulated a small treasure trove of human experience from which many, especially aspiring teachers, can benefit. It is the literary genre consisting of the autobiographical narratives of classroom teachers who tell in clear prose, rich in detail but unencumbered by jargon, of their experiences with small groups of children over the course of one school year. Notable among these writers are Torey Hayden (1980, 1981, 1988), Mary MacCracken (1981), James Herndon (1968, 1971), and Eleanor Craig (1973).

(MacCracken [1986] later wrote of her experiences working in private practice as an educational therapist.) Herndon writes of his experience with ghetto youth in the public schools, and Vivian Paley (1988, 1990) reports her work with normal preschoolers in a university-based laboratory school.

Careful line-by-line analysis and discussion of these works, which we assume are fairly faithful—if not complete or perfect—reports (from the teacher's perspective) of the events in question allows us to follow teacher-pupil interaction as it spontaneously unfolds, interactions that become comprehensible to teacher trainees via their empathic resonance with the participants, and the application of a theoretical framework they have been studying. With these materials, one can venture alternative hypotheses at the start of an episode and seek, in the unfolding narrative, support or refutation of these conjectures. These readings tend to be more engrossing than the usual academic texts because they reflect real-life situations in all their complexity. They recreate the fabric of daily experience—the mundane, the joyful, the exciting—without avoiding the tragic and the dangerous. Most of these reports deal with emotionally or behaviorally disordered children who have been excluded from regular classes. By studying the experience of these teachers and how they manage to facilitate the learning of these children and foster their rehabilitation, teachers in training deepen their grasp of theory by discovering its capacity to illuminate these narratives and expand their own capacity to resonate empathically with the participants.

One can notice how these writers, as they taught, constantly sought to establish and maintain empathic ties with their charges, how constant was their search for the motive and meaning of perplexing, often bizarre and unruly behavior. These teachers reveal exquisite sensitivity to human relationships, how they begin, how they are maintained, and how in joy or sorrow they sometimes end. We can see how they recognize and respond to the fear, shame, or guilt lying behind a facade of lies, bravado and bullying. In their contacts with parents, they demonstrate their empathic attunement to the plight of troubled adults as well and to cultural and social class differences. On occasion, they reveal a capacity to commit themselves to the well-being of their charges that extends beyond the usual call of duty, sometimes even in violation of school rules. Some children remain on their minds when they are at home in the evening, on weekends, and on vacation. Sometimes they search for runaway children and lure them back from their secret hide-outs, take them on outings with their own families, rush them to hospitals in their own cars when these children have been physically or sexually abused. One need not take from these stories the recommendation that all teachers must be prepared to commit themselves to children in this way. To begin with, most children don't require it, nor can many teachers make such a commitment. But one can at least attend to the role played by such commitment in the lives of the children described in the stories.

During the past ten years, I have used these narratives in the training of teachers, school psychologists, and other clinicians. Following are several brief illustrations of the manner in which these works can be usefully addressed.

Example 1

In *City Kid,* Mary MacCracken (1981), returning to graduate school to get the training necessary for certification as a licensed therapeutic tutor, describes her work with Luke, a seven-and-a-half-year-old boy who had set over a dozen major fires and committed a staggering number of thefts. No teacher had been able to manage him. These are her thoughts upon her first visit to observe him in his classroom. "I peered at him intently, saying his name under my breath, Lucas Brauer, Lucas Brauer, trying to make him real. . . . So now I memorized him, scruffy sneakers, . . . the faded jeans torn at the knees. . . . I could help Luke, now that I found him. I knew I could and he would help me too" (p. 1).

One notices first the intense wish to make contact with this boy, to form a real relationship, to fix him or "hold" him, Winnicott might say, in mind. They will be, for one another, reciprocal self objects. She will help him enhance his competence, and his success in turn will enhance her morale.

Watching him, she is puzzled. "There must be some mistake. . . . How could this child have a record of 24 arrests for arson, theft and truancy? . . . Something was wrong somewhere" (p. 1). What she sees clashes with what she expected to see after reading his file. She struggles with this "cognitive dissonance," attempting to find a theory that will reconcile the existing facts with those she will gather empathically.

After observing the class for several minutes, with increasing impatience, she introduces herself to him and indicates to the teacher that she will take him to work with her in another room. "It was already clear that he did not work and his behavior was negative. What I had to know was why, and I wouldn't find out with a stopwatch. I had to listen to Luke, even when he wasn't talking, and I couldn't do that in a room full of thirty kids" (p. 24). Again we note the determination to make empathic contact; measurement and instrumentation; at least at this point in the relationship, she sees as irrelevant and even as encumbrances.

Alone with him, she reveals her keen interest in a drawing he had been working on instead of paying attention in class—a subtle affirmation. She offers him an opportunity to examine the stopwatch, trusting him not to drop it or throw it, and soon they are involved in a game, he measuring the speed of her responses while doing "'dition" (addition). As their time to be together draws to a close, she explains to him her availability, offers to help him, and seeks his response to her offer. When they arrive at his classroom door, he turns and asks, "When you commin'?"

Clearly a relationship has formed, a connection has been made. Luke has not given up his search for the "good object" or, put self psychologically, Luke is still seeking to resume his interrupted development by involving himself with an empathic structure-building self object.

This account deals, in only a fragmentary way, with the richly detailed narrative that the author provides. When teachers and teachers in training study this material, each group discovers some version of the ideas and formulations offered here, with variations and amplifications too numerous to mention.

Example 2

In *P.S., You're Not Listening*, Eleanor Craig (1973) tells the story of her work with five children. Let us consider how she begins her work with Douglas, a nine-year-old black child whose mother abandoned him and his younger retarded brother when she ran off with her lover. The children's grandmother was located in the south and came north to the city to make a home for the boys.

"Douglas and his grandmother were the first to arrive on opening day. She was a heavy, weary-looking woman, wearing a shabby dress and wrinkled elastic stockings" (p. 1).

When she enters the room she begins, "You Mrs. Craig? Well, Doug's here, but he don't want to come in. He's behind the door. . . .

He scared 'cause he wasn't allowed in no school last year. Some schools you've got! Can't even handle a nine-year-old.''

"'Douglas,' I peeked at the huge boy, all of 100 pounds at age nine, crouched behind the door. 'Come choose a desk, you will have first choice'" (p. 1).

Surely there are many constructive or empathic ways to begin a relationship. When teachers study Craig's way of beginning with Doug, all generally recognize its effectiveness. With additional effort, many come to recognize how extraordinary it is and why. The key is her sensitivity to the most salient aspect of Doug's experience at the moment. It is the experience of oppression, of being powerless and without choice in the matter of introducing himself to his teacher and how he would like her to perceive him. The grandmother "bad mouths" him and calls attention to his record of misbehavior. To respond to the oppressed, to those whose sense of autonomy is being eroded, by offering them a choice, as Eleanor Craig does in offering Doug the chance to choose a desk, is to provide the most empathic response possible.

That Craig was able to respond in this way may or may not reflect knowledge acquired through reading Erik Erikson. We may more safely infer that it is an aspect of her mature self organization whose origin is beyond our capacity to trace. The lesson this episode provides for the teachers who study it is that empathic sensitivity to the salient issues in the encounter facilitate the work. Familiarity with a theory like Erikson's further augments a mature self by enlarging our repertoire of things that might in any one instance be salient, as theories point us toward phenomena presumed to be universal and important. All children struggle with issues of autonomy. When Craig meets Douglas, the autonomy issue is center stage—it is poignant, focal, and accessible.

Example 3

As a final episode, I include the encounter between the aforementioned Mary MacCracken and Luke, which highlights her approach to instruction, in this instance an attempt to help Luke improve his slowly developing reading and language skills. MacCracken is clearly aware of the "token economies" associated with behavioral approaches, familiar with the idea that children differ in the relative efficiency with which they employ various sensory modalities in learning, and conversant with an eclectic array of developmental theories that delineate emotional needs of children. The most notable and consistent feature of her work, however, is her effort to create and maintain empathic contact with the child, which requires, in turn, the most thoroughgoing individualization of instruction. The instructional methods, the fragments of theory that will be applied, the lesson plan that is developed, are all custom fitted to the boy and to the boy's mood and motivational state on any given day. Individualized instruction is not just "one to one," it is one particular one to one particular other one.

While sorting through stacks of first-grade books made available to her for use with Luke, MacCracken thinks to herself, "Books using a phonetic or linguistic approach, which needed good auditory ability, didn't seem right for Luke right now" (p. 88). She reveals to us a great absorption in developing an appropriate instructional plan. At home in the evening, she continues to wrestle with the problem. "It doesn't come. The right way to teach Luke, I mean. I know it's there. I can almost touch it, and then it's gone." By the next morning, however, the plan emerges. "I'd begin with the first half of first-grade words I was sure Luke knew, and that were in large type. I'd glue each page on a piece of heavy cardboard and then cut them up and Luke could use the words in his stories. That way there were no 'dippy' pictures and no 'baby book', and, more important, success was sure" (p. 88). Self-esteem and its enhancement is currently a hot topic in education. It reflects, however, as MacCracken evidences, a bit of wisdom developed long ago.

At each of their meetings, MacCracken has for Luke a lesson plan of six items beginning with Best Thing, Worst Thing. "Luke's telling me the best and worst things that happened to him since I last saw him gave me a quick check on where he was and what he needed. It also encouraged his use of language" (p. 89). These last two sentences in and of themselves define the essence of empathic instruction.

It is my hope that this limited account may stimulate wider interest in these documents. Those who favor quantitative proof of efficacy of methods may find these reports disappointing, as would those who favor "high-tech" approaches to the problems of education. Students of these narratives, attending to the qualitative shifts and incremental gains week by week, month by month, can draw their own conclusions about the efficacy of these teachers and the unique combination of theory, technique, and self embodied in their empathic teach-

230   CHARLES SALTZMAN

ing approaches. Many of these children, on the recommendation of the authors as well as the independent judgment of other teachers involved with these children, get promoted, or "mainstreamed." Others make less progress and continue in special education classes. Of interest is that the academic improvement occurs even though the instructional activities and technical interventions necessary to accomplish this are not reported at great length. In this regard, however, one notices a genuine individualization of instruction, each child works on the tasks necessary for him or her, at a pace dictated by the child's capacity to learn.

When we attend to the lengthy case presentations in *Turnabout Children,* however, in which MacCracken (1986) reports on her work as an educational therapist, we can study in great detail the technique of a master. She achieves her successes, incidentally, with the simplest of materials and the most familiar, most venerable of instructional techniques. One can notice, too, in her work an empathic range that encompasses the pain, fears, and disappointments of the parents of these children.

The narratives of Hayden and Craig include life-threatening encounters, chaotic, violent outbursts, which afford us an opportunity to dwell on their causes and to notice how they might be successfully managed. Exquisitely sensitive solutions and even glaring blunders are reported unselfconsciously, without prideful gloating or regretful apology.

It should be clear that there exists a variety of empathic approaches to the education of children. The teachers who have provided these autobiographical accounts can serve as exemplars for those aspiring teachers favoring such an approach. We may be more successful with this and the next generation of children with school difficulties if we can match our zeal for putting computers in the school with an energetic quest to find, train, and place in classrooms more Torey Haydens, Mary MacCrackens, and Eleanor Craigs.

Linda A. Cozzarelli, M.A.

18

An Intersubjective Approach to Teaching and Learning Psychotherapy

failure to acknowledge disruptive feelings in supervision interferes with teaching and learning psychotherapy and can affect the professional self-esteem of both supervisor and supervisee. Avoiding examination of such feelings, which include anger, disappointment, frustration, helplessness, and lowered self-confidence, neglects the emotional components of supervision and often leads to an emphasis on the intellectual, rational aspects. As a result, a disruption in the process may occur between supervisor and supervisee, causing both to feel unsuccessful.

Professional and personal self-esteem are less differentiated for those in the helping professions because the instrument of practice is the self. Success or failure is often viewed as a reflection of one's own character and level of functioning. An important aspect of the therapist's professional self depends on his unique, specific way of helping and seeking help (Ekstein and Wallerstein, 1958). This duality is also reflected in the supervisory relationship.

Supervisor and supervisee bring to the process their individual styles and vulnerabilities regarding themselves as teacher and as student. Their interaction is colored by the fabric of their own internal experiences. Understanding the interplay between two differently organized subjective worlds coming together around the common goal of teaching and learning gives us an additional dimension for understanding the supervisory relationship.

Intersubjectivity (Atwood and Stolorow, 1984) is a process involving a dialogue between two personal universes. In psychoanalytic therapy, the goal of the dialogue is to illuminate and to identify the meaning systems that connect different parts of the patient's internal world into an intelligible whole. These meaning systems are organizing principles based on past experiences which continue to unconsciously and automatically shape an individual's experience and conduct. The patient's experience of the therapist and his activities are co-determined by his own and the therapist's organizing principles. The therapist's organizing principles shape not only his countertransference response but his therapeutic interventions. Eventually, the patient's unconscious organizing activity is understood within the context of the meaning that the therapist's activity acquires.

In this interplay, two situations, intersubjective conjunction and intersubjective disjunction, repeatedly arise (Atwood and Stolorow, 1984). Intersubjective conjunction occurs in instances in which the internal configuration structuring the patient's experience gives rise to expressions of behavior and feelings that are assimilated into closely similar configurations in the internal life of the therapist. Intersubjective disjunction occurs when the therapist assimilates the patient's material into configurations that alter the patient's subjective meaning. Whether or not these situations facilitate or obstruct the therapy depends on the therapist's capacity to decenter from his own organizing principles and empathetically grasp the actual meaning of the patient's experience. If self-awareness is reliably present for the therapist, the corresponding or differing subjective worlds of patient and therapist can be used to promote understanding and insight. Without decentered self-awareness, introspection, and empathy, conjunctions and disjunctions can impede the therapeutic process.

Adapting the intersubjective model to supervision, the supervisor and the supervisee come together around the shared professional goal of teaching and learning psychotherapy. The supervisee's experience of the supervisor and his activities are unconsciously patterned according to his preformed themes regarding learning, and by the supervisor's responses. The supervisor's responses are shaped by his experience of the supervisee and his own organizing principles, which shape his view of teaching and learning and of the supervisee. There is mutual influence occurring unconsciously and automatically. Intersubjective conjunctions and disjunctions repeatedly arise. In this model, it is important that the supervisor be able to immerse himself in the supervisee's professional life, be self-reflective, decenter from the process and reflect on the supervisee's issues in learning and reactions to teaching. The supervisor assesses the supervisee's expectations of himself, his strengths and weaknesses as a therapist, his openness about himself as a learner. Through introspection and empathy, he tries to understand how he might be influencing the supervisee's reactions, feelings, and behavior, and to assess what factors can be gleaned from this to help the supervisee understand patterns that organize his professional functioning. A unique interplay occurs between the subjective worlds of supervisor and supervisee that influence the supervisory process and, if understood, has the potential to facilitate learning. Intersubjectivity, as applied to the supervisory process, emphasizes the mutual influence of the two participants and the dual role of teaching and learning. Within this context, the supervisor must use the process to develop a balance between helping the supervisee learn and the patient progress.

Any learning process recapitulates earlier learning experiences and stimulates related narcissistic needs and issues. In the supervision of psychotherapy, those of focal importance are the wish for omnipotence and perfection—the professional grandiose self (Brightman, 1984–1985). The narcissistic vulnerabilities regarding this structure reemerge in the unmastered and stressful condition characteristic of the beginning phase of a relationship. Both supervisor and supervisee may wish to be omniscient, benevolent, or omnipotent as teacher, learner, and therapist. Each may wish for the other, or the supervisory process per se, to provide needed self-object experiences, which lead to feelings of well-being (Kohut, 1971). The need for feelings of well-being may be so prevalent that more painful feelings are avoided.

The following are clinical examples illustrating the application of these ideas to teaching and learning in supervision.

Example 1

An experienced supervisor, Mr. A., was assigned to consult with Mrs. F., a student in an advanced training program, on her work as a beginning supervisor. The consultation had a stressful beginning. Mrs. F. had canceled a number of the initial sessions on short notice, and then she asked to change the time of the consultative sessions. Although Mr. A. was aware of his anger with Mrs. F., he justified it to himself and to other teaching staff in terms of the inconvenience the cancellations caused. The beginning was further stressed by Mrs. F.'s chronic tardiness. Mr. A. confronted the situation directly and aggressively, enumerating the last-minute cancellations, request for a time change, and tardiness as signs of resistance to learning. In response, Mrs. F. apologetically described pressing personal problems. She also emphasized her wish to continue in the program. Mr. A. felt guilty about his anger. He also felt manipulated by Mrs. F. He did not examine these feelings or attempt to understand their meaning to the supervisory process. Instead, Mr. A. tried to continue his work with Mrs. F., unaware that each had become defensive in the teaching-learning process.

Another circumstance affecting the consultation was their knowledge that other beginnings between students and faculty in the program had gone smoothly. This further compounded their defensiveness, making both less open to sharing their work and their feelings with colleagues. Mr. A. felt like a poor teacher, Mrs. F. like a difficult learner. Mr. A. coped with the painful loss of his professional self-esteem by continuing to avoid experiencing and reflecting on his painful feelings and focusing on Mrs. F.'s inadequacies. In parallel, Mrs. F. coped with a difficult supervisory relationship by focusing on her supervisee's culture rather than on the supervisory process.

Sensing Mr. A.'s impatience and lack of enthusiasm with their work, Mrs. F. brought him a psychosocial study about her supervisee's culture. Mrs. F. stated that another faculty member had read it and found it valuable. Rather than focusing on Mrs. F.'s need to bring in such a book and discussing her supervisory experiences in the program, Mr. A. said he could not read the book. Mr. A. felt angry and frustrated. His refusal to read the book, in contrast to his colleague's willingness, made him feel ungenerous and malevolent. Mr. A.'s inability to focus on the difficult process with Mrs. F. paralleled her inability to focus on the difficult process with her supervisee. A mutual avoidance of negative issues occurred. This avoidance and Mrs. F.'s chronic lateness, which she explained was a characterological problem, made Mr. A. feel helpless and intensified his anger.

Narcissistic issues for each were heightened, with both of them trying to maintain their professional self-esteem. Mr. A. emphasized theory and dynamic formulations in the consultation, which had little impact on Mrs. F.'s learning. Mrs. F. focused on her knowledge of her supervisee's culture, which prevented her from learning from the process. Each one's knowledge was a source for self-idealization and professional self-esteem. Both felt a lack of interest in what they had to offer. Mrs. F.'s need to not be known and to not risk uncertainty was in conflict with Mr. A.'s wish to know and to teach.

With the book as a stimulus, Mr. A. began to acknowledge and reflect on these feelings. Decentered self-awareness enabled him to realize that Mrs. F.'s behavior symbolized her fears and anxieties about her professional self and that similar professional issues were stimulated in himself. As this process occurred, Mr. A.'s feelings of inadequacy, lessened. He was able to focus more on the process, acknowledging that, perhaps, the unstated feelings and issues that clouded the beginning of their work together were continuing to interfere with the process. Mr. A. talked about the importance of risk taking and the need to feel safe in order to understand the complex nature of psychotherapy and teaching and learning. This enabled Mrs. F. to begin to describe more of her supervisory work. Her supervisee also canceled supervisory sessions and avoided talking about the process with her clients. She continued, however, to attribute the supervisee's behavior to cultural influences. Mr. A. focused on identifying possible additional meanings of the supervisee's behavior. As Mr. A. began to reestablish his own narcissistic equilibrium, he was able to examine more closely his own feelings about his work with Mrs. F. and to seek the help and support of colleagues. Mrs. F. began to take small steps toward acknowledging her own painful feelings.

This example illustrates an assault on the grandiose self of student and teacher, followed by loss of professional self-esteem and the subsequent attempts to defend against painful feelings by denial, anger, and omnipotence. The consultant experienced the student's behavior as hostile and devaluing. These feeling states, which Mrs. F. unconsciously feared, subjectively organized her experiences relating to teaching and learning. Mr. A.'s experience of these feelings was so intense that they created an imbalance in his own narcissistic equilibrium. His need to protect himself was such that he temporarily suspended his ability to be reflectively self-aware and to decenter himself from the experience. Instead, his own unconscious organizing principles were called into play and a conjunctive experience occurred, which, when not understood, interfered with both the consultative and supervisory processes. Had Mr. A. been able to acknowledge and understand his feelings, he might have realized that not only was his professional self under assault, but also that of Mrs. F.

The beginning, then, might have focused on how Mrs. F. handled stress and acknowledged that beginning a new professional relationship was stressful. Narcissistic issues, such as fears of not being valued, appreciated, or being good enough, which are often stimulated in the beginning phase of a learning relationship, could have been identified. Focusing on these feelings and on the relationship may have minimized the defensive maneuvers of both, addressed more directly the interference with learning, and provided a model for supervision. It would have emphasized that in teaching and learning, professionals have an impact on one another and that this impact mutually affects professional self-worth and the achievement of a shared goal. Instead, issues of anger, power, and control were avoided, and feelings of narcissistic vulnerability prevailed.

Example 2

Miss M. was a student in an advanced training program. Professionally less experienced and established than her colleagues, she began the case-consultation component of her unit on supervision by apologizing for having one supervisee, a beginning therapist. Contrasting herself to the other students, she stated that she would be discussing beginning issues while her colleagues were presenting more complex ones. She worried that the consultant would be bored. Mrs. Z., the consultant, felt that Miss M. was indirectly expressing her anxiety about competition, envy, and belonging, feelings characteristic of beginning a new training program. Most of all, she felt that Miss M. feared being a disappointment to herself as well as to Mrs. Z. The consultant immediately began to address these issues.

First, Mrs. Z. addressed the inequity between Miss M. and her peers, which Miss M. said was unimportant, but added that she would catch up. Mrs. Z, acknowledged that ambition and competitiveness were natural feelings, especially in training programs. When the issue of boredom was raised, Miss M. stated that a supervisor of a beginning therapist was not very interesting to an experienced consultant. Mrs. Z. stated she was willing to work at whatever level was necessary to help her develop supervisory skills. She added that beginning professional relationships was stressful. Each time a new beginning occurred with a patient, teacher, or supervisor, issues about ourselves are raised. Perhaps being interesting was one such issue. Miss M. showed visible relief.

Mrs. Z.'s awareness of Miss M.'s professional narcissistic vulnerability and her lowered self-esteem was helpful in understanding her defensiveness and her strong need to look to others to explain her shortcomings and enhance her self-esteem. Mrs. Z. was also aware of other reactions to Miss M., which she needed to understand and monitor. She experienced Miss M. as self-effacing in her disclaimers about not knowing and about being inexperienced. Mrs. Z. sensed Miss M.'s underlying anger and envy.

In consultation, Miss M. was very task oriented and focused on the supervisory process. However, she sounded hopeless and helpless as she described her supervisee's setting and clients, a setting that offered short-term therapy to vulnerable multiproblem clients. Mrs. Z. asked about the experience of supervising such difficult cases. Miss M. denied any difficulty, including feelings of helplessness and hopelessness. As the process emerged, it was apparent that Miss M.'s goals for her supervisee were inappropriate for the circumstances. Mrs. Z. asked what might be realistic goals in their work so that the experience could be useful for Miss M., her supervisee, and the clients. She added that it was important to acknowledge the limitations of the situation and the supervisee's professional level of development, as well as the feelings engendered in assessing ways in which one can help and how this conflicts with one's own professional aspirations. During this process, Mrs. Z. was monitoring her own goals and aspirations for Miss M., as well as those of Miss M. for herself.

As these issues were discussed, Miss M.'s feelings of competitiveness, envy, and self-devaluation emerged. In part, her feelings were displaced onto the issue of the supervision of short-term, crisis-oriented therapy versus long-term, psychodynamic therapy. In part, she experienced her supervisee's level of development and work as unimportant and elementary, clear reflections of her feelings about herself. The overwhelming nature of the cases supervised further added to feelings of inadequacy. A tension developed between the demands of advanced training, Miss M.'s level of skill, and her professional aspirations. Aware of this, Mrs. Z. tried to modulate Miss M.'s expectations and to emphasize that every new situation presented a new challenge. Issues of competitiveness and envy were also broached.

Miss M.'s solution to dealing with her inadequate professional self was to find a more advanced therapist to supervise. She was not chosen by several prospective supervisees. Her sense of self-worth was so threatened she could not examine the process. In her ongoing work, there was also difficulty focusing on the process. When attempts were made to focus on a particular interaction, Miss M. angrily replied that, had she not been interrupted, she would have addressed that point. The erosion of her sense of competence and professional self-worth led to these maladaptive maneuvers. Mrs. Z. gently tried to help Miss M. look at these issues. While she stated that she was grateful to Mrs. Z for being helpful, she also responded by becoming more self-effacing and more self-critical. Mrs. Z. felt that these behaviors were attempts at denying her unexpressed anger.

Miss M. began to work with an experienced therapist, who had difficulty accepting patients' intense self-object needs and dealing with their negative feelings. She often denied her meaning to her patients and failed to explore the meaning of cancellations or precipitous terminations. Attempts to help Miss M. explore the meanings of the supervisee's behavior and to use her own feelings as an aide to understanding the supervisory process were gratefully acknowledged, but not implemented. Miss M. wanted to be liked and admired, and to achieve this, she avoided difficult issues. In parallel, Miss M. overtly expressed her idealization of Mrs. Z. The idealization felt inauthentic, and Mrs. Z. speculated that it was an attempt to keep the relationship intact. Miss M. also made statements indicating that she felt she and the consultant were alike, a further indication of her need for a mirroring relationship. In response, Mrs. Z. was aware of not wanting to fulfill this need and of wanting to psychologically separate herself from Miss M. She further speculated that Miss M.'s state of intense need made Miss M. ashamed and angry, perhaps because she felt that she would have to compromise herself to have her needs met. Given this understanding, Mrs. Z. approached the inauthenticity of the idealization by more actively addressing the disappointments and frustrations in their relationship and in Miss M.'s relationship with her supervisee.

Unexpectedly, the supervisee ended supervision with Miss M. No attempt was made to understand how or why the decision was reached. Miss M.'s self-esteem was shaken, but she was also less defended. This enabled her to begin to examine her role in the process. Mrs. Z. focused on the supervisee's inability to respond to her patient's needs and to work with their angry feelings. She drew a parallel between Miss M.'s need for the supervisee, the meaning she had to her in the program, and the supervisee's patients' intense self-object needs. Both sets of needs might have been similarly experienced by the supervisee and frightened her. To protect herself, she withdrew from Miss M. much in the way she allowed patients to withdraw from her.

Mrs. Z. further speculated that the supervisory relationship had become so important that it was difficult for Miss M. to be aware of the negative feelings involved. Her wish to have a positive relationship, her need for idealization, and her inability to discuss the negative caused aspects of the relationship to feel inauthentic. This also paralleled the consultative relationship. These realizations caused Miss M. to feel depressed and worried about her ability to be successful. Her defensiveness continued to lessen, however, and progress was made in the modification of the professional grandiose self. She more easily placed herself in the role of a learner. Difficulties in learning were addressed. Idealization of Mrs. Z. was more appropriate. These shifts enabled Mrs. Z. to feel more genuine and, therefore, more empathetic in her responses to Miss M. Mirroring, validating, and admiring Miss M.'s capacities served to bolster her self-esteem.

This vignette illustrates the consultant's ability to use her self-reflective capacities and to focus on how her behavior and feelings helped her understand and influence Miss M.'s experience and responses to the supervisory process. Fears of rejection and criticism and the need for idealization produced a false professional self, which led to inauthentic responses and avoidance of negative feelings. This was Miss M.'s organizing principle as she entered the beginning phase of a new learning experience.

Ekstein and Wallerstein (1958) have stated that those teachers who have needs for acceptance by students may avoid issues regarding anger, power, and control. Furthermore, needs may arise that lead to viewing students as extensions of the professional self, as projection of power, and as validation for one's skill. These needs and affective states may lead to conjunctive and disjunctive experiences between teacher and student. For learning to occur, the impact and meaning of these experiences on the supervisory process must be assessed. The intersubjective framework is one way to recognize and understand these feelings so that they can be used to facilitate teaching and learning.

Edward P. Kaufman, M.S.W.

19

Understanding the State

of Beleaguerment—

THROUGH A CLINICAL VIEW

OF THE CINEMA

he purpose of this paper is to help to understand "the state of beleaguerment" encountered and experienced by many educators. Over the course of a number of years, I have served as a consultant to various schools and individual teaching and supervisory professionals regarding the impact of this phenomenon. The state of beleaguerment is manifested by an intense feeling of frustration with regard to the ability to accomplish the professional's goal of satisfactorily educating an individual student or small groups of students. Included in this are frustrating experiences with students who are either gifted or "normal," as well as students who have special needs. In addition to the feeling of frustration, educators experience a lowered sense of self-esteem, feelings of incompetence, haplessness, and, in extreme instances, a hopelessness with regard to their professional identity.

Further, even though the professional may be aware intellectually that other colleagues have expressed similar thoughts and feelings, they feel a particular onus, a sense of professional failure in terms of their students. The feeling of aloneness in this dilemma is quite understandable, since inherently the teacher bears the main responsibility for transmitting ideas, concepts, and information to his students in a singular, autonomous role.

One of the things I have found useful is to demonstrate to the educator that he is not alone, that it is a phenomenon that is culturally recognized and frequently dramatized in the broadest way in film portrayals. These film portrayals of teachers, while describing this state of affairs, unfortunately do not offer clear-cut solutions to this problem. Rather, they illustrate the singularity of the responsibility placed upon the teacher.

These films demonstrate through their vivid imagery, the universality of the state of beleaguerment as a normally occurring part of the educator's subjective experience. The cinema, which can be used as a visual textbook, serves as documentation for the examination of the recurrence of the state of beleaguerment and the context in which it occurs. Specifically, it arises in relation to the teacher's coping with his student's transitory or fixed resistance to learning. Education is more than just the transmission of information; it also offers new perspectives and frames of reference to the learner. It is in relation to the latter that skepticism and resistance are introduced by the student. When films about teachers or the educational experience are considered in aggregate, as I have done in this paper, the continuity of theme clearly defines that they are not alone in the experience of beleaguerment. The realization of the ubiquitousness of their experience relieves teachers of self-blame and self-doubt and restores their capacity for self-empathy and reflection. The relief provides a respite that is a means to an end, that is, the reestablishment of empathy and understanding of the student's anxiety vis-à-vis his educational experience. It can be helpful to the educator to understand these anxieties, which may be related to developmental issues, as described by Beaumont (1989); to emotional conflicts, as defined by Pearson (1952); or to neurophysiological interferences as in learning disabilities (Garber, 1988). Thus, the student's reliance on the educator to master his learning task becomes paramount and exacerbates his tensions around felt dependency, deficiencies, and complex issues regarding the formation of relationships.

The idea behind this presentation is to look at the cinema for a model of indirect support for the educator. Writers, drawing documentation from infant research by observing infants, do not recommend this observation as a task for their readers. Similarly, I am not recommending that educators rush to their neighborhood movie theater to view films as a means of solving the educational dilemmas that befall them. The motion picture provides supportive data in demonstrating the universality of the state of beleaguerment, the perceptions and misperceptions of teachers, and the educational struggles and concerns of their students. They do not provide the usually conceptualized means of support vis-à-vis demonstrations of educational philosophy, technique, methodology, and theory. They portray educators coping with the challenge of educating their students, who come from a wide variety of circumstances, cultures, and socioeconomic environments. Whether the milieu is the classroom or outer space, the dynamics of the learning situation remains the same.

After reviewing a multitude of films, it appears that the medium reflects society in that there are no clear examples of support given to educators. In the movie *To Sir with Love*, the school principal tells the Sidney Poitier character, who is about to undertake his first teaching assignment, "We will support you all we can but once you step foot into that classroom, you're there on your own and by yourself." This principal was simply identifying the phenomenon that is universal for educators around the world whether in primary or secondary school, public or private system, or regular or special educational classrooms. The satisfactions that the cinema teachers derive seem to come from winning the hearts and minds of their students, as in *Goodbye, Mr. Chips, The Prime of Miss Jean Brodie, Mrs. Miniver, Wildcats, Hoosiers, Blackboard Jungle, To Sir with Love, Teachers,* and *How Green Was My Valley.* Occasionally these films portray a pat on the back from a colleague, the occasional support of a father-figure administrator, but in the main they focus on the interrelationship between the student and the teacher. What happens? How do the beleaguered heroes or heroines handle their dilemmas? They incant "one for the Gipper" (*Knute Rockne*), and win state championships in karate (*Karate Kid*), or basketball (*Hoosiers*), they marry their deaf-mute student (*Children of a Lesser God*); they give up on education, as Quantrell did, and become legendary outlaws leading their own band of raiders (*Quantrell's Raiders*); they get drunk like Nick Nolte did in *The Teachers*; they die peacefully in their sleep dreaming of thousands of children they've taught, as Robert Donat did in *Goodbye, Mr. Chips*, or, like Socrates, they drink hemlock.

Film portrays the writers', directors', and actors' visions of their teachers and, in a wide variety of movies, there are constant references and transferences to the teacher. These are either warmly (and sometimes too ideally) portrayed or punctuated with bitter, mocking satire. We are seen as brave pioneers and visionaries, all-wise, all-knowing, all-caring; or as brutal buffoons; or as comic characters described by Woody Allen thus: "Those who *can*, do; those who *can't*, teach; those who can't teach and those who are failures at all of the above were assigned to my school." We are the mentors who helped Luke Skywalker become a Jedi Knight and defeat the intergalactic dictatorial empire. We are rabbis and priests whose wise words changed the lives of all we counseled. We are drill sergeants who make men out of boys and lead them successfully through battle. We are the gunslingers with the golden hearts who teach the young boy or girl we encounter how to shoot straight and defend a code of ethics of honesty, honor, and bravery. We are the people who counsel on the joy and pain of life and the virtues of love and hope for tomorrow. The conflicts we must face as teachers are generally of a Faustian nature. While teaching our pupils, we are sometimes a bit shell-shocked, battle-weary, libidinally bombarded as Alan Ladd was in *Shane* and are tempted to sell our souls to the devil, or, if you will, quit to take a higher paying job! In juxtaposition, other films savagely refer to teachers as self-aggrandizing sadists, exploiters of their students' "real genius" and thieves who steal their scientific ideas. Additionally, they are seen as interfering with adolescent growth and development, misunderstanding and admonishing the would-be Tom Sawyers, misperceiving and depreciating the Huckleberry Finns, and degrading and overprotecting the budding, vivacious Becky Thatchers. When attempts at a balance between these extremes is struck, we are seen romantically as providing *Tea and Sympathy*.

Thus, these films dramatize (often unconsciously) our analytic perspective of child development: the oral stage with its references to primary and secondary narcissism and the concomitant idealizations, punctuated by images of the all-good, wise, and caring mother or the all-bad and frustrating mother; the anal phase with its struggle for control and mastery over the body; the establishment of separation-individuation and with it, the joy of autonomy; the phallic phase with its pride in body achievements and discovery of creative capacities; the oedipal phase with its triangulated relationships; the latency phase, in which the child sublimates his sexual curiosity about his own body and the bodies of others into the joy of learning about various bodies of knowledge; and finally, the genital phase with the full blossoming of the capacity for tenderness and love.

As already stated, film tends to reflect the recollections of its artists organized around their own educational experiences. It does not serve our purpose, which is finding a way of meeting the needs of the teachers of needy children. What it does, in a most immediate and evocative sense, is emphasize the profound impact that the educational experience and, in particular, the educators have made on their students. It is basically told through the students' perspective, although the teacher may be the leading character. What these films describe is the ambivalence that has been with us since Adam and Eve about change and knowledge. Teachers are initially perceived as the proverbial "serpent" against whom a variety of defenses must be used. They are the Greek messengers who bring the truth about how the battle goes and who, in one's imagination, must be put to death. Freud weathered the storms of criticism and professional ostracism as he attempted to educate the world about psychoanalysis. In film, as in reality, even kindly Mr. Chips was assaulted by his students' hazing as he initially began to engage them in an educational experience. This experience of educational resistance is beautifully reflected in the poem "For the Brilliant Students of My Dreams" by Harold Wyndham (1985), excerpted below:

> I step into the room,
> Their ready eyes nail me and freeze.
> I call roll, throw in Napoleon, Alexander the Great, Hitler.
> They do not bat an eyelash.
> I stomp up and down, rant, shout out Whitman and Blake.
> . . . .
> They quiver, stiffen, and hold unblinking.
> . . . .

I strip naked, and do jumping jacks.
They smile, three degrees above deadpan.
Now I am furious! I pull out my crowbar!
I smash the desk to splinters!
I attack the walls!
. . . .
For the last straw I light my atom bomb and blow the entire
    room to cinders.
I step over the rubble, picking and poking with my axe handle.
. . . .
Defeated, . . .
I pull out my sword for hari-kari.
Beneath the mount of broken skulls, arms, fingers, filters
    a meek voice:
"Mr. Wyndham? Will this be on the final?"

In order to fully comprehend the beleaguerment of teachers, one must examine the dynamics of the students as it relates to this experience within the educator.

One of the profound paradoxes that teachers of needy students encounter is the defenses that their students erect against receiving that which they need most. For example, the junior college teacher is frequently bedazzled by the learning blockades creatively introduced by the very student who has just explained poignantly that he needs the information contained in his classes in order to progress with his educational and vocational aspirations. The learning-disabilities teacher not infrequently finds himself engaged in a vigorous struggle with his students' denial of their LD problem.

In both instances, these defenses serve to protect the students' narcissism against either the emotional experience or the cognitive recognition of a deficit. These defenses further protect the students against their need to depend on their teacher to correct, remediate, and overcome this deficiency. Students who use learning defenses and who, by other criteria, may be seen as psychologically well developed may display phenomenologically, and often in a transitory manner, some of the features of a behaviorally disordered student. Both groups experience the learning situation and the formation of a learning alliance and relationship with the teacher as painful. The "behavior-disordered" students have, early in their lives, perceived fear and pain in the process of developing relationships. These children and adolescents often convert this fear unconsciously into externally perceived sadomasochistic interactions with significant people in their environment. This externalization makes the internal pain appear to come from the outside. It thus protects these students from dealing with the memories of their initial disappointments, conflicts, or painful interactions with their environment. Thus, past hurts are perceived as coming from contemporary sources.

It is dealing with these learning defenses that makes for the beleaguerment experienced by the teacher of needy children. The needs of these students are more easily satisfied. Freud (1909) stated that the task of education is "to enable the individual to take part in culture and achieve this with the smallest loss of original energy" (libidinal energy). The aim of education according to Whitehead (1967) is to present knowledge, not as a dry abstraction but rather to vitalize it, attaching it to real life applications. For example, a student wants and needs information on a given subject; for the teacher, this request is relatively easy to meet. A student wants and needs a special method of education in an area in which we are trained; again, the task is seemingly simple and straightforward. A student wants and needs a positive relationship with a concerned, informed, caring adult; that is certainly within our nature and professional ideals to provide. Instead, the phenomena we deal with is the students' defense against their experiencing pain and helplessness in the learning relationship. If the defense is working properly, the student experiences relatively little pain and we, the teachers, absorb the feelings of pain and helplessness.

The initial countertransference response to the students' externalization is to experience ourselves as incompetent and painfully inadequate to meet the task. Clearly, what the educator is experiencing is the student's pain regarding his own sense of inadequacy, which has been projected into the teacher. Further, the student with anxieties about special learning needs frequently feels that he is the only one of his peers who has a learning problem. This projected feeling of aloneness forms the basis for earlier described feelings of onus (that he or she is the only one experiencing difficulties in educating his or her students). What the student and the teacher are experiencing vis-à-vis aloneness is analogous to two sides of the same coin. As we are able to identify and analyze this as a projection of the students' inner anxiety, we are able to contain these projections and resume the tasks and aims of education.

The movies have consistently explored the character and dynamics of people who seem to have a proclivity either to unconsciously seek out painful relationships or who inject pain into their relationships. These films are different from the ones that state that love will prevail despite the pain that one may go through while trying to achieve it. Or that with it, one can endure and overcome a variety of hardships. The latter group of films describes part of our cultural preparatory folklore and mores, socially extended to our growing and developing children and adolescents, as well as reaffirming them to the adults in the audience. The former have been studied by serious moviemakers throughout the world as enigmatic and unique, but not unfamiliar, existential experiences. The acceptance and curiosity about these films suggest a preoccupation and interest on the part of filmgoers as if these films represent a microscopic aspect of their own lives. Thus, historically we move from the *Blue Angels* of the 1930s to the *Blue Velvets* of the 1980s. The topic has been viewed "through a lens darkly," as well as lenses that permit more light to fall on the subject. Filmmakers have drawn from their palette both comedy and tragedy to illustrate this complex phenomenon.

Thus, we have directors falling into two categories: the tragedians like Von Sternberg, Bergman, and Bertolucci on one hand, and the comedic talents of Chaplin and the poet laureate of painful contemporary relationships, Woody Allen, on the other. The tragedians tend to take a pessimistic approach, reflecting true Shakespearean tradition cautioning that the fatal flaw is indeed fatal. The comedic directors, on the other hand, subscribe to the modern philosophy and ideal that rationality will prevail and that once understanding, either emotional or intellectual, is achieved, the painful situation is remediable. At the end of *Annie Hall*, Woody Allen tells the following anecdote: relationships remind him of the old story of the man who goes to consult his psychiatrist. The man tells the psychiatrist that he is concerned about his brother, who thinks he is a chicken. The psychiatrist, in a nonanalytic manner, asks the man why he has not institutionalized his brother. The man replies, "Because we need the eggs!" Allen pays tribute to the importance of relationships; that is, although they may be irrational and crazy, "we all need the eggs!"

A film I will examine in detail, which explores the subject in a light but insightful manner, is Frank Oz's musical remake (1986) of Roger Corman's 1950 cult classic *Little Shop of Horrors*. This film, like the original, works on many different levels. It is a homage to, and a self-parody of, the science fiction genre of the cold-war era. Those films depicted our hopes, fears, and fantasies regarding the impact of the alien presence, either malevolent or benign, on the American way of life. Through its intelligent and witty lyrics, the film sings of the American dream of the 1950s, much of which is still applicable today. Like all good science fiction, it uses fantasy to address contemporary problems, in this instance, the impact of urban poverty and man's exploitation of nature and his fellow human beings. It even takes a momentary glance at the problems and magical fantasies of school drop-outs. Basically, it is the story of a boy, a girl, and a plant!

The hero, Seymour, is "an orphan child of the streets." Mr. Muschnik, the owner of a skid-row flower shop, had allowed Seymour, as a child, to take shelter in the basement of the shop. Muschnik's attitude toward his employee, Seymour, is that he is like a marine, there to serve. Seymour does this unquestioningly, since he expects little more from life and relationships than pain. He has a capacity to care tenderly for plants, suggesting an earlier nurturing relationship in his life.

Seymour has two dreams: one is to leave skid row and the other is to be loved by the beautiful and seemingly unattainable Audrey, the cashier of the flower shop. Audrey shares with Seymour the same expectation of pain being part of relationships. Her father abandoned the family when she was a child, and her mother was "poor." In her search for a father figure, she would follow a man and, in her words, "whenever he snapped his fingers" she'd say "sure." Audrey's philosophy regarding relationships is the personification of our psychoanalytic understanding of one of Harlow's primate studies.

Harlow demonstrated that even a barbed-wire negative object is better than no object at all. Audrey, like Seymour, is exploited by the people in her environment. Her boyfriend, Dr. Orrin Schrivello, is an oral-sadistic dentist. Audrey is attracted to Seymour's gentleness but feels undeserving of his love. Ironically, both Seymour and Audrey alternately encourage each other to seek better lives. Clearly, Seymour and Audrey are individuals who unconsciously tend to repeat rather than remember the early experiences of pain and loss. The use of repetition-compulsion defends them against the evocative memories by placing the pain of the past into present-day experiences. As if to underscore this point and to distinguish it from those individuals who perversely and consciously seek and derive pleasure from pain, the filmmaker includes a satiric, full-blown sadomasochistic scene. Enter a dental patient who, with thinly veiled ecstasy in his voice, implores Dr. Schrivello to perform a "long, slow, deep root-canal job." It slowly dawns on the dentist that his patient is having orgasmic delights with each maniacal procedure that he thrusts upon him. In true sadistic fashion, he stops the procedure and thus acquits himself as a paragon of sadism by denying pleasure to the masochistic patient.

Seymour's and Audrey's lives change after Seymour purchases an exotic plant. He christens the plant "Audrey II" in honor of his love for Audrey. Audrey II is placed on display, and a curious public begins to patronize the store. This brings financial and public acclaim to both Seymour and the store, but the road to Oz is littered with stumbling blocks because Audrey II begins to exhibit symptoms of a failure-to-thrive child. Seymour accidentally discovers that his new "baby" has a rare appetite for hematological delights. Seymour assumes his customary position in relation to the objects of his world and literally becomes finger food to his young suckling. Prior to this discovery, Seymour sings his lament "Please Grow for Me," which could well describe some teacher's experiences with their students. Excerpts from his lament follow:

> I've given you sunshine; I've given you dirt;
> You've given me nothing but heartache and hurt.
> I'm begging you sweetly; I'm down on my knees . . .
> Please grow for me.
> . . . .
> I've given you southern exposure to get you to thrive;
> I've pinched you back hard like I'm supposed to;
> You're barely alive.
> I've tried you on levels of moisture from desert to mud;
> I've given you grow lights and mineral supplements;
> What do you want from me . . . blood?
> I've given you sunlight, I've given you rain;
> Looks like you're not happy 'less I open a vein.
> I'll give you a few drops if that will appease;
> Now, please, please grow for me.

Thanks to Seymour's hand feeding, Audrey II thrives and metamorphosizes from the helpless, hungry infant into a Mephistophelean creature. In this form, Audrey II offers Seymour the world on a half-shell—Venus incarnate, Audrey I. Seymour is initially appalled by

Audrey II's bloodthirsty proposition but is seduced by Audrey II into partaking in a primal scene experience activating Seymour's oedipal revenge and rescue fantasies. Through a comedy of terrors, Dr. Schrivello and Mr. Muschnik accidentally become victims of Audrey II's voracious appetite. Dr. Schrivello's disappearance leads to Audrey's confession to Seymour about her feelings of guilt because she had harbored secret death wishes toward the dentist. Seymour, emboldened by her confession, declares his love for her through a serenade of impassioned ardor. Audrey overcomes her fear and joins him in a romantic duet.

Later in the movie Audrey II reveals its true identity to Seymour as the mean, green mother from outer space who is bad and wishes to control and devour the world. The fear of a devouring and controlling introject or internal representation of the object is an idea used by object relations theorists and ego psychologists. The concept explains the perception of pain in interpersonal relationships in individuals who have severe problems in this area of their lives. At the conclusion of the film, Seymour rescues Audrey from the monster, defeats the devil in battle, and the two of them live happily ever after in Audrey's dream house.

In the movie, we see people who associate pain with relationships. These dynamics are significant issues but are only of focal concern when they interfere with the learning alliance. The pain that we, as teachers, deal with is stimulated by the utilization of defenses against these perceptions on the part of our students in the learning situation. As stated earlier, it is dealing with this phenomenon that makes for the sense of beleaguerment within the teacher of needy children. In following the process, the disruption of the teacher occurs when the externalization of the student's feelings of pain and helplessness is absorbed rather than contained by the professional's ego. The experiencing ego's sense of beleaguerment is felt by the educator as coming from inside of him. When this happens, the affective experience is that the teacher feels he is inadequate in meeting the task and that he is the helpless one in the student-teacher dyad. However, when the educator's observing ego is free to reflect upon the situation, it is clearly seen that this is the student's defense and not the educator's problem. There is an exquisite cinematic example of this in a sequence of scenes in George Lukas's *The Empire Strikes Back* (1980). The interchange takes place between Luke Skywalker, the young hero of the "Star Wars" trilogy, and the ultimate teacher, the 800-year-old Jedi master, Yoda. In the initial dialogue between Yoda and Luke, Luke implores Yoda to take him under his tutelage to complete his training as a Jedi knight. Despite his skepticism of Luke's motivation, Yoda cautiously agrees to train him. During the training, Luke erects some learning defenses that impinge upon his ability to involve himself in a task requiring intense mental concentration. His internal tensions disrupt this process. Rather than deal with his own sense of helplessness, Luke assaults Yoda by depreciating his words and accuses Yoda of asking the impossible. The beleaguered Yoda levitates a seemingly immovable object, demonstrating both to himself and to Luke the efficacy of his educational orientation. The astonished Luke exclaims in awe, "I can't believe it!" Calmly, Yoda replies, "That is why you failed!"

When teachers in the cinema are confronted by their students' defenses against their needs, they all seem to borrow a line from Dylan Thomas—they "do not go gentle into that good night; they rage and rage against the dying of the light." Their anger becomes an organizing force and they rail against the system, sometimes against the students, and then have breakthroughs of miraculous insight. These insights lead to innovative teaching methods and unique ways of reaching the troubled student. In juxtaposition, it is rationality, knowledge, and understanding that is the organizing factor in the working through of the problems that confront us in our work. In applying psychoanalytic concepts to the field of education, Freud taught us to analyze pain, and Winnicott (1965) taught us, vis-à-vis the holding environment, to contain the pain. From both, we have learned never to overlook the educational goals. While this process goes on, we struggle to maintain our identification with our educational ego ideals. We employ learning on behalf of ourselves and our students and, as a result, always remain students ourselves. Further education is a means of enriching our understanding and fulfilling our commitment to our professional identification and ideals.

This professional identification has been formed by positive learning experiences and relationships with our own teachers and may be based on the original ones, that is, our parents, or with people who are euphemistically called "significant others" in our lives. It is the pleasure that we derived from these experiences that sustains our ability to cope with every classroom adventure. This pleasure is more than simply the association with significant objects in our lives; it is a separate and independent force that has long detached itself from those important relationships. Specifically, it is the pleasure in mastering a task that is sometimes arduous. It is also the pleasure that we derive from our own creative endeavors. We have, as Ekstein (1969) has stated, moved in the course of our own growth and development from the playing with toys to the playing with thoughts and new ideas. In other words, the teaching and learning experience has become a product of the process of sublimation, and so the cycle is complete. As mentioned earlier, Freud stated that the task of education is to enable the individual to take part in culture and to achieve this with the smallest loss of original energy. To this he added that culture is the product of sublimation. This, essentially, is the process that our educational institutions organize themselves around.

The teacher of students in need fortifies himself with knowledge, understanding, and openness to new experiences. There are moments, however, when most of us "need the eggs"; that is, someone else with whom to share these experiences and thoughts. The structure and new demands placed on our educational systems and, in turn, on the individual educators preclude opportunities for teachers to come together and to share with one another their concerns about their individual students. The time-efficiency studies used for evaluation preclude the old format of a free period, the pause in the day's occupation that was once known as the teacher's hour when colleagues met informally, exchanged ideas, and gave mutual support to one another. The teacher's lounge, as we once knew it, has almost become an anachronism. I am therefore suggesting the formation of the peer study group, either self-led or with a consultant as a replacement for the informal supportive process. These group meetings would afford the opportunity for old and new friends and colleagues to get together and share their experiences and exchange ideas. These types of discussion groups have been valuable to members of allied professions, such as social work and psychology.

In the initial phase of these peer groups, it is to be anticipated that the teaching professional may experience the group in a parallel process. Specifically, like their students, their reliance on others for problem solving may evoke anxiety and pain, fear of criticism, or exposure of self-perceived deficits. It is important for the group ethos that the focus deemphasize specifics of techniques and educational orientation. Beleaguerment impacts on educators regardless of teaching style or philosophy. The focus of this group is designed to relieve an educator of his anxiety regarding his sense of loss of autonomy and fear of colleagial criticism. It further enables the educator to use the group for resolving his sense of beleaguerment through the noncompetitive, supportive atmosphere and enables him to refocus on the student's learning problems.

In summary, I have attempted here to identify, define, and explain the dynamics involved in the educator's feeling of beleaguerment, which is described as a reaction to his student's learning resistances. The examples from the cinema were aimed at demonstrating that this is not a singular experience felt by the educator, but rather a culturally recognized phenomenon. Further, examples were used from the movies to describe those individuals who have the expectation of pain in relationships, and distinguish them from those who receive perverse pleasure from pain. Additionally, it is suggested that an understanding of the learning resistances enables the educator to feel relief from the sense of beleaguerment. Finally, the use of professional support groups is recommended as a means of helping teachers clarify and understand the teaching dilemmas that befall them in the course of their work. As Wittenberg (1983) notes, in the everyday course of events, one of the tasks the teacher performs "may be thought of as resembling the parental function: That is, to act as a temporary container for the excessive anxiety of his students at points of stress. It will mean that he will experience in himself some of the mental pain connected with learning, and yet set an example of maintaining curiosity in the face of chaos, love of truth in the face of terror of the unknown, and hope in the face of despair" (p. 60). This process is intensified with children and adolescents who have special learning needs and problems, students who unconsciously experience the need for relationship inherent in the learning alliance as painful. They thus bring to the learning situation additional apprehension which affects the educator and the educational experience.

In closing, I would like to apply a concept from clinic to classroom. Ekstein (1984) has said that in dealing with the troubled child, it is not always possible to function as a string to a kite, but that at least we can serve as the kite's tail. With this tail even the untethered kite is given some balance and can remain upright while being buffeted by storms until the prevailing winds become calm, allowing the kite to descend, more or less intact, gently back to earth.

Bibliography

Introduction

Barrett, M. (1986) Private Communications.

Barrett, M. & Trevitt, J. (1991) *Attachment Behavior & The School Child: An Introduction to Educational Therapy,* Tavistock & Routledge, London & N. Y.

Caspari, I. (1974) *Learning and Teaching, Collected Papers.* 7AET, 3 Templewood, London W138BA.

———— (1978) Educational Therapy in V. Varma, ed. *Psychotherapy Today.* Constable Publisher, London.

Donaghue, Dennis (1983) *The Arts Without Mystery,* quoted 1991 in Harvard Educational Review, Greene, Maxine, Texts and Margins, p 27, V. 61, #1.

Eisner, Elliot W. (1979) *The Educational Imagination,* Chapter 11, p. 190, McMillan, N.Y.

Field, Kay (1977) *A Psychoanalytic Contribution to Education,* Journal of the Philadelphia Association for Psychoanalysis. Vol. IV, No. 1, 1977, pp 21–43.

Greene, Maxine (1986) *In Search of a Critical Pedagogy,* in Harvard Educational Review, V. 56(4) pp 427–441.

Jones, Richard (1968) *Fantasy and Feeling in Education,* Harper and Row, New York.

Ungerleider, Dorothy (1979) *History of Educational Therapy,* in The Educational Therapist, V. 1(1). The Publication of the Association of Educational Therapists, Encino, California.

Chapter 1

Basch, M. (1988). *Understanding Psychotherapy: The Science Behind the Art.* New York: Basic Books.

Broucek, F. (1982). Shame and its relationship to early narcissistic developments. *Int. J. Psycho-Anal.,* 63:369–378.

Darwin, C. (1872). *The Expression of the Emotions in Man and Animals.* Chicago: University of Chicago Press, 1965.

Kohut, H. (1971). *The Analysis of the Self.* New York: International Universities Press.

———— (1977). *The Restoration of the Self.* New York: International Universities Press.

———— (1984). *How Does Analysis Cure?* Chicago: University of Chicago Press.

Nathanson, D. L. (1987). A Timetable for Shame, In D. L. Nathanson, ed., *The Many Faces of Shame,* New York: Guilford Press, pp. 1–63.

Papousek, H. & Papousek, M. (1975). Cognitive Aspects of Pre-verbal Social Interaction Between Human Infants and Adult, *Parent-Infant Interaction* (Ciba Foundation Symposium). New York: Associated Scientific Publishers.

Tomkins, S. (1962–1963). *Affect, Imagery, Consciousness* Vol. I & II. New York: Springer.

———— (1970). Affects as the primary motivational system. In: *Feelings and Emotions,* ed. M. B. Arnold. New York: Academic Press, pp. 101–110.

———— (1981). The Quest For Primary Motives: Biography and Autobiography of an Idea, *J. Person & Soc. Psychol.* 41:306–329.

White, R. (1960j, Competence and the psychosexual stages of development. In: *Nebraska Symposium on Motivation,* ed. M. R. Jones, Lincoln Nebraska: University of Nebraska Press, 8:97–141.

Chapter 2

Dewald, P. (1987), *Learning Process in Psychoanalytic Supervision.* New York: International Universities Press.

Ekstein, R. & Wallerstein, R. S. (1958), *The Teaching and Learning of Psychotherapy.* New York: Basic Books.

Feynman, R. (1985), *Surely You're Joking. Mr. Feynman!* New York: Norton.

Fleming, J. & Benedek, T. (1966), *Psychoanalytic supervision.* New York: International Universities Press, 1983.

Kohut, H. (1971), *The Analysis of Self.* New York: International Universities Press.

———— (1976), Creativeness, Charisma, Group Psychology, *In The Search of the Self*, ed. P. Ornstein. New York: International Universities Press, 1978.

———— (1977), *The Restoration of the Self.* New York: International Universities Press.

Moraitis, G. (1988), Presentation to the Chicago Psychoanalytic Society: Transference Repetitions and the Pursuit of Novelty.

Pajak, E. (1981), Teaching and the Psychology of the Self, *American Journal of Education*, 90:1–13.

Rapaport, D.(1960), Psychoanalysis as a Developmental Psychology. In *The Collected Papers of David Rapaport*, ed. M. Gill. New York: Basic Books, 1967.

Stern, D. (1985), *The Interpersonal World of the Infant.* New York: Basic Books.

Stone, W. & Whitman, R. (1977), Contributions of the psychology of the self to group process and group therapy, *International Journal of Group Psychotherapy*, Vol. 27, 343–359.

Thomas, A. & Chess, S. (1977), *Temperament and Development*, New York: Brunner/Mazel.

Von Bertalanffy, L. (1967), *Robots. Men and Minds.* New York: George Braziller.

Wolf, E. (1989), A Psychoanalytic Self Psychologist Looks At Learning, In: *Learning and Education: Psychoanalytic Perspectives.* ed. K. Field, B. Cohler & G. Wool, Madison, CT: International Universities Press, pp. 377–394.

Chapter 3

Beaumont, A.M. (1988), The effect of loss on learning, London: *Journal of Educational Therapy*. Forum for the Advancement of Educational Therapy.

Bettelheim, B., & Zelan, K., (1981), *On Learning to Read*, New York: Knopf.

Bowlby, J. (1988), *A Secure Base: Clinical Applications of Attachment Theory.* London: Routledge.

Britton, R. (1989), *The Oedipus Complex Today.* London: Karnac Books.

Caspari, I. (1976), *Learning and Teaching*, London: Forum for the Advancement of Educational Therapy.

Klein, M. (1931), A Contribution to the Theory of Intellectual Inhibition, in *Love, Guilt and Reparation*. London: Hogarth Press (1975).

Klein, M. (1946–63), *Envy and Gratitude*. London: Hogarth Press (1975).

Sinason, V. (1988), Smiling, swallowing, sickening and stupefying; the effect of sexual abuse on the child, *Psychoanalytic Psychotherapy*, 3:2: 97–111.

Chapter 4

Ainsworth, M. D. S. & Wittig, B. A. (1969), Attachment and Exploratory Behavior of One Year Olds In a Strange Situation, in B. M. Foss (ed.) *Determinants of Infant Behavior*, Vol. 4, London: Methuen; New York: Barnes & Noble.

Bick, E. (1968), The Experience of the Skin in Early Object Relations, *International Journal of Psycho-Analysis*, 49: 484–486.

Bowlby, J. (1969), Attachment, *Attachment and Loss*, Vol. 1 (2nd edition 1982), London: Hogarth Press; New York: Basic Books; Harmondsworth: Penguin (1971).

———— (1973), Separation: Anxiety and Anger, *Attachment and Loss*, Vol. 2 of London: Hogarth Press; NY: Basic Books; Harmondsworth: Penguin (1975).

———— (1980), Loss: Sadness and Depression, *Attachment and Loss*, Vol. 3, London: Hogarth Press; New York: Basic Books; Harmondsworth: Penguin.

———— (1988), *A Secure Base: Clinical Applications of Attachment Theory*. London: Routledge.

Main, M., Kaplan, N. & Cassidy, J. (1985), Security in Infancy, Childhood, and Adulthood: A Move to the Level of Representation in I. Bretherton and E. Waters (eds.), Growing Points in Attachment Theory and Research, *Monographs of the Society for Research in Child Development*, Chicago: University of Chicago Press Vol. 50: Serial 209: 66–104.

Sroufe, L. A. (1983), Infant-Caregiver Attachment and Patterns of Adaption in Pre-School: The Roots of Maladaption and Competence, in M. Perlmutter (ed.) Minneapolis: University of Minnesota Press, pp. 41–81.

Stern, D. (1985), *The Interpersonal World of the Infant*. New York: Basic Books.

Winnicott, D. W. (1965), *The Maturational Process and the Facilitating Environment*, New York: International University Press pp. 15–83, pp. 166–171.

——— (1971), *Playing and Reality*, Tavistock Publication, London.

Chapter 5

Barrett, M. & Trevitt, J. (1991), *Attachment Behavior And The School Child: An Introduction To Educational Therapy*, London: Tavistock/Routledge.

Bowlby, J. (1977), The making and breaking of affectional bonds, *The British Journal of Psychiatry 130*, pp 201–210.

Caspari, I. (1974), Educational Therapy in V. Varma (ed.) *Psychotherapy Today*. London: Constable.

Freud, S. (1926), Inhibitions, Symptoms and Anxiety, *Standard Edition* London: Hogarth Press, 1974, 20: 77–175.

Winnicott, D. W. (1965), *The Maturational Process and the Facilitating Environment*, New York: International University Press pp. 15–83, pp. 166–171.

Chapter 6

Adams, J. (1989), Prenatal exposure to teratogenic agents and neurodevelopmental outcome, *Research in Infant Assessment* (pp. 63–72), N. Paul (ed.), White Plains, New York: March of Dimes Birth Defects Foundation.

Als, H. & Duffy, H. (1989), Neurobehavioral assessment in the newborn period: Opportunity for early detection of later learning disabilities and for early intervention, *Research in Infant Assessment* (pp. 127–152), N. Paul (ed.), White Plains, New York: March of Dimes Birth Defects Foundation.

Bryan, T. (1991), Assessment of social cognition: Review of research in learning disabilities, *Handbook On The Assessment of Learning Disabilities: Theory. Research. and Practice*, (pp. 285–312), H. L. Swanson (ed.), Austin, Texas: Pro-Ed.

Cable, B. (1981), *A Study of Play Behavior in Learning Disabled and Normal Preschool Boys*, an unpublished doctoral dissertation,

Northwestern University, Evanston, Illinois.

Carlisle, J. F. & Johnson, D. J. (1989), Assessment of school age children, *The Assessment of Learning Disabilities* (pp. 73–110), L. B. Silver, (ed.), Boston, MA: College-Hill Press.

Carrow-Woolfolk, E. & Lynch, J. I. (1982), *An Integrative Approach To Language Disorders in Children*, Grune & Stratton, New York.

Donahue, M. (1983), Learning disabled children as conversational partners, *Topics in Language Disorders*, 4(1), 15–27.

Federal Register 42(163), August 1977.

Gray, D. & Kavangh, J. (1985), *Biobehavioral Measures of Dyslexia* Parkton, Maryland: York Press.

Hallgren, B. (1950), Specific dyslexia ("congenital wordblindness"): A lenical and genetic study, *Aca Psvchiatrica Scandinavia*, (Suppl. 65).

Johnson, D. (1987), Nonverbal learning disabilities, *Pediatric Annals*, 16(2), 133–144.

Johnson, D. & Blalock, J. (1987), *Adults with Learning Disabilities: Clinical Studies*, Grune & Stratton, Orlando, Florida.

Johnson, D. & Croasmun, P. A. (1991), Language assessment, *Handbook on the Assessment of Learning Disabilities: Theory, Research, and Practice*, (pp. 229–48) H. L. Swanson (ed.), Austin, Texas: Pro-Ed.

Johnson, D. & Myklebust, H. (1967), Learning Disabilities: Educational Principles and Practices, Grune & Stratton, New York.

Kavanagh, J. & Truss, T. (eds.) (1988) *Learning Disabilities: Proceedings of the National Conference*, Parkton, Maryland: York Press.

Keogh, B. K. & Bess, C. R. (1991), Assessing temperament, *Handbook on the Assessment of Learning Disabilities: Theory, Research, and Practice*, (pp. 313–330), H. L. Swanson (ed.), Austin, Texas: Pro-Ed.

Masland, R. & Masland, M. (1988), *Preschool Prevention of Reading Failure*, Parkton, MD: York Press.

Myklebust, H. R. (1954), *Auditory Disorders in Children*, Grune & Stratton, New York.

Pennington, B. (1989), Using genetics to understand dyslexia, *Annals of Dyslexia*, 39, 81–93.

Raviv, D. (1987), *Self-Image of Learning Disabled Adolescents: It's Relation to Severity, Time of Diagnosis and Parental Perceptions*, an unpublished doctoral dissertation, Northwestern University, Evanston, Illinois.

Roth, F. P. & Clark, D. M. (February 1987), Symbolic play and social participation abilities of language-impaired and normally developing children, *Journal of Speech and Hearing Disorders*, 52(1), 17–29.

Salvia, J. & Ysseldyke, J. E. (1988), *Assessment is Special and Remedial Education* (4th ed.), Boston: Houghton Mifflin Company.

Sigel, I. (1971), Language of the disadvantaged: The distancing hypothesis, *Language Training in Early Childhood Education* (pp. 60–78), C. S. Lavatelli (ed.), ERIC Clearinghouse of Early Childhood Education: The University of Illinois Press.

Silver, L. B. (ed.) (1989), *The Assessment of Learning Disabilities: Preschool Through Adulthood*, Boston: A College-Hill Publication.

Swanson, H. L. (1991), *Handbook on the Assessment of Learning Disabilities: Theory, Research, and Practice*, Austin, Texas: Pro-Ed.

Wechsler, D. (1974), *Wechsler Intelligence Scale for Children—Revised*, New York: The Psychological Corporation.

——— (1989), *Wechsler Preschool and Primary Scale of Intelligence—Revised*, New York: The Psychological Corporation.

Wiig, E. H. & Semel, E. (1984), *Language Assessment and Intervention for the Learning Disabled* (2nd ed.), Columbus, Ohio: Charles E. Merrill Publishing Company.

Chapter 7

Bion, W. R. (1959), Attacks on linking, *International Journal of Psycho-Analysis*, Vol. 40.

——— (1962), *Learning From Experience*, London. Heinemann.

——— (1967), A Theory of Thinking. I: Bion, *Second Thoughts. Selected Papers on Psycho-Analysis*. New York, Jason Aronson.

Caspari, I. (1974), What is Educational Therapy?, *Therapeutic Education* Vol. 4, No. 2.

——— (1976), Play and Learning, *Therapeutic Education*, Vol. 8., No. 1

Caspari, I. (1976), *Troublesome Children in Class*, Routledge & Kegan Paul.

Dowling, E. & Osborne, E. (1985), *The Family and the School*, Routledge and Kegan Paul.

Duve, A. (1965), *The AMS Method*, University of Oslo.

———— (1966), Psykodynamikkoglaering, *Nordisk Psykologi.* 18 Vol. No. 3, pp. 67–75.

———— (1969), Psykologisk intervensjon i kriser, *Nordisk Psykoloqi.* 21 Vol. 1–2, pp. 67–75.

———— (1972/77), *Det forste levearets psykoloai*, Universitetsforlaget, Oslo.

———— (1978), Tidlige psykiske aw ik. *Monoqraphi no. 2. Norsk Psykoloqforeninqs Tidsskrift.*

———— (1980), Oyenbrynene og tidlige psykologiske prosesser. *Monografi no. 6 Psykoloqforeninqs Tidsskrft.*

———— (1988), The Norwegian educational assessment method, *The Journal of Educational Therapy,* 2, 1–11.

Freud, A. (1948), *The Ego and the Mechanisms of Defense*, The Hogarth Press, London.

Harris, M. (1975), *Thinking About Infants and Young Children*, Clunie Press, New York.

Hartman, H. (1958), *Ego Psychology and the Problems of Adaptation*, New York: Hutt.

Lewin, K. (1936), *A Dynamic Theory of Personality Structure.*

Max, L. & Briskin, G. J. (1960), *The Clinical Use of the Bender-Gestalt Test.* NY.

Meltzer, D. (1960), Lecture Seminars in Kleinian Psychiatry, unpublished.

Murphy, L. B. (1956), *Personality in Young Children*, Vol. 1, New York.

Osborne, E. (1987), *Educational Therapy. The Proceedings of the Conference* Disabilita Psychica e Disturbo Telazione in Alba, 22–23 November 1985, University of Torino.

Rappaport, D. (1952), Projective techniques and the theory of thinking, *Journal of Projective Techniques*, 16.

Taylor, D. (1986), The child as go-between: consulting with parents and teachers, *Journal of Family Therapy.* No. 8.

Winnicott, C. (1963), Face to Face with Children, in *New Thinking for Changing Needs*, Association of Social Workers.

Winnicott, D. W.(1971), *Playing and Reality*, Tavistock Publication, London.

———— (1986), *Home is Where We Start From*, New York: Penguin Books.

Wittenberg-Salzberger, I., Henry, G. & Osborne, E. (1983), *The Emotional Experience of Learning and Teaching*, London: Routledge & Kegan Paul pp. 53–76.

Wittenberg-Salzberger, I. (1970), *Psycho-Analytic Insight and Relationship*, Routledge and Kegan Paul.

Chapter 8

American Psychiatric Association: *Diagnostic and Statistical Manual of Mental Disorders: Third Edition, Revised*. Washington, D.C., American Psychiatric Association, 1987.

Brumback, R. A. & Staten, R. D. (1982), Right Hemisphere Involvement in Learning Disability, Attention Deficit Disorder, and Childhood Major Depressive Disorder, *Medical Hypotheses*. 8, pp. 505–514.

Cantwell, D. P., Carlson, G. A., (eds) (1983): *Affective Disorders in Childhood and Adolescence: An Update*. New York: Spectrum.

Ceci, S. J. (1987), *Handbook of Cognitive, Social, and Neuro-psychological Aspects of Learning Disabilities* (Vol. 2). Hillsdale, NJ: Lawrence Erlbaum Assoc., Inc., pp. 239–249.

Cohen, J. (1985), Learning disabilities and adolescence: developmental considerations, *Adolescent Psychiatry*, 12, pp. 177–196.

——— (1986), Learning disabilities and psychological development in childhood and adolescence, Annals of *Dyslexia*, 36, pp. 287–300.

Colbert, P., Newman, B., Ney, P, & Young, J. (1982), Learning disabilities as a symptom of depression in children, *Journal of Learning Disabilities*. 15, pp. 333–336.

Forness, S. R. (1988), School characteristics of children and adolescents with depression. In Rutherford, R. B., Nelson, C. M., Forness, S. R. (Eds): *Basis of Service Behavioral Disorders in Children and Youth*. Boston: Little, Brown and Co. pp. 177–203.

Freud, S. (1968), Mourning and Melancholia in W. Gaylin (Ed) *The Meaning of Despair*. New York: Science House 50–69.

Glosser, G. & Koppell, S. (1987), Emotional-behavioral patterns in children with learning disabilities: Lateralized hemispheric differences, *J. of Learning Disabilities*. 20(6), pp. 365–369.

Goldstein, D. & Dundon, W. D. (1987) Affect and Cognition in Children With Learning Disabilities, *In* Ceci, S (Ed): *Handbook of Cognitive. Social and Neuropsychological Aspects of Learning*

Disabilities, Vol. II. New Jersey: Lawrence Erlbaum Assoc., pp. 233–249.

Kazdin, A. E. (1988), Childhood Depression. *In* Mash, E. J. & Treadle, L. G. (Eds) *Behavioral Assessment of Childhood Disorders*, 2nd Edition. New York: Guilford Press, 157–196.

Kovacs, M. (1985), The children's depression inventory (C.D.I.) *Psychopharmacology Bulletin.* 21(4), 995–999.

——— (1980/81): Rating scales to assess depression in school-aged children. *Acta Paedopsychiatrica.* 46, 305–315.

Kovacs, M. & Beck, A. T. (1977), An Empirical-Clinical Approach Toward a Definition of Childhood Depression, *In* Schulterbrandt, G., and Raskin, Allen (Eds), *Depression in Childhood: Diagnosis, Treatment, and Conceptual Models.* New York: Raven Press, pp. 1–25.

Livingston, R., M.D. (1985), Depressive illness and learning difficulties: Research needs and practical implications, *J. of Learning Disabilities*, 18(9), pp. 518–521.

Malmquist, C. P., M.D. (1983), Major depression in childhood: Why don't we know more? *J. of Orthopsychiatry*, 53(2), pp. 262–268.

Mokros, H. B, Poznanski, E. O., & Merrick, W. A. (1989), Depression and learning disabilities in children: A test of hypothesis, *J. of Learning Disabilities*, 22(4), pp. 230–234.

Osman, B. B. (1987): Promoting social acceptance of children with learning disabilities: An educational responsibility. *J. of Reading Writing and Learning Disabilities International*, 3(2), pp. 111–119.

——— (1982), *No One to Play With: The Social Side of Learning Disabilities.* Novato, California: Academic Therapy Publications.

——— (1970), *Learning Disabilities: A Family Affair.* New York: Warner Books (paper).

Reynolds & Coates, 1985, Reynolds Adolescent Depression Scale (RADS).

Rie, H. E. (1966). Depression in childhood: a survey of some pertinent contributions. *J. of the American Academy of Child Psychiatry.* 5, pp. 553–583.

Rourke, B. P., Young, G. C., Leenaars, A. A. (1989), A childhood learning disability that predisposes those afflicted to adolescent and adult depression and suicide risk, *J of learning Disabilities.* 22(3), pp. 169–176.

Ruter, M., Tuma, A. H., & Lann, I. S. (Eds) (1988), Assessment and *Diagnosis in Child Psychopathology.* New York: Guilford Press.

Rutter, M. (1975), *Helping Troubled Children* New York: Plenum Press.

Seligman, M.E. P. (1975): *Helplessness: On Depression, Development, and Death*. San Francisco: W. H. Freeman.

Silver, L. B. (1989), Psychological and family problems associated with learning disabilities: Assessment and intervention, *J. of the American Academy of Child and Adolescent Psychiatry*. 28(3), pp. 319–326.

Stevenson, O. T., & Romney, D. M. (1984), Depression in learning disabled children, *J. of Learning Disabilities*, 17, pp. 579–582.

Thompson, R. J. (1986), Behavior Problems in Children With Developmental and Learning Disabilities, *International Academy of Research in Learning*

Wechsler, D. (1974), *Wechsler Intelligence Scale for Children—Revised*, New York: The Psychological Corporation.

Chapter 9

Palombo, J. (1987), Self-object Transference in the Treatment of Borderline Neurocognitively Impaired Children, In: *The Borderline Patient*, Vol. 1, J. S. Grotstein, M. F. Solomon & J. A. Lang, eds. Hillside, NJ: The Analytic Press.

Rice, G., Ph.D. (1989), *Assessing the Child Through his Play and Fantasy*, presented at the International Conference on "Educational Therapy," Chicago, IL.

Stern, D. (1985), *The Interpersonal World of the Infant*. New York: Basic Books.

Chapter 10

DeHirsch, K. (1977), Interactions Between Educational Therapist and Child, *Bulletin of The Orton Society*. Vol. xxvii, pp. 88–101.

Sacks, O. (1985), *The Man Who Mistook His Wife for a Hat*, New York: Summit.

Ungerleider, D. F. (1985), *Reading, Writing, and Rage*. Rolling Hills, CA: Jalmar Press.

Chapter 11

Coles, G. (1987), *The Learning Mystique: A Critical Look At Learning Disabilities*. New York: Pantheon Books.

Fairchild, M. W. & Keith, C. R. (1981), Issues of autonomy in the psychotherapy of children with learning problems. *Clinical Social Work Journal*, Vol. 9, pp. 134–142.

Fajardo, B. (1983), Parenting a Damaged Child; Mourning Regression and Disappointment. (Unpublished manuscript)

Garber, B (1988), The emotional implications of learning disabilities: A theoretical integration, *Annals of Psychoanalysis*, Vol. 16, pp. 111–128.

Haley, J. (1976), *Problem Solving Therapy*, San Francisco: Jossey-Bass.

Kaslow, F. W. & Cooper, B. (1978), Family therapy with the learning disabled child and his/her Family, *Journal of Marriage and Family Counseling*, Vol. 4, pp 41–49.

Konstantareas, M. M. & Homatidis, S. (1981), Stress and Differential Parental Involvement in Families of Autistic and Learning Disabled Children, In: *Advances in Special Education*, Vol. 3, E. K. Keogh (ed.)

Osman, B.B. (1979), *Learning Disabilities; A Family Affair*, Mt. Vernon, NY: Consumers Union

Pollack, J. M., (1985), *Pitfalls In The Psychoeducational Assessment Of Adolescents With Learning And School Problems*. Adolescence, Vol. 20, pp. 479–493.

Shane, E. (1984), Self Psychology: A New Conceptualization for the Understanding of LD Children, *Kohut's Legacy:* Contributions to Self Psychology, P. Stepansky and A. Godlberg (eds.) Hillsdale, NJ: Analytic Press, pp. 191–203.

Silver, L. B. (1974), Emotional and Social Problems of the Families With a Child Who Has Developmental Disabilities, *Handbook on Learning Disabilities*, R. E. Webber (ed.). Englewood Cliffs, NJ, Prentice-Hall.

———— (1984), *The Misunderstood Child: A Guide for Parents of Learning Disabled Children*, New York: McGraw-Hill, International Book Co.

———— (1986), Controversial approaches to treating learning disabilities and attention deficit disorders, *American Journal of Diseases of Children*, Vol. 140, pp. 1045–52

Stern, D. (1985), *The Interpersonal World of the Infant.* New York: Basic Books.

Chapter 12

B., & Mamen, Ph.D.(1985), *Learning Disabilities: Etiology, Diagnosis and Management.* Psychiat. Clin. N. Am., 8:703–720

Fairchild, M. W. & Keith, C. R. (1981), Issues of autonomy in the psychotherapy of children with learning problems, *Clinical Social Work Journal,* Vol. 9, pp. 134–142.

Hunt, R. D., & Cohen, D. J., (1984), *Psychiatric Aspects Of Learning Difficulties.* Ped. Clin. N. Am., Vol. 31, pp. 471–497.

Pickar, D. B. (1988), Group Psychotherapy and the Learning Disabled Adolescent, *Adolescence,* Vol. 23, pp. 761–772.

Pollack, J. M., (1985), Pitfalls in the Psychoeducational Assessment of Adolescents with Learning and School Problems, *Adolescence,* Vol. 20, pp. 479–493.

Silver, L. B. (1989), Psychological and family problems associated with learning disabilities: Assessment and intervention, *J. of the American Academy of child and Adolescent Psychiatry.* 28(3), pp. 319–326.

Ziegler, R. & Holden, L. (1988), Family therapy for learning disabled and attention deficit children, Am. J. Ortho. Vol. 58, pp. 196–210.

Chapter 13

Alschul, S. (1988), Trauma, Mourning and Adaptation: A Dynamic Point of View. In: *Childhood Bereavement and its Aftermath,* ed. S. Altschul. Madison: International Universities Press.

Freud, A. (1965), *Normality and Pathology in Childhood: Assessments of Development.* New York: International Universities Press.

Freud, S. (1917a), Mourning and Melancholia, *Standard Edition,* Volume 14, London: Hogarth Press, pp. 237–258.

Furman, E. (1974), *A Child's Parent Dies: Studies in Childhood Bereavement.* New Haven: International Universities Press.

——— (1986), On Trauma, When is the Death of a Parent Traumatic?

Psychoanalytic Study of the Child, 41:191–208. New Haven: International Universities Press.

Furman, R. A. (1964a), Death of a Six Year Old's Mother During His Analysis, *Psychoanalytic Study of the Child*. 19:377–397. New York: International Universities Press.

———— (1964), Death and the Young Child: Some Preliminary Considerations, *Psychoanalytic Study of the Child*. 19:321–333. New York: International Universities Press.

Garber, B. (1981), Mourning in Children: Toward a Theoretical Synthesis. *The Annual of Psychoanalysis*, 9:9–19. New York: International Universities Press.

Kohut, H. (1971), *The Analysis of the Self*, New York: International Universities Press.

Nagera, H. (1970), Children's Reaction to the Death of Important Object: A developmental Approach. *The Psychoanalytic Study of the Child*. 25:360–400. New York: International Universities Press.

Palombo, J. (1981), Parent loss and childhood bereavement: Some theoretical considerations, Clinical Social Work Journal, 9:1, 3–33.

———— (1985), Treatment of borderline disturbances in a neurocognitively impaired child, Clinical Social Work Journal, 13:2, 117–127.

Pollack, G. (1978), Process and affect: Mourning and grief, International Journal of Psychoanalysis, 59:255–276.

Wolfenstein M. (1966), How is Mourning Possible?, *Psychoanalytic Study of the Child*, 21:93–123, New Haven: International Universities Press.

Chapter 14

Aichorn, A. (1964), *Delinquency and Child Guidance*. New York: International Universities Press.

Basch, M. (1980), *Doing Psychotherapy*. New York: Basic Books, pp. 7–32.

Bettelheim, B. (1988), Education and the Reality Principle, *Surviving*, New York: Vintage Books, pp. 127–142.

Ekstein, R. & Motto, R. L. (1969), *From Learning for Love To Love of Learning*, New York: Brunner/Mazel, pp. 172–215.

Freud, S. (1900), The Interpretation of Dreams, *Standard Edition* London: Hogarth Press, 1974, Vol. IV, pp. 96–122

————— (1912), Recommendations to Physicians Practicing Psychoanalysis, *Standard Edition*, London: Hogarth Press, 1974, Vol. 12, pp. 109–119.

————— (1916–1917), The Introductory Lectures on Psychoanalysis, *Standard Edition*, London: Hogarth Press, 1974, Vol. 15, Lecture #VII, pp. 100–113; Lecture # XXIX, pp. 471–495.

————— (1974) On the Beginning of Treatment (Further Recommendations on the Technique of Psychoanalysis), *Standard Edition*, London: Hogarth Press, Vol. XII, pp. 121–144.

Frost, R. (1951) *The Road Not Taken; An Introduction to Robert Frost*, New York: Holt.

Giovacchini, P. (1986), *Developmental Disorders*, New York: Jacob Aronson.

Harris, I. (1961), *Emotional Blocks to Learning: a Study of the Reasons for Failure in School*, New York: The Free Press.

Kaufman, E. (1985), Things About Borderline Adolescents and Psychoanalytic Psychotherapeutic Techniques for Such Stuff, *Ninety Years of Caring*, Judith Schild, (ed.) Jewish Children's Bureau, Chicago.

Kennedy, H. (1975), Pseudobackwardness, *Psychoanalytic Study of the Child*, Vol. 30, New York: International Universities Press, pp. 279–306.

Klein, E. (1949), Psychoanalytic Aspects of School Problems, *Psychoanalytic study of the Child*, New York: International Universities Press, Vol. 3/4 pp. 369–390.

Lustman, S. (1970), Cultural Deprivation, a Clinical Dimension, *Psychoanalytic Study of the Child*, Vol. 25, pp. 483–502.

Newman, J. (1964), Problems in learning arithmetic in emotionally disabled children, *Journal Am. Acad., Child Psychiatry*, Vol. 3, pp. 413–429.

————— (1973), "He can but he don't" (gifted underachievers), *Psychoanalytic Study of the Child*, Vol. 28, New York: International Universities Press, pp. 83–129.

Pearson, G. (1952), Survey of Learning Difficulties, *Psychoanalytic Study of the Child* Vol. 7, New York: International Universities Press, pp. 322–386.

Peller, L. (1966), Freud's Contribution to Language Theory, *Psychoanalytic Study of the Child*, Vol. 21, New York International Universities Press, pp. 448–467.

Pine, F. (1985), Development of Learning and Behavior in Childhood,

Developmental Theory and Clinical Process, New Haven: Yale University Press, pp. 183–205.

Plank, E. & R. (1954), Emotional Components in Arithmetical Learning as Seen Through Autobiographies, *Psychoanalytic Study of the Child*, Vol. 9, New York: International Universities Press, pp. 274–293.

Sperling, M. (1967), School Phobias: Classification, Dynamics and Treatment, *Psychoanalytic Study of the Child*, Vol. 22, New York: International Universities Press, pp. 375–401.

Sperling, O. (1964), The balancing function of the ego with special emphasis on learning, (Comments on Dr. Sperling's paper by Margaret Little), *International Journal of Psychoanalysis*, Vol. 45, pp. 254–262.

Stern, D. (1985), *The Interpersonal World of the Infant*. New York: Basic Books.

Ungerleider, D. F. (1985), *Reading, Writing, and Rage*. Rolling Hills, CA: Jalmar Press.

Whitehead, A. N. (1967), *The Aims of Education*, New York: Free Press.

Winnicott, D. W. (1965), The Maturational Process and the *Facilitating Environment*, New York: International University Press, pp. 15–83, pp. 166–171.

Chapter 15

Bacal, H. & Newman, K. (1990), *Theories of Object Relations: Bridges to Self Psychology*. New York: Columbia University Press.

Cohler, B. & Galatzer-Levy, R. (1990), Self, Meaning and Coherence in the Second Half of Life, in Nemiroff & Calarusso (eds.) *Advances in Understanding Adult Life*. New York: Basic Books.

Galatzer-Levy, R. (1991), Considerations in the Psychotherapy of Adolescents in A. Slomovitz (ed.) *Adolescent Psychotherapy*, American Psychiatric Association Press. (in press)

Galatzer-Levy, R. & B. Cohler (in press, a) The Psychological Significance of Others in Adolescence: Issues for Study and Intervention in P. Tolpin and B. Cohler (eds) *The Adolescent*, New York: Guilford.

Galatzer-Levy, R. (in press, b) *The Essential Other*, Basic Books.

Garber, B. (1989), Deficits in Empathy in the Learning Disabled Child, in Field, K. Cohler., B. and Wool, G. Field (eds.), *Learning and Education: Psychoanalytic Perspectives*, New York: International Universities Press, pp. 617–637.

Kohut, H. (1971), *The Analysis of the Self*, New York: International Universities Press.

Lachman, F. & Beebe, B. (1990), Representational and Self-object Transferences: A Developmental Perspective, Paper delivered at the 13th Annual Conference on the Psychology of the Self, New York.

Lipton, S. D. (1977), The advantages of Freud's technique as shown in his analysis of the rat man, *Int. J. Psychoanal*, Vol. 58, pp. 255–73.

Rosen, V. (1977), *Style. Character and Language*, S. A. Jucovy, M. Atkin (eds.), New York: Jason Aronson.

Rothstein, A. B., L., Crosby, M., Eisenstadt, K. (1988), *Learning Disorders: An Integration of Neuropsychological and Psychoanalytic Considers.* New York: International Universities Press.

Rourke, B. (1989), *Nonverbal Learning Disabilities*, New York: Guilford Press.

Schwartz, D. (1989) Implications of the Infantile Neurosis For Learning Problems in Childhood, Field, K. Cohler., B. and Wool, G. (eds.), *Learning and Education: Psychoanalytic Perspectives.* New York: International Universities Press, pp. 539–398.

Silver, A. and Hagin R. (1990), *Disorders of Learning in Childhood.* New York: Wiley.

Wolf, E. (1988), Treating the Self: Elements of Clinical *Self-Psychology.* New York: The Guilford Press.

Chapter 16

Boxer, A. (1986) Psychoanalysis and education in the Chicago Public Schools: The Report on a Pilot Project on Staff Development. Paper presented at the 63rd Annual Meeting on the American Ortho-psychiatric Association, Chicago, IL. April 10, 1986.

Britzman, Deborah P. (1986) *Cultural Myths in the making of a teacher: Biography and Social Structure,* in Harvard Educational Review, V. 56, #4, pp. 442–456.

Carnegie Forum on Education and the Economy (1986) A Nation Prepared: Teachers for the 21st Century. The Report of the Task Force on Teaching as a Profession. New York.

Elson, Miriam, (1989) *The Teacher as Learner, the Learner as Teacher,* in Learning & Education: Psychoanalytic Perspectives, Field, K., Cohler, B. J., Wool, G. New York, International University Press, Inc.

Freud, S. (1914) *Some Reflections on School Boy Psychology,* Standard Edition V. 13. Hogarth Press, London.

Howard, Jessica (1989) *On Teaching, Knowledge, & "Middle Ground* in Harvard Educational Review V. 59(2) pp. 226-239.

Jackson, Philip, W., (1986) *The Practice of Teaching,* New York, Teachers College Press.

Kubie, Lawrence, S. (1958) *Neurotic Distortion of the Creative Process,* University of Kansas Press, Lawrence, Kansas.

McDonald, Joseph, P. (1986) *Raising the Teacher's Voice and the Ironic Role of Theory,* in Harvard Educational Review, V. 56, #4, pp 355–378.

Sarason, S. B., Davidson, K., Blatt, B. (1973 & 1986 revision) *The Preparation of Teachers: An Unstudied Problem in Education.* Jossey Bass, New York & London.

Sarason, S. B., (1985) *Caring and Compassion in Clinical Practice,* Jossey Bass, New York & London.

Schon, Donald (1973) *The Reflective Practitioner,* Jossey Bass, New York & London

Silberman, Chas E. (1970) *Crisis in the Classroom,* The Remaking of American Education, Random House, New York.

Stern, D. (1985) *The Interpersonal World of the Infant,* New York: Basic Books.

Zimiles, H. (1987) Progressive Education: On the Limits of Evaluation & the Development of Empowerment. *On Teachers College Record, V. 89(2).*

Chapter 17

Aichorn, A. (1948), *Wayward Youth,* New York: Viking Press.

Basch, M. F. (1983), Empathic understanding: A review of the concept and some theoretical considerations, *J. Amer. Psychoanal. Assn.,* 31: pp. 101–126.

——— (1983), The Concept of "Self": An Operational Definition, in L. Benjamin, G. Noam (eds), *Developmental Approaches to the Self,* New York: Plenum Publishers.

——— (1984), The Selfobject Theory of Motivation and the History of Psychoanalysis, pp. 3–10, in P. E. Stepansky and A. E. Goldberg (eds.), *Kohut's Legacy,* Hillsdale, NJ: Analytic Press/Lawrence Erlbaum Associates.

Bettelheim, B. (1950), *Love is Not Enough*, New York: The Free Press.

———— (1955), *Truants From Life*, New York: The Free Press.

———— (1982), *On Learning to Read*. London: Thames and Hudson.

Bettelheim, B., and Zelan, K., (1981), *On Learning to Read*, New York: Knopf.

Brenner, C. (1973), *An Elementary Textbook of Psychoanalysis*, revised edition, New York: International Universities Press.

Craig, E., (1973), *P. S. You're Not Listening*, New York: Signet, New American Library.

Ekstein, R. & Motto, R. L. (1969), *From Learning for Love To Love of Learning*, New York: Brunner/Mazel, pp. 172–215.

Erikson, E. (1950), *Childhood and Society*, New York: W. W. Norton & Company.

Friedman, L. (1987), Tool and Method Pride, Kohut Memorial Lecture, San Diego (audiotape).

Hayden, Torey (1980), *One Child*, New York: Avon.

———— (1981), *Somebody's Else's Kids*, New York: Avon.

———— (1988), *Just Another Kid*, New York: Avon.

Herndon, J. (1969), The Way It's Spozed To Be, New York: Bantam Books.

———— (1971), *How To Survive In Your Native Land*, New York: Bantam Books.

Holzman, P. (1970), *Psychoanalysis and Psychopathology*, New York: McGraw-Hill.

Kernberg, O. (1976),Object Relations Theory and Clinical *Psychoanalysis*, New York: Jason Aronson.

Kohut, H. (1971), *The Analysis of the Self*, New York: International Universities Press.

———— (1977), *The Restoration of the Self*, New York: International Universities Press.

———— (1984), *How Does Analysis Cure?* Chicago & London: The University of Chicago Press.

MacCracken, M. (1981), *City Kid*, New York: Signet Books, Div. of New American Library, Inc.

———— (1986), *Turnabout Children*, New York: Signet Books, Div. of New American Library, Inc.

Paley, V. G. (1988), *Bad Guys Don't Have Birthdays*, Chicago: University of Chicago Press.

———— (1990), *The Boy Who Would Be a Helicopter*, Chicago: University of Chicago Press.

Piaget, J. (1952), *The Origins of Intelligence in Children*, New York: International Universities Press.

Rapaport, D. (1967), *The Structure of Psychoanalytic Theory*, Monograph No. 6 (Vol. II, No. 2), New York: International Universities Press.

Redl, F. (1966), *When We Deal With Children*, New York: The Free Press.

Redl, F. & Wattenberg (1959), *Mental Hygiene in Teaching*, New York: Harcourt-Brace.

Sizer, T. (1989) Restructuring High Schools, Assoc. for Supervision & Curriculum Development, Alexandria, Virginia, Audio Tape.

Tolpin, M. & Kohut, H. J. (1980), The Disorders of the Self: The Psychopathology of the First Years of Life, S. Greenspan and G. Pollock, *The Course of Life. Vol. 1. Infancy and Childhood*, Washington, D. C., U. S. Dept. of Health and Human Services.

Vygotsky, L. S. (1962), *Thought and Language*, Cambridge, MA: M. I. T. Press.

———— (1978), *Mind in Society: The Development of Higher Psychological Processes*, Cambridge, MA: Harvard University Press.

Chapter 18

Atwood, G. E. & Stolorow, R. D. (1984), *Structures of Subjectivity: Explorations in Psychoanalytic Phenomenology*. Hillsdale, NJ: The Analytic Press.

Brightman, B. K. (1984–85), Issues in the training experience of the psychotherapist, *J. Psychoanal. Psychoanalysis* Vol. 10, pp. 293–317.

Ekstein, R. & Wallerstein, R. S. (1958), *The Teaching and Learning of Psychotherapy*. New York: Basic Books.

Kohut, H. (1972), Thoughts On Narcissism and Narcissistic Rage, *The Psychoanalytic Study of the Child*, New York: Quadrangle Press 27: 360–440.

Stolorow, R. D., Brandchaft, B.,& Atwood, G. E. (1987), *Psychoanalytic Treatment: An Intersubjective Approach*. Hillsdale, NJ: The Analytic Press.

Chapter 19

Beaumont, M. (1993) "Reading Between the Lines: The Child's Fear of Meaning," *Emotions and Learning Reconsidered,* Gardner Press, New York.

Blanchard, P. (1946), Psychoanalytic Contributions to the Problems of Reading Disabilities, *Psychoanalytic Study of the Child,* New York: International Universities Press, pp. 163–187.

Buxbaum, E. (1964), The Parents Role in the Etiology of Learning Disabilities, *Psychoanalytic Study of the Child.* New York: International Universities Press, pp. 421–427.

Dervin, D. (1985), *Through a Freudian Lens Deeply. A Psychoanalysis of Cinema.* New Jersey: The Analytic Press.

Ekstein, R. (1984), The Treatment of a Borderline Adolescent: *Cross Generational Communication,* Unpublished paper presented in Chicago, IL.

Ekstein, R. & Motto, R. L. (1969), *From Learning for Love To Love of Learning,* New York: Brunner/Mazel, pp. 172–215.

Freud, S. (1909), Family Romances, *Standard Edition,* Vol. IX, London: Hogarth Press, 1958, pp. 237.

―――― (1912–1913), Totem and Taboo, *Standard Edition,* Vol. XII, London: Hogarth Press, 1974, pp. 1–162.

―――― (1939), Moses and Monotheism: Three Essays, *Standard Edition,* Vol. XX, London: Hogarth Press, 1974, pp. 1–54.

Garber, B. (1988), "The emotional implications of learning disabilities: A theoretical integration," *Annals of Psychoanalysis,* vol. 16, pp. 111–128.

Greenberg, H. R. (1975), *The Movies On Your Mind,* New York: Saturday Review Press/E. P. Dutton and Co., Inc.

Griffith, R. & Mayer, A. (1957), *The Movies,* New York: Simon & Schuster.

Harris, I. (1961), *Emotional Blocks to Learning: a Study of the Reasons for Failure in School,* New York: The Free Press.

Hellman, I. (1954), Mothers of Children with Intellectual Inhibitions, *Psychoanalytic Study of the Child,* New York: International Universities Press.

Klein, M. (1931), A contribution to the theory of intellectual inhibition, *International Journal of Psychoanalysis,* Vol. 12:2, pp. 206–218.

McDermott, J. F. Jr. & Lum, K. Y. (1980), Star Wars: The Modern Developmental Fairy Tale, *Bulletin of the Menninger Clinic.* Vol. 44, pp. 381–390.

Pearson, G. (1952), Survey of Learning Difficulties, *Psychoanalytic Study of the Child.* New York: International Universities Press, pp. 322–386.

Peller, L. (1966), Freud's Contribution to Language Theory, *Psychoanalytic Study of the Child*, New York: International Universities Press pp. 448–467.

Shipman, D. (1982), *The Story of Cinema*, New York: St. Martin's Press.

Sperling, O. (1964), The balancing function of the ego with special emphasis on learning, (Comments on Dr. Sperling's paper by Margaret Little), *International Journal of Psychoanalysis*, Vol. 45, pp. 254–262.

Stern, D. (1985), *The Interpersonal World of the Infant.* New York: Basic Books.

Ungerleider, D. F. (1985), *Reading. Writing and Rage.* Rolling Hills, CA: Jalmar Press.

Whitehead, A. N. (1967), *The Aims of Education*, New York: Free Press.

Winnicott, D. W. (1965), *The Maturational Process and the Facilitating Environment*, New York: International University Press pp. 15–83, pp. 166–171.

———— (1971), *Playing and Reality*, Tavistock Publication, London.

Wittenberg, I., et. al, (1983), *The Emotional Experience of Learning and Teaching*, London: Routledge & Kegan Paul, pp. 53–76.

Subject Index

Name Index

Adams, J., 80
Adler, A., xvi, xvii
Aichorn, A., xiii, xxvi, xxxviii, 165, 219
Ainsworth, M., 4, 46
Als, H., 80
Altschul, S., 151
Atwood, G., 188

Bacal, H., 172
Barrett, M., ix, xv, xix, xxiv, xxviii, xxx, xl, 4, 45, 53, 195
Barsch, R., xxxviii, xxxix
Basch, M., ix, xvi, 3, 6, 167, 219
Baygood, L., xx
Beaumont M., ix, xvi, 4, 34, 42, 242
Beck, A., 92
Beebe, B, 172
Benedek, T., 14, 29
Bensdorf, J., xix,
Bensdorfs, The W., xx
Berkman, M., xx
Bernsfeld, S., xiii, xviii, xxvi
Bess, C., 73
Bettelheim, B., xiv, xxvi, xxxix, 35, 161, 164, 219
Bick, E., 47
Blalock, J., 74, 81
Blatt, B., xxxiii, 202, 205
Bonaparte, M 7 xxvi
Borenstein, L., xix
Bowlby, J., xv, xvi, xxxi, 3, 38, 45, 47, 49, 55
Boxer, A., xix
Brazelton, T, 7 128
Brenner, C., 218
Brightman, B., 233
Britton, R., 37, 44
Britzman, D., 192
Brown, R., xix, x., 80
Broucek, F, 8

Brumback, R., 93
Bryan, T., 78
Burlingham, D., xxvi
Buxbaum, E., xiii

Cable, B., 76
Campbell, D, xxx
Carlisle, J., 74
Carrow-Woolfolk, E., 77
Caspari, I., xxviii, 35, 57, 195
Cassidy, J., 49
Chess, S., 17
Child, C., 205
Childress, B., xix
Clark, D., 76
Cohen, J., 91
Cohler, B., 172
Colbert, P, 90, 92
Coles, G., 126, 131
Cozzarelli, L., ix, 188, 231
Craig, E., xvi, 224, 226
Croasmum, P., 74
Crosby, M., 171

Darwin, C., 7
Davidson, K., xxxiii, 202, 205
DeHirsch, K., xxxviii, 117, 119
Dewald, P., 29
Dewey, J., xiv
Donoghue, M., xL 78
Duffy, H., 80
Duve, A, M., ix, xxiv, xxvii, xL 67, 82, 83, 195

Eisen, M., ix, xvii, xix, 112, 126
Eisen, S., ix, 112, 139
Eisenstadt, K., 171
Ekstein, R., ix, xiii, xxxix, 14, 29, 118, 167, 170, 219, 232, 240, 253
Eldens, The R., xx
Elson, M., 199